The Bilingual Revolution Series

Speaking the World

Multilingualism and Cultural Fluency in the Professional World

Edited by

Mehdi Lazar and Fabrice Jaumont

CALEC – TBR Books
New York – Paris

Copyright © 2025 by CALEC

All rights reserved. No part of this publication may be reproduced, distributed, or transmitted in any form or by any means without prior written permission.

TBR Books is a program of the Center for the Advancement of Languages, Education, and Communities. We publish researchers and practitioners seeking to engage diverse communities on education, languages, cultural history, and social initiatives.

CALEC – TBR Books
750 Lexington Avenue, 9th floor
New York, NY 10022
USA
www.calec.org | contact@calec.org
www.tbr-books.org | contact@tbr-books.org

Cover illustration: Gaël Gaborel
Cover design: Toscane Landréa

ISBN 978-1-63607-436-8 (Paperback)
ISBN 978-1-63607-445-0 (eBook)
Library of Congress Control Number: 2024939901

PRAISES

In the ever-evolving tapestry of global interaction, *Speaking the World: Multilingualism and Cultural Fluency in the Professional World* is a pivotal exploration of the intersection between language, culture, and professional success. It unravels how multilingualism extends beyond mere communication while unlocking diverse cultural perspectives and fostering international collaboration. This work is essential for professionals and academics, offering a comprehensive understanding of the indispensable role of linguistic and cultural skills in today's world.
    – Professor Teboho Moja, New York University and University of South Africa

With artificial intelligence now doing our translations easily and virtual meetings in English giving a superficial – and wrong – impression that we are all similar, it has never been so tempting to avoid language learning. *Speaking the World: Multilingualism and Cultural Fluency in the Professional World* makes a compelling and timely case for the importance of language beyond the immediate practical needs of communication as a gateway to a more profound sensitivity to culture. The book takes us on a stimulating journey to explore different perspectives on how language ability and cultural fluency are complementary skills to improve our understanding of our international partners. This understanding is the precondition to integrating across differences, turning those differences into professional opportunities, and countering the divisive tendencies of our times. A thought-provoking and important book.
    – Claudia Mueller, Affiliate Professor for Intercultural Leadership, ESCP Business School

Navigating the intricacies of our globalized society requires more than just linguistic ability; it demands a deep cultural understanding. *Speaking the World: Multilingualism and Cultural Fluency in the Professional World* masterfully captures this essence, exploring how multilingualism and cultural acumen shape the modern professional landscape. This book is an invaluable resource for anyone seeking to comprehend the multifaceted role of language and culture in our increasingly interconnected world.

— Dr. Jane Flatau Ross, International Educator and Author of *Two Centuries of French Education in New York*

Speaking the World: Multilingualism and Cultural Fluency in the Professional World is a beacon in exploring global communication and cultural dynamics. It delves into the heart and shapes our understanding of the world and how cultural fluency becomes a bridge to new opportunities in the professional sphere. This book is not just an academic achievement; it is a crucial guide for navigating the rich tapestry of our global society.

— Darcey H. Hale, Former Head of School, The International School of Boston

We live in a time defined by global interconnectedness. *Speaking the World* stands out as an essential guide for navigating the complexities of today's international landscape. This book masterfully highlights the importance of multilingual communication and cross-cultural understanding as critical assets in our global economy. Insightful analysis and practical recommendations highlight how the journey toward cultivating these competencies must begin early, extending beyond the classroom to include rich, immersive cultural experiences, ultimately contributing to building a better world. Multilingualism and cultural competencies are no longer luxuries for the well-traveled; they are essential for our survival as a species.

— Noumane Rahouti, Ph.D., Lecturer at Sultan Qaboos University

Born and educated in Germany, I moved to France over a decade ago to start working as a professor of Entrepreneurship at a French business school. When my children were quite young, I developed a deep interest in how learning languages and new cultures impact kids and young adults. *Speaking the World: Multilingualism and Cultural Fluency in the Professional World* is an invaluable resource, addressing many of my questions and prompting me to consider new ones. Chapters 3 and 11, which explore multilingualism's intersection with neurodiversity and artificial intelligence, are particularly insightful. I highly recommend this book and hope it sparks widespread discussion, innovative ideas, and meaningful policy development in this vital area.

– Professor Martin Kupp, ESCP Business School

Speaking the World: Multilingualism and Cultural Fluency in the Professional World is a compelling "call to action" on the imperative of multilingualism in our increasingly interconnected global landscape. Almost 50 years since Edward Said's seminal work Orientalism critically examined Western perceptions of non-Western cultures, this volume adeptly navigates us through the complexities of cultural competence in the face of rapid globalization. Using a broad and impressive body of evidence on the benefits of multilingualism, the authors present a cogent argument for reevaluating our approach to education, multiculturalism, and the intricate interplay of language and culture in daily life. This work not only challenges readers to develop multilingual proficiencies but also advocates for their application in fostering cross-cultural dialogue and collaboration. It stands as an essential contribution to the discourse on global communication and understanding. I, for one, say thank you, merci, zikomo.

– John William Bray, Educator, Director of Learning, iArticulate

Brilliant and a must-read! *Speaking the World: Multilingualism and Cultural Fluency in the Professional World* is indeed a masterclass for anyone seeking to understand and navigate the complexities of our globalized economy. It is a revolutionary guide for entrepreneurs and professionals to develop the critical assets of multilingual communication and cross-cultural understanding.

– Ashish Jaiswal, DPhil (University of Oxford), educationist and author of Visionary Thinking

Although I arrived "late" to international education, in the past decade, I have been fortunate to experience firsthand, across contexts and continents, how learning and communicating through more than one language shapes children's developing understanding of, connections to, and engagement in the world. *Speaking the World: Multilingualism and Cultural Fluency in the Professional World* provides invaluable insights from varied disciplines and regions into how language acts as a bridge for building intercultural competence. Its critical and richly-referenced exploration of global competencies and bilingual education offers essential guidance for educators (and parents), preparing young people to become global leaders and professionals to act on and thrive in an undeniably interconnected world. This collection offers compelling reading for anyone committed to helping develop the next generation of culturally fluent global citizens.

– Shelley Paul, Founder & Lead Consultant, Second Circle

ACKNOWLEDGEMENT

As we bring to fruition the comprehensive work *Speaking the World: Multilingualism and Cultural Fluency in the Professional World*, we are filled with deep gratitude and a profound appreciation for the myriad of individuals and groups who have contributed to this endeavor.

First, we thank every author who shared their insights, research, and experiences in this volume: Sergio Adrada-Rafael, Dina Rosa Agyemang, Gaspard Belhadj, Françoise Bougaeff, Laurence Champomier, Victorien Coquery, Fatou Alhya Diagne, Megan Diercks, Gabrielle Durana, Lama Fakih, Isabelle Finger, Tobechukwu Precious Friday, Michele Gerring, Eric Hertzler, Md. Zubair K. Khan, Joanna Greer Koch, Elena Korzhenevich, Hélène Leone, Xiaojin Niu, Armineh Petrossian, Steven J. Sacco, Marta Sachy, and Pascal Vallet.—your contributions have been the pillars upon which the strength of this book rests.

We sincerely thank Alexandra Erman, Marylène Fage, Dave Margulius, Jean-Marc Merriaux, and Louise Roussel for graciously participating in our interviews and sharing their insights on multilingualism in the professional world. Their perspectives have been invaluable, and their contributions greatly enrich our understanding of the role of languages in global workplaces.

Special gratitude is extended to Toscane Landréa and Isabella Lobo, whose meticulous proofreading ensured the clarity and coherence of our collective voice. Your dedication and attention to detail have brought clarity and polish to our work.

We also thank the Board of Directors of the Center for the Advancement of Languages, Education, and Communities. Your support, guidance, and unwavering belief in the importance of our mission have been a source of constant inspiration and motivation.

To our families, our deepest gratitude. Your understanding, patience, and endless encouragement have been our bedrock. You have shared in our challenges and celebrated our achievements, offering love and support through every step of this journey.

Finally, this acknowledgment would only be complete by mentioning the broader community of language educators, learners, and advocates. Your passion and commitment to multilingualism and cultural fluency drive change in our world, and this book is a testament to that collective endeavor.

In conclusion, *Speaking the World* is not just the product of our efforts but a symphony of diverse voices and perspectives. It reflects a shared vision and collective commitment to fostering a more linguistically and culturally fluent world.

Mehdi Lazar & Fabrice Jaumont

Table of contents

Preface
Darla K. Deardorff 1

Introduction: Unlocking the potential of multilingualism and cultural fluency in the professional landscape
Mehdi Lazar and Fabrice Jaumont 3

PART 1. Multilingualism, cultural fluency, and global competencies 19

Chapter 1 – Cultural intelligence in the professional world
Armineh Petrossian 21

Chapter 2 – Multilingualism: What history tells us
Victorien Coquery 29

Chapter 3 – Navigating global competencies: Insights from the OECD
Eric Hertzler 52

Chapter 4 – The multilingual advantage in the global contemporary workplace
Mehdi Lazar 66

PART 2. Empowering students 71

Chapter 5 – Are U.S. college graduates culturally ready to work abroad? A survey study
Sergio Adrada-Rafael 73

Chapter 6 – Revitalizing for relevancy and representation: The revisioning of a multilingual and multicultural teacher education program
Joanna Greer Koch 82

Chapter 7 – Educational projects of the Mission Laïque Française:
Interview with Jean-Marc Merriaux
Gaspard Belhadj and Mehdi Lazar 93

Chapter 8 – Multilingualism and neurodiversity in the
contemporary world
Laurence Champomier 97

Chapter 9 – Dual-language programs in Southern Florida: A model
for potential reforms to instruction for English language learners in
Arizona, with implications for students' professional success
Michele Gerring 109

PART 3. Empowering organizations 123

Chapter 10 – Navigating the benefits and challenges of
multilingualism and cultural fluency in Silicon Valley:
Myths and reality
Isabelle Finger 125

Chapter 11 – The four dimensions of global leadership
Mehdi Lazar 135

Chapter 12 – Could international schools be the incubators for
culturally competent organizations?
Françoise Bougaeff 147

Chapter 13 – Multilingualism and cultural fluency within
multinational corporations operating in Francophone Africa:
Implications for French-language programs
Steven J. Sacco and Megan Diercks 159

Chapter 14 – Prospects and challenges of incorporating
multilingualism and multiculturalism into the higher education
system in Bangladesh: A case study
Md. Zubair K. Khan 169

Chapter 15 – Understanding the shortage of French-language
teachers in Canada
Hélène Leone 179

PART 4. Empowering citizens 191

Chapter 16 – Multilingualism in the age of artificial intelligence
Pascal Vallet 193

Chapter 17 – Empowering youth to shape the digital narrative of the African continent: WikiAfrica Education's experience
Dina Rosa Agyemang, Fatou Alhya Diagne, Tobechukwu Precious Friday, Elena Korzhenevich, and Marta Sachy. 205

Chapter 18 – Multilingualism for all: From dream to reality in public policy
Gabrielle Durana 220

Chapter 19 – Multilingualism in Lebanon
Lama Fakih 226

Chapter 20 – The missing link between global competence education and Chinese laborers' life abroad
Xiaojin Niu 233

PART 5. Reflections 243

Marylène Fage, Organizational Change Manager at Bosch 245

Alexandra Erman, Chief People Officer at BforeAI 248

Louise Roussel, Senior Relationship Manager at KeyBank 251

Dave Margulius, Co-founder of Quizlet 253

Conclusion: Embracing multilingualism and cultural fluency – charting the path forward
Mehdi Lazar and Fabrice Jaumont 256

Guide for educators and parents: Fostering multilingualism and cultural fluency 265

References 287

About the authors 323

About TBR Books 331

Preface

Dr. Darla K. Deardorff,
Chairholder of the UNESCO Chair of Intercultural Competences at Stellenbosch University (South Africa)
Research fellow at Duke University (United States).

In an era of heightened global interconnectivity and subsequent societal polarization, the importance of multilingualism and cultural fluency cannot be overstated. These competencies are not simply "add-ons" to the professional world; they are essential tools for navigating the complexities of today's interconnected yet divided realities as people are faced with connecting across differences on a daily basis. *Speaking the World: Multilingualism and Cultural Fluency in the Professional World*, expertly edited by Mehdi Lazar and Fabrice Jaumont, comes at a pivotal moment in this global discussion. This book offers a rich and timely exploration of the profound impact of language and cultural navigation on professional life, diplomacy, education, and beyond.

As someone who has spent much of my career researching and addressing intercultural competence and global learning within higher education, I am particularly encouraged by the themes addressed in this much-needed volume. The contributors highlight that multilingualism is far more than merely an advantage. Regardless of the context of one's work, be it in international business, academia, or government, the ability to communicate successfully across languages and differences presents opportunities for collaboration, teamwork, and learning from one another. More importantly, multilingualism allows for deeper cultural understanding and mutual respect, which are essential in ultimately fostering global cooperation and addressing grave challenges confronting us as humans.

Intercultural competence, or cultural fluency, as the term used in this volume, is viewed as equally essential as multilingualism. My research has indicated that language alone is not enough to develop intercultural competence. Instead, such competence must be intentionally addressed and involves key elements such as perspective-taking, open-mindedness, and listening for understanding (instead of response). This is particularly true since there are cases of "fluent fools" - those who may know the grammar and vocabulary of another language but are interculturally incompetent in navigating within the culture. Thus, intercultural competence and cultural fluency become about navigating the complexities of human interaction and relationships in a way that is respectful and adaptable. This book demonstrates that such cultural fluency enhances our ability to build meaningful, lasting relationships across divides by preventing misunderstandings and creating environments where diversity can truly thrive.

In this volume, Lazar and Jaumont have brought together diverse perspectives on how multilingualism and cultural fluency intersect in various sectors, from early education to professional development. The insights provided here illuminate the pathways for cultivating these essential competencies while also addressing the significant challenges that must be overcome, such as equitable access to language education. Given the increased global migration trends, multilingualism and intercultural competence will become all the more crucial, not just for migrants but also for host cultures. Thus, as we look to the future, language and intercultural competence will only continue to grow in importance - in the workplace as well as in daily life. The ability to understand and communicate across cultures and differences remains key for human flourishing and belonging, the promotion of peace, and the social integration of all within truly inclusive societies. This book is ultimately a call to action to embrace multilingualism and cultural fluency as we recognize our shared humanity in which we are all interconnected and interdependent, a world in which we must learn to live together as fellow humans sharing this planet.

Introduction: Unlocking the potential of multilingualism and cultural fluency in the professional landscape

Mehdi Lazar and Fabrice Jaumont

In today's globalized economy, multilingualism and cultural fluency have become critical assets. The demand for advanced personal and professional competencies, such as multilingual communication and cross-cultural understanding, is at an all-time high in the professional world. The shift towards remote work, coupled with increasing demographic and cultural diversity in many countries, has further emphasized the importance of multilingualism and cultural fluency. These skills are essential for overcoming language and cultural barriers across various industries and company cultures.

Consequently, cross-cultural management and intercultural leadership have become critical in modern business practices following the growing integration of economies and cultures. At the same time, the evolving context of the increasingly global nature of our human activities has not been adequately represented in traditional business literature and education at large. Even with the importance of multilingual abilities and cultural fluency for global leaders, the journey towards cultivating these competencies for all begins with preparing future professionals. The importance of incorporating language learning and cultural studies from an early age cannot be overstated, as it sets the foundation for a comprehensive understanding of various cultural dynamics. This preparation is not limited to the confines of a classroom; it encompasses exposure to diverse cultures, whether through study abroad programs or engagement with diverse local communities. Such experiences ignite curiosity about the world and nurture a comprehensive understanding of various cultural dynamics. For professionals, the imperative of upskilling is also evident. Such enhancement can be attained through participation in language courses, workshops focusing on cultural competence, and engagement in international assignments. Employers have a crucial role to play by providing the necessary resources and time for language learning and cultural training, thereby supporting individual growth and contributing to broader organizational and societal development.

This shift demands leaders and professionals across all levels to develop new skills and perspectives, equipping them to navigate and thrive in diverse international environments effectively. These skills are not confined to mere language proficiency; they extend to understanding cultural nuances and sensitivities, crucial for successful global interactions. They involve a unique mindset characterized by openness, adaptability, and an appreciation for diverse perspectives. Beyond specialized fields like diplomacy or translation, multilingual and culturally fluent individuals are increasingly valued across various sectors for offering fresh perspectives and innovating "outside the box." Their ability to bring diverse perspectives is a crucial driver of innovation and progress in the globalized economy.

Multilingual and culturally fluent individuals often become exemplary global citizens, equipped to engage deeply with diverse cultures and international issues. Their unique skills enhance decision-making and problem-solving processes, making them indispensable in a world where business and cultural boundaries are constantly converging. Their skills enable them to actively seek and understand varying perspectives, thus broadening their worldviews. This ability is particularly beneficial in global economies where individuals fluent in two or more majority languages have a competitive advantage. They are adept at communicating in diverse markets and understanding multiple cultural contexts, which is invaluable in international business, diplomacy, and global networking.

Global companies have been at the forefront of this effort, capitalizing on and driving globalization over the past decades. For these companies, effectively navigating global business requires employees to possess a blend of cultural knowledge—including insights into various cultural norms, communication styles, and interaction methods—along with practical skills. These competencies are essential for success in international environments and across cultural boundaries. Additionally, cosmopolitan views have fueled the growing demand for global citizenship education, fostering intercultural and mutual understanding.[1]

At the crossroads of all these perspectives, multilateral organizations such as UNESCO, OECD, and the Council of Europe have produced policies and programs reinforcing the need to develop multilingual abilities, cultural fluency, and global competence. UNESCO, for example, defined intercultural competence in 2013 as relevant knowledge about cultures and general knowledge about the issues that arise when members of distinct cultures interact. They include receptive attitudes that encourage settlement and contact with other people, as well as the skills needed to draw on this knowledge and these attitudes when interacting with others from different cultures.[2] Similarly, progress has been made in raising awareness of the benefits of mastering a heritage language for the last twenty years. Mastering a heritage language opens further communication channels and demonstrates cultural competence, balancing heritage language proficiency with other languages relevant to one's professional field.

As we can see, the outlook on multilingual skills and cultural fluency has changed dramatically in the past two decades. Whether for mutual understanding, international collaboration, economic development, or business and trade enhancement, tourism, societies, organizations, and individuals increasingly recognize the social and economic benefits of multilingualism and cross-cultural abilities. The common thread in all these various perspectives and efforts is the recognition that cultures are the essence of human diversity, shaping our identities, values, and worldviews. Cross-cultural abilities, therefore, enable individuals to interact efficiently and appropriately across different cultural contexts, either to foster mutual respect and collaboration or to work on a global scale. To do so, mastering languages provides deeper insights into cultures, allowing for a more profound understanding and appreciation of diverse perspectives. This is, in summary, what the research says.

---

[1] Appiah (2006).
[2] Leeds-Hurwitz (2013).

Essential skills for navigating cross-cultural challenges in the global professional world—What the research says

In the 1980s, Hofstede's innovative work[3] pinpointed several crucial skills for navigating diverse cultures that remain relevant today. These include respecting others, avoiding judgment, acknowledging the limits of one's perspectives, showing empathy, being adaptable, allowing everyone a chance to speak, and tolerating ambiguity. Repeatedly, articles in professional journals have included the most relevant and informative segments about how to lead across borders or the value of cultural diversity in professional settings. Since Hofstede's seminal research, an increasing body of work assembled relevant and sound research often grouped under the term "cross-cultural management," representing cross-cultural ability research in management schools worldwide and its dissemination in the professional world. Research in cross-cultural management generally falls under two categories. On the one hand, researchers investigate the role and practices of global managers and the challenges revolving around global leadership management. On the other hand, researchers investigate the characteristics of cultures, cultural variables, and the fundamentals of cross-cultural interactions.[4]

In the first category, the literature highlights how managers now lead teams globally and must quickly assess and integrate across distinct cultures and into new cultural contexts. Besides the need to speak other languages, adapt one's behavior across cultural differences, and work effectively and successfully in diverse cultures, this strand focuses on the strategical, organizational, and managerial aspects of working on intercultural or global teams. It recognizes that diversity in virtual global teams or culturally diverse groups can be beneficial and challenging. Indeed, contextual diversity significantly enhances creativity, decision-making, and problem-solving in teams, and groups with higher contextual diversity produce better quality work and more innovative solutions. In short, creative teams are

---

[3] Hofstede (1980).
[4] Kluckhohn et al. (1961); Hall et al. (1990); Schwartz (1992); Hampden-Turner et al. (2004).

diverse, and culturally diverse teams can help deliver better outcomes than less culturally diverse teams.[5] Of course, the benefits of contextual diversity outweigh the challenges,[6] but culturally diverse teams require specific competencies to manage or participate in.

Consequently, many researchers investigate the roles and responsibilities of global leaders, including how to prevent and handle conflicts in multicultural teams, how to coach, establish rapport, and communicate effectively with international teams, how to manage tension in teams or between global headquarters and local offices, or how to navigate complex organization designs such as matrix and network structures.[7] Similarly, some researchers note the importance of thinking about organizational interculturality beyond a national prism. In other words, 'intercultural' is not always synonymous with 'international.'[8] That is to say that each organization will have its own culture, which is a blend of one or several national cultures, but also the culture of the groups working or belonging to the organization (those will be subcultures, for instance, based on religious, regional, or other characteristics), and the organizational culture itself.[9]

In the second category, research questions include how best to deal with intercultural contexts and what cultural variables are present in workplaces and work-related situations. The GLOBE (Global Leadership and Organizational Behavior Effectiveness) study[10] is a perfect example of this strand, as it aims to explore the relationships among societal culture, organizational culture, and leadership effectiveness across different countries. Researchers in this field aim to uncover how conflicting norms, different assumptions or values, communication, and management styles and preferences can make cross-cultural collaboration challenging and prevent multicultural teams from reaching their full potential. In return, they show how this ability to understand cultural differences and change

---

[5] Jang (2018).
[6] Taras et al., (2021).
[7] Henson (2016); Thomas & Peterson (2017); Reiche (2021).
[8] Frame & Sommier (2020).
[9] Nahavandi (2002).
[10] House et al. (2004).

one's behavior, heavily influenced by culture, requires a particular skill set and mindset. Andy Molinsky calls this capacity global dexterity,[11] or the ability to adapt one's behavior in a foreign culture successfully.

Doing so often requires one to leave their comfort zone. People's attitudes, values, or thought systems vary significantly, and cultures heavily influence beliefs and habits of mind.[12] Of course, various cultures shape individuals, and we are all the combination of a layering of influences ranging from national or regional cultures to generational, social, or even organizational cultures. This shaping is profound, as culture heavily influences beliefs, habits of mind, and behaviors in professional settings.[13] Nevertheless, even if our individual experiences shape us alongside our culture, culture shapes how we see and interact with the world, teaching us what is considered correct or best. Consequently, in the book, we will define culture, which includes a large and complex ensemble of beliefs, habits, references, conditioned behaviors, or "hidden codes" as a "shared system"; in that sense, culture is learned through socialization and influences our thoughts and feelings.[14]

Over the past twenty years, many authors have studied the impact of cultural differences on teams or performance, particularly by identifying cultural variables.[15] Cultural variables significantly impact how people work and behave in professional settings. They are based on the world's cultural patterns and influence what some researchers have identified as a particular organizational and management style sometimes called the national organizational heritage.[16]

These variables can include context communication,[17] relation with personal space or time, power distance and leadership styles,

---

[11] Molinsky (2013).
[12] Nisbett (2003).
[13] Hofstede (1997).
[14] Hofstede et al. (2010).
[15] Meyer (2016); Clark (2008); Wagner et al. (2014).
[16] Nahavandi (2002).
[17] Hall (1976).

ways to handle ambiguity,[18] or 1 leadership styles,[19] to name a few. The main takeaway is that independent of the model used, cultural values shape personal behaviors, tangibly affecting teams' and organizations' culture, actions, and performance.

Consequently, cultural differences have been widely covered, and understanding cultural differences is now recognized as crucial. Authors like Erin Meyer[20] stress the importance of navigating cultural differences to manage and lead effectively globally. In this context, recognizing the cultural factors that share human behavior allows managers and professionals to analyze the reasons for others' behavior, leading to strategically increased effectiveness.[21] Similarly, Bennett's Developmental Model of Intercultural Sensitivity describes how people progress from ethnocentrism to embracing cultural differences.[22] To go along with this idea of being more culturally fluent, other authors insist on professionals developing a "global mindset"[23] or a set of critical cognitive capabilities necessary to navigate the challenges and opportunities of our global realities while transforming them into personal and professional options. For those authors, global professionals combine an openness to and awareness of diversity across cultures and markets with a propensity and ability to synthesize this diversity. Linda Brimm[24] has been focusing on what she described as the "global cosmopolitan mindset," or a desire to learn and to understand the world from a local and a global point of view, the ability to be creative, and the extension of one's linguistic and cultural knowledge.[25] Other researchers, such as Livermore, highlight cultural intelligence's importance in working effectively with people with different backgrounds.[26] Nevertheless, one red thread in all those authors' work is the importance of language

---

[18] Hofstede (1996).
[19] Hampden-Turner & Trompenaars (2004).
[20] Meyer (2016).
[21] Ibid. (2016).
[22] Bennett (2004).
[23] Murtha et al. (1998); Harverston et al. (2000); Jeannet et al. (2000); Levy (2005); Gupta et al. (2008).
[24] Brimm (2018).
[25] Ibid.
[26] Livermore (2015).

abilities, which is well known amongst cognitive psychologists and some key attributes essential to culturally sensitive and competent individuals. Those key attributes are developed further in the annexes of the book and include skills such as open-mindedness, adaptability, empathy, and curiosity.

Exposure to multiple languages and cultures increases open-mindedness, cultural sensitivity, and resilience. Language acquisition encourages individuals to understand and appreciate different viewpoints, develop resilience in overcoming challenges, embrace diverse perspectives, or adjust to various environments.

The interrelation between multilingualism and cultural fluency

In the last twenty years, the advantages of being multilingual have become increasingly apparent in various societies. Due to demographic changes, migrations, new educational programs, or professional incentives, the knowledge, use, and regular learning of more than one language, whether in personal, academic, or professional spaces, have increased regularly.

In today's global economy, the ability to communicate, especially in another language, is a significant advantage. Multilingual workers are now recognized as able to help navigate language and cultural barriers and differences in various industries and company cultures more efficiently. In a world where cultural differences can tremendously affect organizations and teams, as we have shown before, the enhanced ability to navigate cultural nuances is highlighted as an asset. In that context, more and more school systems worldwide are increasing their language instruction programs or creating bilingual programs to prepare students for a global future, recognizing the importance of multilingualism and the increasing number of multilingual individuals worldwide.[27]

Multilingual education is also expanding globally, with immersion programs gaining popularity since the second half of the 20th century and flourishing in many cities worldwide. Canada's immersion programs in North America started as early as the 1960s,

---

[27] Grosjean (2021).

and from there, multilingual education spread to the United States, which is now considered a very efficient education model. Besides the many benefits of multilingualism, it is proven to enhance an individual's cognitive flexibility[28] as they possess multiple words for the same object, concept, or idea. Multilingual individuals also demonstrate improved executive function and multitasking abilities[29] compared to monolinguals, a greater willingness and aptitude for learning an additional language,[30] and enhanced analytical skills in language comprehension.[31] Children who study a second language tend to achieve higher scores on verbal standardized tests[32] and outperform their monolingual counterparts in math and logical reasoning skills[33]. Given all the benefits of multilingualism, multiple stakeholders are now involved in multilingual education advocacy, from groups protecting minority languages[34] to states aiming for internationalization or unity.[35]

The many benefits of multilingualism also include the less-researched development of intercultural competence. Intercultural competence can be defined as "the ability to communicate effectively and appropriately in intercultural situations based on one's intercultural knowledge, skills, and attitudes."[36] Intercultural competence is mainly - but not only - developed through language instruction, and many authors consider language acquisition and intercultural competence to be interrelated or even a "two-way competence."[37] In other words, multilingualism, particularly in education, is linked to linguistic and cultural acquisition. When students or individuals learn other languages, they develop a deeper understanding of different cultural perspectives, including their own, enhancing their intercultural competence. This competence refers to

---

[28] Kroll & Rossi (2024).
[29] Antón et al. (2019).
[30] Baker (2014).
[31] Grey et al. (2017).
[32] Stewart (2005).
[33] Blom et al. (2017).
[34] Jaumont (2017).
[35] García et al. (2017).
[36] Deardorff (2006a), p. 247.
[37] Chen & Hélot (2018), p. 172.

communicating culturally appropriately, demonstrating appreciation and understanding for others, and maintaining an open and respectful attitude. Achieving a high level of intercultural competence requires students to dedicate ample time not only to mastering another language to a sufficient degree but also to exploring, explaining, investigating, and reflecting on various cultural groups' perspectives, values, and beliefs. As students acquire language and culture, they discover other cultures using authentic resources, often through reading but not always, and can compare similarities and differences between cultures. This cultural exploration offers insights and perspectives about the profound impact of culture on attitudes and worldviews. This process leads to a deeper understanding of others and an appreciation for differences and helps develop qualities such as flexibility, adaptability, cultural humility, empathy, and respect. At the same time, by cultivating broader knowledge of other cultures, one comes to appreciate one's own culture better and benefits from enhanced self-awareness.

Empowering all actors to benefit from multilingualism and cross-cultural abilities

More stakeholder groups have been involved in developing multilingual and cross-cultural abilities in individuals in the last decades. They now include states promoting internationalization and more programs seem to revolve around a rationale that provides global and local benefits for individuals, shifting the target of multilingual programs from minority to majority groups at the individual and collective levels. Consequently, in addition to the debate around teaching methods or the shortage of highly qualified teachers,[38] the politics of multilingualism can add issues in implementing and managing multilingual programs. In that sense, this book aims to help promote multilingualism and cultural fluency and support all individuals and organizations interested in exploring, encouraging, and engaging in multilingualism and cultural fluency to do so.

---

[38] Agirdag (2013).

This book's authors acknowledge the tension between the many approaches to multilingualism and intercultural competence. For instance, schematically, UNESCO supports upskilling in those areas, intending to promote mutual understanding and an emphasis on preserving and promoting linguistic diversity while, on the other hand, the OECD approach to multilingualism and global competencies focuses on the practical advantages of multilingualism in enhancing individuals' ability to participate effectively in a globalized world. The OECD emphasizes multilingualism's economic and professional benefits. It provides a comprehensive understanding of how proficiency in multiple languages can contribute to success in international business, diplomacy, and other global endeavors while helping countries develop their economies. In this approach, multilingualism is seen as a tool for increasing competitiveness and promoting economic growth in a globalized marketplace, while UNESCO promotes cultural and linguistic preservation, appreciation, and diversity.

This book recognizes the importance of multilingualism and cultural fluency, validating the experiences and efforts of those proficient in multiple languages. It acknowledges the tension between the UNESCO and OECD approaches but also realizes that areas of overlap and constructive collaboration exist between them. This book, hence, proposes a balanced approach, valuing the goals of language diversity and cultural preservation, with objectives of team effectiveness, economic development, and the advancement of multilingualism policies and practices.

Speaking the world: unlocking multilingualism and cultural fluency

In *Speaking the World*, we delve into the realities, opportunities, and challenges of being multilingual and culturally fluent in today's and tomorrow's professional world. This book addresses two main questions: Why are multilingualism and cultural fluency relevant in the professional world, and how can we effectively prepare current and future professionals to be multilingual and culturally fluent? The authors of this collective volume offer various insights into different multilingualism and multiculturalism practice models. The chapters cover different world areas, disciplinary approaches, and languages. This book also provides insights into developing multilingual and multicultural teams as a strategy for diverse thoughts and means to achieve more meaningful results.

Our book's comprehensive exploration is centered around critically examining multilingualism's pivotal role in the global professional landscape and the insightful inquiry into the interplay between linguistic diversity, cultural fluency, and economic growth. It delves into whether multilingual capabilities confer a competitive edge for professionals and global economies. Furthermore, it evaluates the essentiality of cultural fluency alongside linguistic skills in the workplace, society, and school, distinguishing between intercultural competence, cultural intelligence, global competence, and multilingualism and their relationship with cross-cultural competencies.

The book scrutinizes educational frameworks, questioning their capacity to equip students for the global marketplace, the necessity of bilingual education for future readiness, and the factors influencing the development of multilingual curricula and the possibility for all learners to be multilingual. It critically assesses the qualifications and methodologies of educators that bolster multilingual programs, the outcomes that uphold democratic values and human rights, and the specific linguistic proficiencies that unlock global opportunities, thereby providing a nuanced understanding of the challenges and dynamics shaping multilingual education policy and practice. The book also addresses how individuals from various backgrounds can become more linguistically and culturally competent. Examples taken from diverse contexts in the Middle East, Africa, Europe, and Asia bring forth the need to train citizens and workers to play crucial roles in fostering understanding and collaboration across diverse work environments and societies. A reflection on the role of artificial intelligence on language acquisition and language usage, or multilingualism through history, allows readers to expand their perspectives and look at multilingualism through a wider lens.

This book draws on the expertise of a diverse group of authors, each contributing unique insights into the multifaceted nature of multilingualism and cultural fluency. It focuses on our capacity to empower others and ourselves, inspiring a sense of motivation and determination. Revolving around five main sections, it first examines multilingualism, cultural fluency, and global competencies. In the second section, we investigate how to empower students to become multilingual and culturally fluent individuals, igniting a sense of inspiration. In the third section, we focus on ways to empower organizations to be more inclusive and value multilingualism and interculturalism, fostering empowerment. In the fourth section, we turn to citizens, investigating ways to develop more multilingual and multicultural societies, encouraging a sense of community. Finally, the fifth section allows different voices from the professional world to share their views, thoughts, and experiences on multilingualism and cultural fluency, promoting shared learning and growth.

In the book's first section, Armineh Petrossian emphasizes the importance of cross-cultural intelligence, a critical component of professional success in a globalized world. Victorien Coquery revisits the portrait of famous creative historical figures, focusing on their multilingualism and multiculturalism. Mehdi Lazar identifies four traits that give multilingual individuals a competitive edge in the professional world. Finally, Eric Hertzler highlights the importance of the OECD's work on global competencies.

In the book's second section, Sergio Adrada-Rafael investigates whether U.S. college graduates are genuinely prepared to work abroad, assessing their cultural readiness through a survey study. Joanna Greer Koch discusses the revitalization and relevance of multilingual and multicultural teacher education programs, offering insights into the evolution of teaching in diverse linguistic settings. An interview with Jean-Marc Merriaux, General Director of the MLF, done by Gaspard Belhadj and Mehdi Lazar explores various aspects of the educational project of the Mission Laïque Française (MLF) and its relevance in our world. Laurence Champomier wonders how our professional world could be even more inclusive for neurodiverse, multilingual individuals. Michele Gerring presents a model from Southern Florida's dual-language programs, suggesting potential reforms for English language learners with broader implications for professional success.

In the third section, we inquire into our capacity to empower organizations. Isabelle Finger navigates the complexities of multilingualism and cultural fluency in the high-tech corridors of Silicon Valley, debunking myths and presenting the stark reality. Mehdi Lazar offers insights into the four critical dimensions of global leadership. At the same time, Françoise Bougaeff raises a compelling question about how to shape culturally competent organizations, focusing particularly on examples drawn from international schools. Steven Sacco and Megan Diercks discuss the implications of multilingualism within multinational corporations operating in Francophone Africa, highlighting the significance of French-language programs. Md. Zubair K. Khan examines the prospects and challenges of incorporating multilingualism and cultural diversification in higher education, focusing on South Asia with a case study in Bangladesh. Hélène Leone tackles the challenge of Canada's nationwide shortage of qualified French-language teachers, a critical issue in maintaining bilingual education.

In the fourth section, we investigate how to empower citizens to become more linguistically and culturally fluent. Pascal Vallet develops the challenges of language translation and intercultural understanding in a world driven by artificial intelligence. An intriguing collective chapter by authors from the Moleskine Foundation and Fondazione Aurora delves into empowering African youth to shape the digital narrative of their continent. This topic resonates deeply with the book's theme, emphasizing the power of voice and representation in a multilingual context. Gabrielle Durana explores the future of professional multilingualism and its role in promoting equity. Lama Fakih's chapter on multilingualism in Lebanon provides a fascinating look at a nation where multiple languages coexist as part of its identity. Finally, Xiaojin Niu bridges the gap between global competence education and the real-life experiences of Chinese laborers abroad.

In the fifth section, the book is further enriched by interviews and reflections from individuals like Alexandra Erman from BforeAI, Louise Roussel from SVB Bank, Marylène Fage from Bosh, and Quizlet co-founder Dave Margulius, adding personal narratives and practical insights to the academic discourse. These diverse voices are included to ensure a comprehensive and inclusive understanding of the topic, making the audience feel valued and part of the conversation. Those interviews have been used as illustrative points and narrative elements about being a multilingual and multicultural professional, further emphasizing the importance of diverse perspectives in shaping the discourse.

Finally, the discourse on multilingualism and cultural fluency highlights their indispensable role in shaping professionals adept in their fields and equipped to navigate and contribute to a diverse and interconnected global landscape. The path toward a multilingual and culturally fluent future involves concerted efforts across educational institutions, workplaces, and policy frameworks to foster a world where linguistic and cultural diversity is acknowledged, celebrated, and leveraged for collective progress and understanding. This emphasis on the value of linguistic and cultural diversity in collective progress and understanding is designed to make the audience feel enlightened and appreciative of the richness it brings to our global society. Furthermore, one need not be multilingual or multicultural to be interested in the world as extensively to be professionally successful.

Being multilingual or multicultural, however, does offer a particular window to the world. Even more, a sliding glass door allows one to see the extraordinary diversity of human experience more clearly and exit one's circumstances to enter someone else's view of the world and engage with it on a deeper and richer level.

In support of this vision, we have included a comprehensive guide designed for teachers and parents to foster multilingualism and cultural fluency among students and children. This guide blends theoretical insights with practical strategies, providing activities, discussion prompts, and resources to engage learners actively. Integrating these elements informs and inspires educators and parents to create environments where curiosity about languages and cultures can thrive. Whether used in a classroom or at home, this guide is a valuable tool to prepare the next generation for success in an increasingly diverse and interconnected world.

PART 1.
Multilingualism, cultural fluency, and global competencies

Language is the means of getting an idea
from my brain into yours without surgery.
– Mark Amidon

Chapter 1 – Cultural intelligence in the professional world

Armineh Petrossian

The world is becoming increasingly interconnected and interdependent with a drastic surge in modern technology, improved communication tools, and advanced transportation systems. This interconnection and interdependence have shrunk economic boundaries and potentially increased culturally based conflicts. In today's globalized world, professionals and students face linguistic challenges when communicating with people worldwide.[39] Therefore, a position in industry, sciences, or academics no longer demands strictly interacting with those nearby but with partners from around the country and the globe.

Cultural intelligence has become critical in achieving global understanding and characterizing the 21st century.[40] Today's social fabric is meshed with diverse cultures in pluralistic societies.[41] Furthermore, enhancing one's cultural fluency allows one to develop cultural intelligence. This involves learning about cultural norms, such as whether to shake hands, and transforming our mindset and behavior. This capacity is necessary to achieve global reach and communicate or work efficiently in diverse workplaces. In this context, learning another language for communication purposes and developing listening skills to understand global social issues better and enhance one's cultural intelligence is crucial.

As global competition intensifies, cultural intelligence has emerged as a critical source of long-term competitive advantage in the global economy. A rapidly developing world demands that future generations master skills such as languages, global thinking, cultural fluency, and cultural intelligence to be successful and compassionate leaders.[42] In a global setting, cultural intelligence helps individuals

---

[39] Ng et al. (2009).
[40] Thomas & et al. (2008).
[41] Bernardo & Presbitero (2018).
[42] Earley & Peterson (2004).

work successfully across cultures and in culturally diverse situations.[43] A culturally intelligent person understands cultural differences and is capable of empathizing and interpreting the differences as a native would.[44] Of course, a person can acquire cultural intelligence by being exposed to experiences in other cultures, such as traveling, studying abroad, or interacting with someone from that culture.[45] By learning a different language, individuals will also learn about the cultures that share that language, thus integrating a tolerance for people's differences into their identities.[46] With that in mind, in this chapter, we will explore cultural intelligence, why it matters in the professional world, and how it can be sustained, mainly through learning other languages.

The link between multilingualism and cultural intelligence

Today, global companies face the challenges of intercultural differences within their workforce and business dealings.[47] Moreover, many global leaders rely on their cultural awareness to improve their leadership and elevate their relationships with others.[48] In addition, human interaction in our global economy encompasses diverse cultures, religions, and socioeconomic backgrounds beyond many people's comfort zones.

Developing the capacity to communicate and understand varied perspectives to become culturally competent has become paramount for many individuals and countries.[49] By learning a different language, individuals can learn about the cultures that share that language, acquire cultural competency, and have the potential to integrate a tolerance for people's differences into their identities and communicate effectively in various contexts.

---

[43] Presbitero (2017).
[44] Earley & Mosakowski (2004).
[45] Crowne (2008).
[46] Pufahl & Rhodes (2011).
[47] Earley & Peterson (2004).
[48] Baker (2012).
[49] Ang et al. (2007).

An education emphasizing the acquisition of at least two languages hence has the potential to promote positive values, help students take responsibility for their actions,[50] raise awareness of social justice, identity, and cultural diversity in developing intercultural understanding.[51] Learning a second language could bridge the gap in cultural understanding and provide learning strategies for respecting and understanding cultural differences. Indeed, the relationship between language acquisition and cultural awareness allows for building a better understanding of global ethics and cross-cultural empathy.[52] In the 21st century, learning another language has become integral to many countries' curricula, even though cultural intelligence is an area that does not remain elusive for many.[53]

Therefore, in many education systems, the fundamental meaning of curriculum and instruction must adapt to and recognize societal changes by accepting the significant advantages of a real bilingual or multilingual education.[54] Bilingual and multilingual children and individuals not only have equal or higher phonological awareness, vocabulary, grammar, literacy, and reasoning capacities than monolingual peers but also have a higher level of cultural consciousness.[55] They also reflect a higher performance of executive function, which is the ability to manage cognitive processes such as working memory, reasoning, task flexibility, and problem-solving.[56] Therefore, learning another language is beneficial at any age.[57]

The correlation between language acquisition and cultural intelligence allows us to understand cross-cultural empathy and social and emotional intelligence better, which relate and interact directly with one's level of cultural intelligence.[58] Emotional

---

[50] De Lissovoy (2011).
[51] Korzilius et al (2017).
[52] Contini & Maturo (2010).
[53] Ng et al. (2009).
[54] Carstens (2015).
[55] Li et al. (2016).
[56] Esposito & Baker-Ward (2013).
[57] Earley & Peterson (2004).
[58] Crowne (2009).

intelligence is the ability to acknowledge and recognize one's own emotions and those of others and the aptitude to use intelligence in making choices accordingly. Conversely, cultural intelligence is the capacity to function in multiple cultures efficiently. Cultural intelligence, therefore, compared to emotional intelligence, is the added focus and ability to navigate diverse cultural environments easily.

Technological advancements have made the world a smaller place to live, with increasing interactions among its citizens. Cultural and language differences shape how we view others and ourselves. Given this phenomenon, the human brain can adapt when it detects similarities. By adjusting, the brain guides us toward better social behavior in diverse cultural settings, which allows individuals to display cultural intelligence. As language and culture mesh together in mastering a language, values, and perceptions of the world will change over time, thus cultivating a global awareness of culturally intelligent beings.[59] Therefore, acquiring another language is central to developing intercultural awareness and provides the fundamentals to train culturally intelligent individuals over time.[60] As one learns or practices a language for many years, the language learning process becomes a positive factor that allows the language learner to understand, empathize with people, and behave appropriately and effectively with people from diverse cultures.[61]

Compared to 56 percent of Europeans, only 17 percent of Americans speak more than one language proficiently.[62] In a global economy, second language instruction needs to be seriously addressed by many educational systems. While English is considered a world language, second and third languages must be taught in schools and made accessible to all adults to prepare individuals to succeed as global citizens and professionals in the 21st century. Language learning and awareness will develop individuals' cultural

---

[59] Della Chiesa (2010).
[60] Abbott et al. (2004).
[61] Ng et al. (2009).
[62] Tochon (2009).

intelligence, which will, in turn, be composed of four components: metacognitive, cognitive, motivational, and behavioral.[63]

The four areas of cultural intelligence

Cultural intelligence is a term that is often at the forefront of globalization, diversity, and cross-cultural awareness.[64] Today, our classrooms, workplaces, and boardrooms are composed of an increasing number of diverse individuals. One needs to navigate many intercultural scenarios daily.

Culture is "the belief systems and value orientations that influence customs, norms, practices, and social institutions, including psychological processes (language, caretaking practices, media, educational systems) and organizations (media, educational system). All individuals are cultural beings and have a cultural, ethnic, and racial heritage. Culture has been described as the embodiment of a worldview through learned and transmitted beliefs, values, and practices, including religious and spiritual traditions. It also encompasses a way of living informed by the historical, economic, ecological, and political forces on a group. These definitions suggest that culture is fluid and dynamic and that there are universal cultural phenomena and culturally specific or relative constructs."[65] Culture, therefore, is a group of people's shared social beliefs and values. A multicultural person can relate to many or several cultures. Intracultural refers to people of one culture interacting with people within the same culture; conversely, intercultural refers to the ability to interact between or among people of different cultures.[66]

Cultural competencies are a general term for over three hundred concepts related to cultural competence, such as self-awareness and cultural empathy.[67] Meanwhile, cross-cultural ability means the ability to communicate effectively across many cultures. In a

---

[63] Pufahl & Rhodes (2011); Contini et al. (2010); O'Rourke et al. (2016).
[64] Thomas et al. (2008).
[65] American Psychological Association (2003), p. 380.
[66] Presbitero (2017).
[67] Ang et al. (2015).

globalized world, cross-cultural intelligence is the ability to function competently with others despite cultural differences.[68] Cultural intelligence allows individuals to connect and work effectively across cultures.[69] This ability is formed with the following four factors: metacognitive, cognitive, motivational, and behavioral,[70] and can be measured by Ang, Van Dyne, and Koh's cultural intelligence scale.[71] Those four critical areas are central to the development of cultural intelligence.[72]

Metacognition is the ability to process information to understand cultural differences.[73] Individuals with high metacognitive cultural intelligence are aware of their thinking processes. They can adapt their views and question cultural assumptions in intercultural interactions.[74] As an example of a metacognitive exercise, Sternberg identified several characteristics of core mental processes: recognizing the existence of a problem, defining its nature, finding solutions to resolve the issue, and allocating, defining, and evaluating solutions to the problem.[75]

Cognition relates to the process of learning about different cultures and cross-cultural interactions[76] through self-awareness and knowledge of one's social environment. An example would be knowing one's cultural background and being conscientious of how this can shape one's viewpoints for understanding other cultures.

The motivational aspect of cultural intelligence is a person's ability to learn and function in cross-cultural situations.[77] This component requires a more significant commitment to staying engaged and adjusting to new cultural settings.[78] Not giving up too

---

[68] Sieck et al. (2013).
[69] Crowne (2009).
[70] Al-Dossary (2016); Schlägel & Sarstedt (2016).
[71] Ang et al. (2006).
[72] Macnab & Worthley (2010).
[73] Crowne (2008).
[74] Macnab & Worthley (2010).
[75] Sternberg (1985).
[76] Earley & Mosakowski (2004).
[77] Macnab & Worthley (2010).
[78] Crowne (2008).

soon when encountering challenging situations in intercultural dealings is an example of the motivation component.[79]

Finally, the behavioral component demonstrates a person's ability to adjust their behavior when interacting with people of different cultures.[80] For example, a person with elevated levels of behavioral cultural intelligence may change their communication manners to interact more effectively with people from diverse cultures by using appropriate words, correct tone of voice, body language, and facial expressions.[81] Depending on the depth and extent of exposure to other cultures, individuals will eventually reduce their cultural gaps and increase their cultural intelligence. Cultural intelligence will emerge as the leading skill in developing global leaders through one's ability to self-analyze, learn from experiences, and develop language and cultural aptitude.[82]

Conclusion: Cultural intelligence in the professional world

Cultural intelligence is a person's ability to connect and work across cultures.[83] It emerged as an essential, influential, and transformative element in today's globalized world. Cultural intelligence can be acquired by being exposed to experiences in other cultures through four critical areas: metacognitive, cognitive, motivational, and behavioral. This is crucial for understanding the importance of multilingualism and its impact on cultural intelligence, particularly when learning to think differently.[84]

Thinking differently expands initial knowledge and perspectives and enriches learning. For professionals to compete in a multicultural and globalized world, speaking more than one language is not an option anymore but an imperative. Cultural intelligence, therefore, cannot be considered in a vacuum, as it depends on

---

[79] Li et al. (2016).
[80] Crowne (2008).
[81] Earley & Mosakowski (2004).
[82] Barner-Rasmussen et al. (2014).
[83] Crowne (2009).
[84] Goh (2012).

multilingualism.[85] Learning additional languages is critical, and teaching children a second language early is the best course. Multilingualism allows individuals to communicate with a larger population and makes them more competitive in a global job market. It is proven that being multilingual allows one to easily communicate in a multicultural setting, accept and value diversity, listen, develop empathy, be more creative, adapt to diverse situations quickly, and have less of a challenge learning additional languages.

Moreover, the relationship between language acquisition and cultural intelligence allows us to understand global ethics and cross-cultural empathy better. As language and culture mesh together in mastering a language, values, and perceptions of the world will change over time, thus cultivating a global awareness of culturally intelligent beings.[86] Change is not easy, but it is inevitable. Some countries are more open to change and have a higher level of adaptability than others. Nevertheless, all societies are partly responsible for bringing about change for the better of students, citizens, communities, and organizations.

An old Armenian proverb states, "Kani lezou guides, aynkan mart es," which translates into "You embody as many people as the number of languages you speak." In a simplified manner, this proverb summarizes and reaffirms the changes we must see in current and future leaders.

---

[85] Zentella (2009).
[86] Della Chiesa et al. (2012).

Chapter 2 – Multilingualism: What history tells us

Victorien Coquery

"It is in Latin that I have administered the empire; my epitaph will be incised in Latin on the walls of my mausoleum on the banks of the Tiber, but it is in Greek that I have thought and lived."[87] Would Hadrian have been the same emperor if he had spoken only one language? The words that Marguerite Yourcenar lends him in her novel *Mémoires d'Hadrien* suggest not. The writer paints a portrait of a complex man: an excellent soldier. He initially hid his taste for Greek authors; an inventive legislator, he was flexible and tolerant as long as he could remain effective; supreme leader of the Roman Empire, he received the title of Philhellene from the Athenians. To sort and label everything about him as Greek or Roman would most of the time be artificial; to assert that this or that quality came from Greek or Latin would be risky and reductive; to explain his entire life and deeds by his bilingualism would be excessive. However, it is hard not to see that this dual influence sheds a singular light on a vibrant character's contrasts, nuances, and finesse. Indeed, as Hadrian shows us, being bilingual is not just about speaking two languages: it is about being *between* two languages, having to negotiate the place to be given to each, not adding them up in one's memory but combining their resources and knowing how to use each one at the right moment. Faithful to the intense power of Caesar and Augustus described by Roman historians, Hadrian also relied on Greek Stoics to guide his life and poets to transform his beloved Antinous into a god.

Not all multilinguals are lucky enough to rule the Roman Empire. Not all bilinguals are as brilliant as Hadrian was. Multilingualism is not a determinism nor the promise of an exceptional destiny. Nevertheless, it is worth looking back in history

---

[87] Yourcenar (1951).

to see if speaking or reading several languages does not consolidate other qualities. Firstly, finesse; as the meanings of the Greek word *logos* suggest, a language is also a system of thought; to speak several languages is to open to multiple ways of thinking, to consider different points of view, and to grasp more nuances. Then, there is creativity: To master a language is to possess the cultural memory it carries and the centuries of history deposited in its words. As Charles Baudelaire said, "To manage a language skillfully is to practice a kind of evocative sorcery."[88] Each language has music, poetry, and images, a breeding ground for artists and creators. Finally, tolerance: Learning a language means having the patience to say less precisely what you could say easily in your language; it means having the humility of taking a step towards the other that no automatic translator can do for you.

Multilingualism, a school of finesse, creativity, and tolerance: This is the hypothesis this chapter wishes to put forward for reflection in the light of historical examples. It would be illusory to draw up a composite portrait of the multilingual individual, as each case is unique: People speak or write French and English, Turkish or Chinese, whether they have been doing so since childhood or not, with varying degrees of proficiency and in a variety of situations. The idea of a standard portrait that erases differences would close our eyes to the notion that makes the subject so interesting: that of the gap—the gap between languages, between oneself and others, between the written and the spoken word. To be multilingual is to have to constantly negotiate a complex and changing gap, to be understood as well as possible while making the most of this richness; it is to tame the very notion of difference, to feel closer to that which is distant from us, the distance depending on the step we are prepared to take.

However, does this prove that speaking languages develops our curiosity or that the curious are interested in languages? Does mastering languages make us more subtle, or does it make us virtuosos of valuable tools but not enough to think well? Does history also have simpler multilinguals, such as the Germanic enslaved people captured by the Romans to dig mines? As for the

---

[88] Baudelaire (1869).

multilingualism of Caesar, Mussolini, and Amin Dada, it preserved them in no way from intolerance. Conversely, language is not the only gateway to multicultural competence: Not all readers of Russian novels are Russian speakers, nor can all children with a passion for Egyptian gods decipher hieroglyphics.

It is important to remain cautious and avoid systemic thinking on such a complex subject. Historical facts can give us a pragmatic approach to the subject. At a time when multilinguals account for an estimated 60% of the world's population, it would be a pity not to look in the rear-view mirror of history. If this chapter introduces new perspectives for analyzing multilingual experiences and makes its benefits more evident, it will have achieved its goal.

Multilingualism as a school of finesse

Being able to translate or speak a language is certainly not enough to define intelligence. Children aged four to six learn languages more quickly than adults. We can also know languages as a daily need without realizing the conceptual richness they open. The 16th-century French and Portuguese explorers of America understood this well: To form interpreters between themselves and the native peoples, they took illiterate street children and placed them with a tribe for a few years; when the sailors returned, the children spoke both languages. The latter were called *truchements*: the word became synonymous with intermediary.[89] This reflects the low regard for Multilingualism beyond its technical value. For most people, its practical value outweighed its value in terms of more remarkable finesse.

It would also be too easy to draw from history an example of a language prodigy like Jean-François Champollion to list the languages he mastered. His genius was deciphering hieroglyphics, not mastering so many languages, even if his passion for languages led him to his discovery. A gift for languages can quickly become sterile if it is not put into practice, caught up in the technical virtuosity of the tools that languages are. The polyglots William Jones, Giuseppe Mezzofanti, and Emil Krebs, brilliant though they were,

---

[89] Havard (2019).

did not leave the same mark as Champollion. Developing uncommon finesse presupposes something more than Multilingualism and is not a function of the number of languages one knows.

Michel de Montaigne is a case in point for whom Latin, Ancient Greek, French, and Gascon were paths of access to turns of thought rather than scholarly passions. In his *Essais,* he writes: "Que le gascon y aille, si le français n'y peut aller."[90] When, in the common language, he lacks the words to express a precise idea, he takes the liberty of using Gascon words. The Latin and Greek verses that punctuate his speech, often inserted into his French syntax, show that thoughts, often moral, seem better summed up in Latin while 16th-century French enabled him to develop his reasoning. Montaigne provides the names of very few authors he quotes; we can see that he seeks precision rather than erudition. Each language has nuances: French says *connaissance*, sometimes *savoir*, whereas English always says knowledge. However, it has only one word for liberty and freedom and none for success.

Philosophers have often used foreign languages as external points of view on the language of their thought or as reservoirs of concepts. Friedrich Nietzsche notes the temporal distance provided by ancient languages: "I do not know what meaning classical studies could have for our time if they were not untimely—that is to say, acting counter to our time and thereby acting on our time and, let us hope, for the benefit of a time to come."[91] We could make the same point for today's languages in space: A new language gives access to new nuances and a more complex worldview. Trivial examples are the number of words to describe snow in Inuit, cheeses in French, and kinds of pasta in Italian. We should not forget the effects of etymology, such as culture, in German *Bildung,* word-for-word training, while French and English retain the agricultural metaphor of Latin. Moreover, let us not forget polysemy: Nietzsche is interested in the Greek *archê*, which is both *beginning* and *command*;[92]

---

[90] Montaigne (1580).
[91] Nietzsche (1874).
[92] Nietzsche (1873).

what appears to us as two meanings in one word was, in fact, only two effects of meaning for a single concept; every language has its associations of ideas.

Being multilingual also means knowing that words are not things. It means breaking away from the obviousness of our native language to take a fresh look at the world and understand it more objectively. Suppose there is an international science language. In that case, researchers also think in their native tongue, like Galileo navigating between Italian and Latin and Einstein between German and English, among other languages. But we must be wary of drawing too direct a conclusion: Einstein used to say that he thought beyond words,[93] which is not to say that speaking languages did not accustom him to the reflex of thinking *differently*. Indeed, let us not forget that scientific concepts are defined with the help of natural language. When the French mathematician Nicolas Bourbaki created the concept of barrel spaces,[94] he first thought of wine barrels. Language carries images and metaphors, all models in which the world is conceived. Today, voices are being raised to highlight the danger of monolingual sciences.[95] Marie Curie was fluent in three languages renowned for their complexity: Polish, Russian, and French. The relationship between science and multilingualism merits further research.

It is worth noting, however, that the contribution of multilingualism may not be so evident in all areas. Beyond its day-to-day usefulness, it benefits the Mediterranean merchant of the Middle Ages more than the Paris St-Germain soccer player transferred to a Spanish club. Commercial exchanges require mutual trust and understanding more deeply rooted in language than the technical gestures of a sporting discipline. It would seem helpful to emphasize the principle of synergy: Multilingualism only brings added value if implemented in a relevant context that will enhance it—that is, a context in which multilingual competence is not just helpful in expressing oneself but a context in which it multiplies

---

[93] Jakobson (1982).
[94] Bourbaki (1971).
[95] Jaime (2022).

another competence. This is the case in the social sciences, and even the exact sciences, where defining concepts is crucial. Business and diplomacy questions exchanges, equivalence, reciprocity, bridges between cultures, and negotiating values. In the case of soccer, multilingual competence is undoubtedly more helpful to the coach, whose profession relies heavily on the use of the spoken word. He could take advantage of cultural differences: coach in English, *entraîneur* in French, and *allenatore* in Italian, respectively, refer to the ideas of guide, pace, and strength.

Despite this, research continues to confirm the value of teaching languages from childhood onwards.[96] Multilingual children receive a more complex experience that tends to make their brains more plastic and more able to adapt to novelty and what differs from their familiar world in all domains. The bilingual path has been the foundation of classical studies since ancient Rome. Rome was a bilingual society, including at levels less affluent than Hadrian's. Roman teachers were often Greek slaves; bilingual Latin-Greek textbooks have survived; Romans from good families never missed a study trip to Greece, like Cicero in Rhodes; and reading Lysias and Demosthenes was crucial to mastering the art of speech in the context of trials.[97] Both languages—*utraque lingua*, to say it like the Ancients in the singular[98]—are the key to the whole of knowledge and even to the whole of society, as since Alexander, Greek was the language of exchanges in the East. Bilingualism was so natural that Julius Caesar said his last words—"You too, my son"—in Greek rather than in his native language, Latin.[99] For a Roman, studies conducted solely in Latin would have been incomplete.

Studies based on ancient languages lasted long after the fall of the Roman Empire. Latin remained the language of clerics and scholars in the Middle Ages and the basis of elite courses until the 20th century, in an overly exclusive way that lost its flavor. The absence of frequent oral use has led to these languages becoming so-called dead

---

[96] Byalistok (2017).
[97] Marrou (1948).
[98] Dubuisson (1981).
[99] Suetonius (c. 120).

languages: a course in grammar and translation, where the preoccupation with technical precision risks losing the taste for language to the most sizable number. Indeed, true multilinguals do not translate Spanish into English or German into Russian: They handle their languages like a carpenter handles his tools; they do not analyze each word after "putting it in order" and giving it a grammatical label. Most of the time, they rely on intuition rather than technical analysis. To teach exclusively through grammar is to risk confusing multilingualism with elitism, a narrow vision. Even in modern languages, the benefits of multilingualism are sometimes obscured by didactic archaisms, while pedagogies that emphasize the cultural and social skills opened by language are emerging.[100]

However, as early as the 17th century, thinkers such as John Amos Comenius placed modern languages at the heart of studies without denying Latin. Born in the Czech Republic, he studied in Germany, taught in Poland, and spent the rest of his life in exile in Holland.[101] For him, speaking several languages—if possible, more than two—was the condition for access to universal knowledge: he calls it theosophy, i.e., wisdom from God. Since the return of Christ was imminent (1668 or 1672 were possible dates), men had to try to understand one another and remedy the confusion that had existed since Babel. Comenius had experienced the violence of the Thirty Years' War head-on: Even if the violence was linked to religious conflict, he believed that languages could facilitate understanding of others. Wittgenstein later wrote, "The limits of my language mean the limits of my world."[102] We can infer that what we cannot say escapes us and leads to frustration, which can lead to violence. For Comenius, languages do not end in themselves: speaking a language gives me access to other people's worldviews. It enables me to see our common humanity behind the veil of cultural differences. His aims can be seen in his method: To arrive at words, he starts with images, the shared experience; to teach these words, he writes dialogues and situation scenarios; his progressive pedagogy

---

[100] Gohard-Radenkovic (2004).
[101] Courrier de l'UNESCO (1957).
[102] Wittgenstein (1921).

guides the student from images to the thoughts of the great authors. Our language textbooks are already there. It is a pity that the few fantasies of his millenarian visions led greats like Denis Diderot to ridicule him as a delusional mystic and cause him to lose the credit he deserves. The growing importance of multilingualism today leads UNESCO and historians of ideas to redress this misunderstanding.[103]

Comenius' wish for universal education may not have been fulfilled, but the courts of Europe unknowingly applied his principles. During the modern era, diplomatic missions were the preserve of the nobility: among the sovereigns of Europe, it was essential to understand each other. Marriages often followed treaties signed after wars: Louis XIV married his Spanish cousin Maria Theresa of Austria; Louis XV married Marie Leszczynska, a Pole; Louis XVI married Marie Antoinette, an Austrian. In his early years, the future Louis XVI received a comprehensive education from Monsieur du Berry: in addition to various physical and scientific subjects, he learned Latin, German, Italian, and English.[104] Why teach the future king of France languages when French was the official language of diplomacy at the time? Moreover, it was a fashionable language from Catherine the Great's Russia to Benjamin Franklin's America.[105]

Languages give access to the intimacy of a culture, to the interiority of a people, to the original version of a discourse or reflection. Without seeking to explain everything in this way, we can risk the idea that each language is the bearer of a particular state of mind, in which the organized character of German is opposed to the taste for the exceptional in French and the pragmatism of English, so simple to conjugate. Multilinguals feel this state of mind more than they can explain, but they would only have one if languages were strictly equivalent. In this sense, languages foster intercultural competence and foster mutual understanding.

Reflections on education in the Age of Enlightenment culminated more than a century later in the Third Republic's reforms of compulsory public education. At the same time as diminishing the

---

[103] Caravolas (2009).
[104] Girault de Coursac (1995).
[105] Fumaroli (2001).

influence of regional languages to unify the nation, the Republic gave the most considerable number of people access to knowledge previously reserved for the elite. Against tensions with Germany, modern languages became an issue of power: The French noticed that they were falling behind their neighbors.[106]

Let us delve into the essence of finesse: Languages do not necessarily make us smarter, but they enrich our understanding with more nuances. The debate on whether curiosity fuels language learning or vice versa can be set aside. Instead, let us focus on the virtuous circle: The more we delve into languages, the more we learn about others, and the more our world becomes transparent and precise. This language-learning journey empowers us, making the benefits of languages more pronounced.

Children's faster language learning abilities undoubtedly owe this to reasons linked to brain development and their leisure time. However, their curiosity about the world, adaptability, and imagination are particularly noteworthy. In a way, they lead by example, inviting us to connect imagination and the gift of language and explore the links between multilingualism and creativity.

Multilingualism as a school of creativity

Seeing languages as a way of learning to be creative is surprising at first sight. Languages are normative and prescriptive: they have their rules, their conjugations, their declensions, their exceptions, and their conventions. Poorly mastered grammar threatens us with misunderstandings: In French, it is the sometimes-subtle step between *vous* and *tu*, masculine and feminine. It is the negation that can reverse the meaning of a sentence. Learning a language requires care, listening, and attention rather than reinventing the rules. Languages require repeated effort instead of the painter's fantasy or the poet's inspiration.

Nevertheless, poetry in the West begins with a multilingual text. Homer's Greek epics contain lexical and syntactic elements from

---

[106] Dubois (2017).

various dialects, including Aeolian, Dorian, and Ionian.[107] Several hypotheses have been put forward: These dialects reflect the travels of the aede, who recited his poems as he went from village to village; they reflect oral transmission in a variety of regions; they are an aesthetic choice on the part of the poet. Whatever the case, the richness of Homer's language offers a diversity worthy of Ulysses' travels. It is singular that the people who referred to all foreign languages by the word "barbarian"—implying that foreign languages are an incomprehensible suite of sounds—should have taken as their constant reference a poet with such a mixed language.

The history of English literature begins with a multilingual. The London poet Geoffrey Chaucer wrote in Latin and Anglo-Norman French, as did the literati of the 14th century; however, he gave the English language literary dignity with *The Book of the Duchess*, a tribute to Blanche of Lancaster, and his other works, including the famous *Canterbury tales*.[108] In Italy, he is thought to have seen the poet Petrarch and the writer Boccaccio, who were not content with Latin. Geoffrey Chaucer lived between languages in the sense that he was able to transfer the literary prestige of Latin and French to English, then the language of the people: He acted as an intermediary, an arbiter, showing the people of his time the English language from a literary and not just a practical angle, giving it a new charm, a new dignity. It took a multilingual to bridge the gap between languages and to ring the bell for English literature. It is also said that he and the French chronicler Jean Froissart were responsible for arranging the marriage of the Englishman Richard II to a French princess: Languages opened him up to original, unusual situations, contributing to his creativity.

In France, the poets of the Pléiade drew their inspiration from Latin and Italian. Literary creation rarely occurs *ex nihilo*: it comes from revivals, transpositions, and cross-fertilizations. "Cueillez dès aujourd'hui les roses de la vie," Pierre de Ronsard advises Hélène,[109] just as Horace said to Leuconoé: "Seize the day, without trusting the

---

[107] Haug (2007).
[108] Crépin (2004).
[109] Ronsard (1578).

world to tomorrow."[110] With the requisite cultural transpositions, commonplaces pass from one language to another, gaining a new nuance with each passage. Joachim du Bellay, known as the author of the manifesto *Défense et illustration de la langue française*,[111] published ten years after the ordinance of Villers-Cotterêts, himself authored poems in Latin and borrowed several passages from the *Dialogo delle lingue* by Sperone Speroni,[112] who defended Tuscan Italian against Latin. The very name Pléiade is Greek, as are many of their allusions and references; the sonnet form comes from Petrarch's Italy. Multilingualism allows for permanent cultural transfers.

Before the Pléiade, François Rabelais, a literary pioneer, fearlessly paved the way, not hesitating to enrich the French lexicon by drawing on the languages he knew. His courage and creativity gave us tohu-bohu, a term from biblical Hebrew that refers to the state of the world just created. We owe the renaissance of French to authors like Rabelais who, far from being stuck in their mother tongue, spoke many others, despite the resistance of some, such as the printer Henri Estienne, to the influence of Italian. Rabelais's boldness and innovation continue to inspire us in literature and language.[113] Humanists could borrow words, poetic forms, images, and ideas from this neighboring and related language to enrich and bring their language to life.

Defending French meant exposing it to foreign influences, letting it breathe, enriching it with borrowings that were gradually acclimatized to the language, validated, or rejected by general usage, sometimes tamed, sometimes forgotten. As with English words in today's French, speakers experiment, accepting some words, resisting others, some disappearing in fashion, and others grafting themselves onto the language to the point where their origins are forgotten. Who remembers that French owes the word *soldat* to 16th-century Italian? Multilinguals contribute to these exchanges through which a language breathes, lives, and evolves.

---

[110] Horace (23 BC).
[111] Du Bellay (1549).
[112] Speroni (1542).
[113] Boudou (2001).

Literary creation owes a great deal to them: there is no shortage of examples. Many poets have been translators, such as Leconte de Lisle with Homer, Gérard de Nerval with Goethe's *Faust*, and Charles Baudelaire with Edgar Poe's *Tales of the Grotesque and Arabesque*. Baudelaire translates the word *goldfish* as *Poisson d'Or* instead of *poisson rouge*: such a tasty mistake is a poetic find.[114] The exercise of translation, right down to its sideways steps, shows the gap where the distance from one language to another is measured in diverse ways of perceiving the same objects: it enriches our view. Stéphane Mallarmé was a teacher of English. Paul Verlaine and Arthur Rimbaud spent several bohemian months in England, teaching French. In his prose poem *Aube* (Dawn), Arthur Rimbaud speaks not of a waterfall but of a *wasserfall*, which echoes the verb *s'écheveler* (to dishevel); elsewhere, he borrows words from his Ardennes dialect, as in the *flasche* in *Bateau ivre* (Drunken boat), which replaces the puddle. The foreign word adds a touch of strangeness, like a spice that spices up the rest of the dish: multilingual poets apply the Baudelairean theorem that "the beautiful is always bizarre."[115] They draw on other languages to make their words original, harmonious, and rich in new nuances. Multilingualism opens the way to a particular type of creativity based on cross-fertilization and the interplay of echoes, a point worthy of study.

From words to images, from words to sounds, there is only one step. Renaissance historians have shown the reciprocal influence of architects and poets: Each building is a stone poem with its structure, ornaments, and figures.[116] The influence of Italy led to transfers of knowledge and invitations to artists: At Le Clos-Lucé, Leonardo da Vinci proposed his inventions to Francis I; Louis XIV invited Jean-Baptiste Lulli, who Frenchified his name to Lully. Thanks to Venetian glassmakers, the Hall of Mirrors at the Château de Versailles was built: French agents took advantage of a strike to encourage them to share their secrets. Conversely, several

---

[114] Pécastaing (2011).
[115] Baudelaire (1855).
[116] Pauwels (2002).

17th-century French painters—Nicolas Poussin, Claude Gellé, and Simon Vouet—lived and worked in Italy. André Chastel writes that there would have been no French painting as we know it without Italian painting.[117] Languages were bridges, vectors, tools for the passage of knowledge, styles, and representations from one country to another: The Italian word *disegno,* which designates both *drawing* and *thought,* enabled Nicolas Poussin to formulate his conception of the painter as an intellectual, as opposed to an artisan.

On another level, Vincent van Gogh deserves to be mentioned: the tortuous yet poetic style of his letters written in French invites us to draw parallels with his paintings.[118] In search of the light of the South, this man from the North was looking for an elsewhere, a more profound expression for which the habits, practices, and ways of his time and milieu were insufficient.

Aesthetic trends permeate all the arts, and artists often frequent the same circles. In Montmartre, Guillaume Apollinaire, a French poet of Polish origin, met the Spaniard Pablo Picasso. Claude Lévi-Strauss remarks in his essay *Race et Histoire*[119] that the most refined civilizations, with the most complex technologies, did not have an intrinsic superiority but rather a capacity to embrace outside influences by playing the role of crossroads. This is true of Babylon, Baghdad, Andalusia, Samarkand, Venice, Vienna, Paris, and New York. Nevertheless, are not multilingual crossroads incarnate? In them, languages and cultures intersect, measure, and enrich each other. The parallel between city worlds and man worlds is tempting.

Linguistic richness enriches science and technology. The epic of zero is a fine example of this. If multilinguals were content to seek equivalents from one language to another, European scholars in the Middle Ages would not have adopted the Arab zero borrowed from India. In addition to this new number, *ṣifr,* which gave rise to the French words *chiffre* and *zéro,* Europeans adopted a far more efficient system of writing numbers than the Romans, which would not have allowed mathematics to flourish in the West. Passages from one

---

[117] Chastel (1993).
[118] Coquery (2023).
[119] Lévi-Strauss (1952).

culture to another are not mere transfers but catalysts, revealing new possibilities in the host culture: soon, zero-enabled binary calculation, computing, the Internet, and social networks. Alongside this grand epic, we can envision, on a more modest scale, the countless fertile exchanges of ideas facilitated by the multilingual skills of explorers, the curious, and pioneers. These individuals gained a deeper understanding of others and their visions of the world and championed the vast potential unlocked through such exchanges. In this sense, multilinguals are more than polyglots, and multilingualism is more than a toolbox. It is an open-minded attitude to difference, which means not seeking to systematically reduce it to the known but perceiving its explosive force.

In the political sphere, explosions can be revolutions: the friction of languages sometimes produces sparks. The Founding Fathers of the United States included a considerable number of multilinguals. Benjamin Franklin spoke French, English, and Italian; his impeccable adaptation to the mores of the French court was a determining factor in his influence and Louis XVI's entry into the war on the side of the thirteen colonies. John Adams read the Latin and Greek classics in their original language; few translations were available on this ocean side. He mastered French and traveled to France and the Netherlands, where he negotiated the support of Dutch bankers. Thomas Jefferson, the future American ambassador to France, was also an avid reader of Latin and Greek authors, who were the key to the texts of ancient political philosophy, from Aristotle to Cicero. In a world dominated by monarchies, ancient authors provided the Founding Fathers with models for republics and democracies, from which the Constitution still in force today was written, alongside other influences such as the Englishman John Locke and the Frenchman Montesquieu. The young French Republic also used ancient models to wipe out the monarchy; the Bolsheviks used a German thinker, Karl Marx, to convince the working classes to overthrow the Russian Tsar. Ancient languages provide a step back in time, and modern languages a step back in space.

Benjamin Franklin designed the lightning rod, bifocal spectacles, a reformed alphabet, and a glass harmonica; Thomas Jefferson drew inspiration from Palladio's Italian mansions to design the plans for Monticello, where he maintained his botanical garden; John Adams was also a builder. Multilinguals are often jacks of all trades, and cognitive science research tends to show their versatility and ability to multitask.[120]

At the start of this section, we mentioned the normativity of languages. Let us not forget that constraint itself is fertile since it pushes us to our limits, forcing us to draw on our resources. However, multilinguals also show us that languages are a breeding ground for new combinations and pioneering synergies. In the background, learning foreign languages leads us to develop adaptive strategies and even to question our categories of thought, mainly when the foundations are different, such as between Latin and Semitic languages, Southeast Asian languages, Oceanic or Amerindian languages. Nor should we forget that we experience our discoveries, emotions, decisions, and relationships through language: The plurality of languages is not a purely intellectual phenomenon but a panoply of filters and zooms through which our experience of the world can be multiplied.

We have spoken of multilingual minds as crossroads of languages, but crossroads are not always well-reputed. There are those of the theater, Hecate's in *MacBeth*, and those of comedy, where you risk bumping into Dom Juan. Interpreters are not exempt from suspicion of treason or espionage because they have power over languages that elude us, and kings entrust them with truths that are sometimes more precious than coins. In times of crisis, the foreigner is the designated traitor, the most convincing scapegoat. Is it not at these moments that the multilingual can play the role of cultural link, showing us that the barbarian is none other than an allophone?

Multilingualism as a school of tolerance

The vaccine against intolerance has yet to be found. We know Thomas Jefferson's contradictions, and the fingerprints of black children in the bricks of Monticello remind us that he did not escape

---

[120] Poarch & Bialystok (2015).

all the prejudices of his time. It is easy to think we understand others just because we know some of their words when each person handles language in their own way. The litotes in English politeness, the euphemism in the U.S., and the irony in France are not grasped on the first try. Learning through clichés, such as the Eiffel Tower, a baguette, and a beret as images in the French textbook, or Big Ben and the double-decker bus in the English textbook, is also tempting. It can be tempting to boast about the number of languages one can speak to impress others, while the degree of mastery and finesse in each language is more significant.

These precautions invite us to clarify our topic. We have suggested that multilingualism is mastering and living in or *between* languages. Beyond the technical aspects of finesse and creativity, we can consider the added value of multilingualism—specifically, its ethical significance in building fruitful relationships with people from other cultures. In other words, how can embracing multilingualism educate and inspire us, making us better people? Where can we take multilingualism to nourish our humility rather than our arrogance, emphasizing the importance of humility over arrogance in the context of multilingualism to align with the chapter's goal?

Comparing Marco Polo and Christopher Columbus may provide an initial answer. Both were Italians from multilingual merchant families; both thirsted for the new, for discovery and, let us face it, for riches. Both were looking for a way to the end of the world, and the latter had read many of the former's stories. However, their attitudes toward foreigners differed profoundly. Marco Polo inquired about the names of the places he passed through on the Silk Road, noting them in his notebook; Christopher Columbus gave the islands he landed on a Spanish name. When he arrived in China, Marco Polo placed himself at the service of the great Khan Kubilai, serving as his spyglass pointed at the West, translating Latin and Italian documents for him while feeding his curiosity about Asia. This emphasis on curiosity and listening in Marco Polo's approach highlights the ethical value of well-understood multilingualism.

In contrast, Christopher Columbus wished to spread the Gospel in the New World and kidnapped five hundred Arawaks to sell them as enslaved people in Spain. Marco Polo learned four languages with their alphabets and served as Kubilai's messenger throughout the empire for seventeen years; Christopher Columbus planted the Spanish flag before setting sail again for Europe. This black-and-white picture needs to be qualified: Kubilai was more authoritarian with Marco Polo than the Bahamians were with Christopher Columbus; the balance of power was not the same. Nonetheless, each drew up their model based on curiosity and listening in one case and on the quest for immediate profit in the other.

The New World exploration provided something for humanists to consider, starting with Michel de Montaigne. His encounter with the Cannibals prompted him to decenter, and to him, the apparent cruelty of the warriors of Brazil calls us to realize the even greater cruelty of the Portuguese, who buried their enemies alive up to their heads before riddling them with arrows.[121] "Everyone calls barbaric what differs from his customs."[122] We are always someone else's barbarian, and recognizing that strangeness is merely an effect of perspective invites us to find common humanity beneath the garment of difference. This demonstrates Terence's principle, which heralded the spirit of the Enlightenment centuries in advance: "I am man, and I consider nothing human to be foreign to me."[123] The encounter with the other initiates me into an encounter with the universal.

"I want and intend you to learn the languages perfectly: first the Greek, as Quintilian wants, secondly the Latin, and then the Hebrew for the Holy Letters, and the Chaldean and Arabian likewise; and that you form your style, as for the Greek, in imitation of Plato, as for the Latin, in Cicero."[124] In the educational program outlined by Gargantua for his son Pantagruel, languages are not pretexts for pedantry (that would be the mistake of Thubal Holopherne, who favors quantity of knowledge), but the key to access to the humanities: literature, philosophy, theology. In his following novel,[125] François Rabelais shows that this education opens the door to discussion, to the search for solutions other than violence: Faced

---

[121] Montaigne (1580).
[122] Montaigne (1588).
[123] Terence (Circa 163 BC).
[124] Rabelais (1532).
[125] Rabelais (1534).

with Picrochole's aggression, the enlightened king Grandgousier tries diplomacy and only uses force once this option has been ruled out. Languages teach us patience and the effort to understand others; multilingualism opens the door to an ethic of dialogue. In a debate, we seek to win; in a conversation, we seek a subtle form of pleasure; but in dialogue, we take advantage of our differences to collaborate in the search for a truth or a solution. Multilinguals are predisposed to dialogue because they know how words can be a source of misunderstanding and innovative ideas.

This idea of multilingualism as a gateway to the humanities and, therefore, to ethics is reflected in the idea of the Republic of Letters. From the 15th to the end of the 18th century, the term described a vast network of epistolary exchanges between scholars in Europe and the New World.[126] French, English, German, and Spanish scholars first met in Italian universities; their exchanges continued in Latin correspondence, building bridges between cultures and promoting the circulation of new ideas. The Dutchman Erasmus wrote to the Englishman Thomas More. Since he met his daughter Margaret Roper, who was educated in Latin and Greek, Erasmus considered girls' education helpful. Far from perverting or diverting them from domestic duties, reading the great texts elevates their spirit and virtue, which can only benefit the husband. The exchanges between the brilliant Isotta Nogarola and her master, Guarino of Verona, show that such an idea was far from fashionable. Erasmus' exchanges with the great minds of Europe nurtured his satirical and critical spirit, giving him the perspective to understand humanity and cultural specificities better. The university exchange program that bears his name is aptly named, and the replacement of Latin by the various languages of today's countries only serves to further decentralization and mutual understanding.

To speak several languages is to gradually enter the intimacy of culture, giving oneself the means to grasp it from the inside. If, as Hegel says, it is indeed "in words that we think,"[127] speaking another's language can help me understand their mind's subtleties.

---

[126] Simon (2020).
[127] Hegel (1830).

In *De l'Allemagne*, Germaine de Staël remarks that the French interrupt each other more than the Germans.[128] In German, valuable information comes last, whether the verb at the end of a subordinate in *wenn* or the order of ideas in a compound word like *Kaffeetasse*, "cup of coffee." In French, the essential idea is given right from the start. Germaine de Staël sees this as the origin of French conversation and salon culture.

The nuances of languages alert me to cultural differences: in Hebrew and Arabic, conjugation according to gender; in English, the absence of formal politeness in the second person; in Korean, the seven levels of politeness. Would Chinese patent laws be so flexible if learning Mandarin did not require patiently copying thousands of characters? Language also carries taboos, such as the one that hangs over the number four in Chinese (四) and in Japanese (四), where it is a homophone of the word *death* (死). In Japanese, the word "love" appears only in the translation of English novels in the 19th century.

Knowledge of foreign languages does not invite us to simplistic deductions but to applicable precautions: the "truth" for which Gandhi fought has more to do with *right action* than with the truth of the West based on the Latin *veritas*, the adequacy of reality with discourse. Idiomatic expressions do not always have literal translations: guess how the French say, "to take the French leave?" Of course, *filer à l'anglaise*. Last, language conveys a concept of time, which E. T. Hall has shown to be essential to intercultural understanding between monochronic and polychronic cultures.[129]

Learning a new language also shows us the links and what our language owes to foreigners. To Italian, French owes *bagatelle*, *grotesque*, *citrouille*; to Arabic, *algèbre*, *sucre*, *albatros*; to Persian, *châle*, *jasmin*, *tambour*; to Hindi, *coton*, *shampooing*, *pyjama*. Likewise, learning a language can shed light on specific place names: Gibraltar, Guadalquivir, and Madrid. Portugal's very name comes from Arabic. In the end, foreigners are not so foreign to us. We understand the symbolism of first names, Layla, which means night in Arabic, and Yu, rain in Chinese. Foreign words are no longer buzzing, and

---

[128] de Staël (1813).
[129] Hall (1983).

foreign writing no longer scribbles. Learning Chinese helps us get accustomed to different sounds, which can help us become more sensitive to Beijing opera, which differs significantly from Vienna's or Milan's. The language introduces us to the sensibility of a culture.

The idea that mastery of a foreign language can lead to a better understanding of others and a more tolerant world, already present in the 17th century with Comenius, inspired the project of international schools in the 20th century. The International School of Geneva was founded in 1924 to meet the needs of civil servants working for the International Labour Office, which had been established by the League of Nations. Its founding occurred against the backdrop of the emergence of international organizations aimed at fostering dialogue between nations to prevent a recurrence of the disaster of the Great War. The school initially comprised three teachers and eight students. Other establishments had been created as early as the end of the 19th century: The International College at Spring Grove, open from 1866 to 1889, was born of a reflection on the advantages of multilingual education, based on the idea that young people should be prepared as early as possible for language differences, to avoid them becoming barriers.

International schools sprang up after World War II against corporate internationalization and growing trade. Parents' aims could be pragmatic, such as providing an alternative to the state education system or enabling their children to build up an international network; growing up among pupils from diverse backgrounds and horizons helps to develop an international mindset at an early age, sensitive to cultural differences. The Yew Chung International Schools (from 1932), the European Schools (from 1953), and the United World Colleges (from 1963) are three examples of networks promoting this spirit. Mary Hayden and Jeff Thompson have produced an enlightening summary of these networks for UNESCO.[130] We could see their ancestor in the prestigious Galatasaray Lycée, created in 1868 with Victor Duruy's help at Sultan Abdülaziz's request. The teaching of French and other languages and the welcoming of Muslim pupils and Jewish and

---

[130] Hayden & Thompson (2010).

Christian ones invite some parallels. One could trace this back to the *écoles des jeunes de langues* established by Jean-Baptiste Colbert to enhance French influence in the Mediterranean, which has evolved into today's Institut National des Langues et Civilisations Orientales de Paris (INALCO). Underlying national interests do not erase the desire to take foreigners into account.

In short, multilingualism invites us to be tolerant because it helps us put ourselves in the other person's shoes. By borrowing their language, we put on their garment of words. We take on another voice: some even say another personality as if each language spoken was a role played. The word "person" comes from the Latin *persona*, meaning the theatrical mask that carries the sound of the actor's voice: To speak a language is, therefore, to play a social role without any nuance of falsity. The Portuguese writer Fernando Pessoa, whose surname rightly means "the person," provides a symbolic example: raised in an Irish school in South Africa, he wrote in Portuguese or English, depending on his inspirations. Depending on the situation, he used different heteronyms to express the multiple facets of his personality.[131] Multilingualism can serve as a form of role-play that helps us understand the world, express it, and interact with it more versatilely. It fosters tolerance and appreciation for diverse cultures and situations.

Finally, addressing the other person in their language is an effort, a politeness that no automatic translator can replace. It is a symbolic step, like an offering. Stammering in a new language, experiencing the frustration of words missing to express thought, and feeling like a beginner again, or even an idiot, invites humility and empathy for foreigners for whom learning our language is a daily effort.

Conclusion

As we end our journey, we must emphasize that multilingualism allows neither fast generalizations nor definitive conclusions. Without claiming to be exhaustive, we have attempted to gather examples that may invite reflection, refinement, and research. We

---

[131] Michael (2014).

have grouped these examples according to three benchmark values that can serve as a compass: finesse, creativity, and tolerance. It is incumbent upon us to discern what is anecdotal and what is symptomatic. Furthermore, we should apply our conclusions to our field and observe the relevant synergies.

The professional world is one area where multilingualism can be enlightening, if only because of the ideas underlying the notion of work. In English, *work* emphasizes the result, the finished product, echoing the word *Werk* in German, while in French, the word *travail* comes from the name of a torture instrument. We might also recall the etymology of the word profession, which associates *speech* (Old Latin *fari*) with a public, *official* notion (*pro*): Each profession is defined by rules, certifications, and diplomas, each time taking shape in a particular language that influences its formulation. Multilingualism, therefore, helps to understand professional cultures. Its advantage is that it enables us to grasp the nuances of thought and the underlying images, sometimes unconscious and invisible behind the translation.

Multilingualism is multifaceted: the merchant, the interpreter, the diplomat, the athlete, the tourist, the student, the immigrant worker, the scientist, and the philologist do not all approach multilingualism from the same angle. Multilingualism can be profound, more theoretical, or more lived, more a matter of disinterested passion or well-understood usefulness, and each multilingual profile is unique based on the languages learned or forgotten, with varying degrees of influence from one language on another. Finally, as François Grosjean reminds us, each multilingual uses their language for different purposes and contexts.[132] We can learn another's language to dominate them better or, on the contrary, to understand them better. We can take the story of the Tower of Babel as a symbol of division or, on the contrary, of universal kinship through the memory of an original unity, of which each language is a unique and irreplaceable part. The languages we speak give us access to more nuances and information, but they do not condition our thinking or hinder our freedom.

---

[132] Grosjean (1982).

However, Lawrence of Arabia's character embodies the fear of losing one's identity in the language of the other, of remaining trapped in a *no-man's-land* of in-between languages, in a kind of linguistic schizophrenia.[133] Losing oneself in the other is the significant risk of love—a question especially burning in bicultural couples. On the other hand, in his autobiography *Penser entre les langues (Thinking Between Languages)*, Professor Heinz Wismann paints a picture of a happy and fruitful multilingualism,[134] where the foreign language enables us to see "ourselves as another"[135] and thus become more aware of ourselves in our relations with others. Between these two poles lies a complex spectrum, a geometry of multiple dimensions whose horizons we may never fully grasp.

In any case, the freedom and innumerable potentialities opened by multilingualism create the need for an ethic while simultaneously providing its keys through dialogue, as we have suggested. Multilingualism enables us to interact with a person on multiple levels. Nelson Mandela illustrates it in a sentence: "If you talk to a man in a language he understands, that goes to his head. If you talk to him in his language, that goes to his heart." Multilingualism equips us with more options to refine our interactions with others.

Each of us must reflect on the kind of multilingual individual we aspire to become.

---

[133] Lean (1962).
[134] Wismann (2014).
[135] Ricoeur (1990).

Chapter 3 – Navigating global competencies: Insights from the OECD

Eric Hertzler

We all live in a VUCA environment and face four significant challenges:
1. Protecting our planet and ensuring growth continues to lift billions of people out of poverty;
2. Ensuring maintenance, innovation, and the future of work by maximizing the benefits of future technologies and generative artificial intelligence while minimizing the negative consequences;
3. Managing imbalances and equity by creating an inclusive global economy;
4. Dealing with flows, identity, freedoms, protection, and international cooperation to create more inclusive and sustainable societies.[136]

According to the OECD, this VUCA environment is the framework we must learn to evolve and make the most of it.

In order to live in this interconnected, ever-changing world, the OECD Program for International Student Assessment (PISA) focused on assessing four global competencies for its 2018 data

---

[136] Bennis & Nanus (1987) introduced the VUCA concept to address the leadership and strategic management challenges facing organizations in an ever-changing world.
- Volatility: Refers to the nature and speed of environmental changes. External factors can change rapidly and unpredictably.
- Uncertainty: Refers to the absence of predictability and certainty about the future. Information may be incomplete or changeable, making it difficult to make decisions.
- Complexity: Indicates the multiplicity of factors and interactions that can influence a situation. Situations can be complex, with many interdependent variables.
- Ambiguity: Refers to the difficulty of correctly interpreting situations due to multiple possible interpretations. Information may be contradictory or difficult to interpret.

collection of 15-year-old students.[137] These global skills have since been the subject of some exciting developments, notably in a report by Global Cities and the *OECD Codebook for Global Student Learning Outcomes* published for high school students thanks to a partnership with Harvard Graduate School of Education (Project Zero), supported by the Bloomberg Philanthropies foundation.[138] This report expands on another report, *The Environmental Sustainability Competence toolbox*.[139]

We will examine the contemporary dynamics of global competencies, analyze them, and, lastly, discuss how they are developed professionally.

Historical dynamics of global competencies

Globalization 1.0 to Globalization 4.0

Globalization[140] is in this compression of time and space aimed at overcoming obstacles and barriers, lowering transaction costs, and multiplying exchanges through the implementation of global standards (imposition of the metric system and Greenwich time zones in the 19th century by France and Great Britain, ISO quality standards, diplomatic communication standards, French-English standards, web standards, including specific cultural and linguistic standards seen as a means of prolonging Western cultural domination and in particular the values of Anglo-Saxon Protestantism) with varying degrees of success, as illustrated by the Fordlandia case.[141]

---

[137] OECD (2018).
[138] Tiven et al. (2023).
[139] Borgonovi et al. (2022).
[140] Globalization has been described as an unprecedented compression of time and space, resulting in the intensification of social, political, economic, and cultural interconnections and interdependencies on a global scale (Steger, 2020).
[141] Grandin (2009); Derey (2016).

Since the mid-19th century, we have witnessed four waves of globalization, each accompanied by sociocultural and technological transformations calling for new skills.

Globalization 1.0 runs from the mid-19th century to the First World War. The second industrial revolution, where administrative management thought dominated by Max Weber, Henry Fayol, and Frederick Winslow Taylor, produced a directive management vision in closed systems. This period saw the acceleration of colonialism, which reinforced economic and cultural imperialism, guaranteeing investors' rights to the detriment of democratic rights. The critical skill sought was mass literacy.

At the famous Solvay Conference in 1927, multilingualism was de rigueur.[142] The English language took advantage of the exclusion of Germany and Japan from the League of Nations to impose itself, despite the resistance of French in public international law and international organizations, notably the United Nations, at the end of the Second World War.

Globalization 2.0 began at the end of the Second World War and ended with the collapse of the Eastern bloc, characterized by a bipolar world with market economies dominated by the USA in the West and the growing importance of English on the one hand and the other hand, with planned economies and the ideological domination of the Soviet Union in the newly decolonized states.

Globalization 3.0 from 1989 to the global financial crisis from 2008 to 2012 accelerated the cultural domination of the USA following the collapse of the Soviet empire and created a cross-border financial and virtual space with the advent of a digital world. With the accelerated globalization of value chains, management theorists Clayton Christensen, Gary Hamel, and numerous consultants are promoting agile organizations capable of adapting to ultra-competitive open environments.

---

[142] Gordin (2015).

The challenges of Globalization 4.0[143]

According to Joseph Stiglitz and Dani Rodrik, the last two waves of globalization, as early as 2001, bear the seeds of significant national and global imbalances. Globalization 4.0 is characterized by China—U.S. rivalry, the exponential development of generative artificial intelligence, climate change, and nationalism worldwide. This reflects deep-seated identity crises in a multipolar, polarized world aggravated by the collapse of salaried work. In a volatile environment, acquiring and developing new skills is essential.

- From a geopolitical point of view, a multipolar world requires us to go beyond an ethnocentric, Western world vision. We must first grasp local and global issues to understand and appreciate other people's points of view and worldviews in general.
- From a sociocultural point of view, the dominance of English as a universal language has enabled nations to communicate but not to understand each other. The need for multilingual and intercultural skills emerges.
- From a technological point of view, we live in an increasingly interconnected world. Still, social networks isolate and polarize us: We must engage in open and respectful manners to have effective intercultural interactions.
- From a sustainable point of view, our civilizational models and the methods we live collaboratively show the need to promote collective well-being and sustainable development.

All these challenges have contributed to the definition of new skills: "global" competencies.

United Nations, UNESCO, and OECD promoting "quality education"

To respond to the many challenges facing humanity, such as persistent poverty, lack of education, healthcare, water, and food,

---

[143] "Globalization 4.0 has only just begun, but we are already vastly underprepared for it. Clinging to an outdated mindset and tinkering with our existing processes and institutions will not do." Schwab (2019).

discrimination, violence, weak governance, growing inequality, population displacement, and climate disruption—interdependent, interrelated problems affecting every part of the globe—in 2015, the United Nations defined a reference framework, the Agenda 2030. This agenda applies to all states and public and private institutions in the North and South.

At the heart of this framework are the 17 Sustainable Development Goals (SDGs), successors to the Millennium Development Goals (MDGs) that covered 2000-2015. These goals result from a process that began at the Stockholm Earth Summit in 1972, followed every ten years in Nairobi, Rio in 1992, Johannesburg, and again in Rio in 2012.

2015 marked the convergence between adopting the SDGs, the Addis Ababa Action Plan on Financing for Development, and the Paris climate agreement reached at COP 21. The SDGs are to be implemented by the end of 2030, under the responsibility of each United Nations member state.

SDG 4 on "quality education" affirms the right to education as an inalienable human right. UNESCO considers education a fundamental human right, fostering the full development of the human personality and promoting mutual understanding, tolerance, friendship, and peace.[144]

SDG 4 comprises ten cross-cutting, multidimensional outcome targets. To achieve these goals, United Nations expert groups have defined quantified indicators: Target 4.7 aims to ensure that all students acquire the knowledge and skills necessary to promote sustainable development, human rights, gender equality, a culture of peace, global citizenship, and appreciation of cultural diversity and the contribution of culture to sustainable development.

In 2016, the OECD published a noteworthy report on the framework for analyzing global skills, which was set to be evaluated in the 2018 wave of PISA (Programme for International Student Assessment).

---

[144] UNESCO has published many reports since 2001 on cultural differences and the importance of education in acquiring global skills. See the Reference section.

The OECD's work has been taken up at the European level by the Council of Europe, with the introduction of a Cultural Competence Index in 2018.[145]

OECD Global Competency Analysis is an approach focused on secondary education.

Definition and implementation in the 2018 PISA report

The OECD's four global competencies, which are multidimensional by nature, encompass the ability to:
1) Examine local, global, and intercultural issues;
2) Understand and appreciate the perspectives and worldviews of others;
3) Engage in open, respectful, and effective intercultural interactions across cultures;
4) Act in favor of collective well-being and sustainable development.

For its 2018 data collection of 15-year-old students, the Program for International Student Assessment (PISA) focused on assessing the global skills needed to live in this interconnected, ever-changing world.[146]

To assess these skills, the PISA 2018 survey relied on two instruments:
1) Cognitive assessment, focusing on students' knowledge and cognitive skills;
2) A set of questionnaire items collecting information directly from students, parents, teachers, and school principals. According to school leaders, teachers, and parents, these items explore students' attitudes, knowledge, skills, the learning opportunities available at school, whether a curriculum is dedicated to global skills, and activities to promote these skills.

---

[145] The Council of Europe Reference Framework on Competencies for Democratic Culture led to further developments and resources.
[146] Ramos & Schleicher (2018).

The OECD's assessment of the global skills of 15-year-old students raises the question of how to develop these skills in an educational context. Teaching these skills requires establishing a common language underpinned by three essential principles.

The first principle for establishing a common language involves pinpointing essential concepts like "common good territory" or "sustainable development." This principle mandates the generalization of such knowledge and encourages deterritorialization, aiming to create a transnational common language transcending specific geographic and disciplinary boundaries. This approach facilitates more transparent and effective communication across different regions and sectors, fostering a shared understanding essential for global cooperation.

The second principle, transdisciplinarity, emphasizes not restricting knowledge to a single discipline. This means breaking down traditional boundaries between fields of study to allow for more comprehensive interactions. By deterritorializing knowledge—freeing it from the confines of specific disciplines—we can foster richer interactions and enhance our understanding of the world's complex interconnections. This approach promotes a deeper understanding and encourages innovative solutions to emerge from integrating diverse perspectives.

The third principle seeks to transform knowledge into a social skill, building upon the foundation laid by the previous principle. It entails utilizing the disseminated knowledge as a basis for "living together" despite differences. This approach demands that we engage with complexity to imbue transversality with meaning and foster interdisciplinarity. Doing so, we deepen our understanding across various fields and enhance our ability to collaborate effectively in diverse social contexts.

Teaching global skills is inseparable from citizenship education for action. Teaching citizenship involves participating in activities and experiences that explore our territory, combining a local and international perspective. Citizen training involves action, experience, and study because the knowledge taught is an educational tool. From this perspective, education aims to build actions that mobilize different actors to develop territorial, intercultural, sustainable, and durable intelligence. Education for citizenship is based on the diversity of cultural models, fostering mutual understanding and the values of friendliness and civility in an open, democratic society. This educational action, initiated by the world's problems, is based on the diversity of cultural models, making the school a social and educational place where the values of friendliness and civility are built in an open and democratic society.

Global competencies from a *Francophone* perspective

During the decolonization movements, Senghor and Césaire created a Francophone space in which universities, member states, and peoples reflected on the richness of their shared heritage. Emerging from the aftermath of colonialism, the Organisation Internationale de la Francophonie is a pluralistic, diverse, and intercultural supranational space grouping 84 states and governments sharing the French language and universal values.[147] Its institutional project is based on university cooperation with players such as the Agence Universitaire de la Francophonie and Senghor University in Alexandria, making education a significant lever for development. As a pluralistic, diverse, and intercultural supranational entity, the Francophonie addresses sustainable development objectives through multilateral cooperation, emphasizing interculturality, education for sustainable development, new technologies, human rights, and the inclusion of vulnerable populations. Over the decades, the French-speaking world has responded to the Sustainable Development Goals through multilateral cooperation, prioritizing intercultural issues, cultural and linguistic diversity, education for sustainable development, new technologies, human rights, the inclusion of vulnerable populations, and gender equality in training and enterprise.[148]

---

[147] Charte de la Francophonie (2005)
[148] The Association des Universités entièrement de langue française was created in 1961, followed by the Agence de coopération culturelle et technique in March 1970, then replaced in 1998 by the Agence Universitaire Francophone. At the Versailles Summit in 1986, the first Francophone

In several African countries, for example, where education needs to be more adapted to the environment to avoid rapid school dropout, developing these skills is much more challenging. Education should consider cultural diversities and values, reinforcing sustainable development and heritage-based conflict resolution. Global competencies, defined in the context of SDG 4, represent an essential lever for achieving these objectives. However, questions remain as to whether these skills are a means of imposing a "Western model" or "Western standards," how they translate into fundamental interactions between individuals, and how they apply to local, global, and intercultural problems. Can multiculturalism and multilingualism strengthen these skills and foster new interactions? These questions underline the need to examine the values, spaces, and contexts in which these skills are developed.

The need to acquire new skills throughout life

In a VUCA context, it is essential to make decision-makers and managers aware of the challenges inherent in a constantly changing environment. Understanding and acknowledging volatility, uncertainty, complexity, and ambiguity can help inform strategic decision-making and change management within organizations, particularly personnel management. In addition, it seems essential to cultivate and develop in the context of globalization 4.0 a set of key competencies such as language skills, critical thinking, creativity, communication, collaboration, management of stress and uncertainty, intercultural sensitivity, technological mastery, particularly in the face of the development of artificial intelligence.

Part of this logic is the development of the skills-based approach through national reference systems and tools (e.g., in France, *France Compétences*,[149] Répertoire National des Compétences et des

---

summit, the member states expressed their desire to be a laboratory of diversity, aiming to think and act together. This brought out a shared determination to meet the challenges of the French-speaking world by focusing on the technologies of the future and involving the various players in modern society.

[149] *France Compétences* created by law no. 2018-771 of September 5, 2018

Certifications RNCP) and international ones (UNESCO, OECD, Council of Europe).[150] The aim is to identify and develop talents through training, support, and deployment within and across organizations.

First, we will examine the philosophical underpinnings of lifelong, global competencies and then present such an approach's managerial and personal necessity.

The importance of acquiring global skills throughout life: Philosophical foundations

Thinking globally, as suggested by Edgar Morin[151] In one of his late books, evokes a vital imperative, recalling the call made as early as the 1930s by the philosopher Jacques Ellul: "Think globally, act locally," which aligns with Patrick Geddes's thinking.[152] René Dubos took up this notion at the first summit on the environment in 1972.[153] According to Morin, it is essential to have a global awareness, a contemporary reaffirmation of the humanistic relationship between the macrocosm (the world as a whole) and the microcosm (the local level). This approach echoes today's challenges, including a globalized economy that subjects all nations to competition for yield and the need to preserve the planet's natural balance. Humanity is facing a countdown, underlining the increasing fragility of the earth as a limited common good, exposed to measurable over-exploitation. In line with their country's economic and ecological policies, each

---

[150] The OECD with its global and environmental competencies; UNESCO (2015); World Trade Organization and International Labour Organization (2017), which presents the results of the Skills for Trade and Economic Diversification (STED) program, shows that skills policies have a key role to play in determining the ability of companies to participate in trade and of workers to find good jobs. The International Labour Organization's skills and employability service also publishes regular reports.
[151] Morin (2015).
[152] "'Local character' is thus no mere accidental old-world quaintness, as its mimics think and say. It is attained only in course of adequate grasp and treatment of the whole environment, and in active sympathy with the essential and characteristic life of the place concerned." Geddes (1915).
[153] Dubos & Ward (1972).

individual contributes to this problem yearly by "consuming" one or more "planet equivalents." This scale of predation, in which the United States occupies a predominant position, encompasses all the world's countries, regarding them as collectively involved and responsible.

Therefore, it is essential to consider these three significant aspects: economic globalization, the issue of sustainable development on a worldwide scale (which is, or should be, self-evident), and the educational scene. This focus on education is based on the premise that it is safer to teach specific values and ethical behaviors to people who are not yet "complete" than to seek to correct or modify adult representations and stereotypes rooted in usage and mores, whether individual or collective.

The importance of global skills throughout life: a managerial necessity

The four global competencies defined by the OECD, in their logical interweaving, are made necessary because of the 2030 sustainable development objectives and would enable precise assessment, like that of schoolchildren, employees, or, more broadly, all adults in the context of lifelong learning. Today, they are included in the ESG (Environmental, Social, and Governance Standard) framework. Here are the four dimensions of these global skills:

- "Acting in favor of collective well-being and sustainable development."

  First, acting in favor of collective well-being and sustainable development is essential. On an organizational and societal level, this refers to policies of social and environmental responsibility (SER) in the spirit of Howard Bowen and, on a personal level, to a personal ethic derived from Protestantism.[154] This skill can be developed daily through individual actions inside and outside organizations. It involves designing actions and assessing their impact.

---

[154] Bowen (1953). For an overview in French, see Le Goff (2010).

Various legal systems, including the European Union, have implemented more or less coercive rules.

- "Understanding local, global, and intercultural issues."
  It is essential to understand how the world is interwoven, the value chains, the relationships between the local and the global, and the connections, and to act accordingly.
- "Understanding and appreciating other people's points of view and visions of the world."
  It is essential to understand other people's points of view and worldviews without lapsing into blissful relativism. You then need to appreciate them in the light of your objectives and personal ethos, the organization, and even the country or territory in which you find yourself.
- "Engage in open, respectful, and effective intercultural interactions."
  This communicative skill is critical in the age of artificial intelligence. To contextualize communication, embrace its multilingual dimension, overcome discriminating representations, and fight against stereotypes.

The development of the intercultural approach in the corporate world became a managerial necessity at the end of the 20th century. It was based on a variety of studies, starting with the vast study by Dutchman Geert Hofstede at IBM in the early 1970s on the impact of culture in the world of work, which gave rise to a profusion of studies based on a quantitative approach aimed at defining "objective" criteria of cultural differences likely to affect the performance of individuals and organizations.[155] Hofstede expanded his approach and developed additional differentiation criteria, influenced by authors such as Fons Trompenaars, Hampden-Turner, Shalom H. Schwartz, and the GLOBE study on cultural approaches to global leadership. Building on this foundation, Erin Meyer later introduced her concepts of "cultural relativism" and the "cultural map," along with eight new criteria for differentiating cultural

---

[155] Over 100,000 questionnaires distributed to IBM subsidiaries worldwide by psychologist Geert Hofstede to measure the impact of culture within organizations. Hofstede (1983).

approaches within companies.[156] A French qualitative approach led by Philippe d'Iribarne has enriched this corpus.[157] Finally, Tsedal Neeley's work for the Japanese multinational Rakuten[158] highlights the importance of a linguistic and cultural policy for organizations with an international strategy.[159] Her work resonates with the approach taken by American universities and those of the OECD's four global competencies, notably in her paper anticipating the COVID-19 pandemic.[160]

This body of knowledge, which is now widely taught in continuing education programs for managers,[161] has impacted the performance of large multinationals and smaller organizations, attracting and keeping their diverse talents, which enables greater agility and adaptability to local realities.[162]

Navigating global competencies in a complex world

The framework put in place by the 38 member states of the OECD,[163] which aims at better policies for a better life, raises the question of common standards, measurement tools to produce data and analyses, and actions on a global scale[164] in a particularly tense context within our societies, directly competing with other models.[165]

---

[156] Meyer (2016).
[157] D'Iribarne (2020); D'Iribarne (1998).
[158] Neeley (2014); Neeley (2017).
[159] Not all companies are interested in this, so it is essential to carry out a self-assessment beforehand. Aleksander (2008).
[160] Neeley (2015b).
[161] In addition to courses, the Label Bienvenue en France program offers intercultural and conversation workshops for both staff and students.
[162] Emirates—Training in cross-cultural communication in the workplace—develop the ability to work seamlessly across cultures.
[163] Colombia and Costa Rica were the two states with the best results.
[164] OECD (2019).
[165] While more than 89 countries took part in the latest PISA survey in 2022, with results published in 2023, and 102 were associated with at least one cycle, global skills were only measured in 2018 without covering India, and since then, neither China nor the Russian Federation has been involved.

Exploring the concept of global competencies means questioning the way we connect to the world. More than 20 years after the introduction of the PISA tests, global skills offer an opportunity to ask about our relationship with knowledge and our perception of the world, not only in secondary and higher education but also in all public and private organizations. In this way, they can help build a better world by promoting tolerance, international cooperation, conflict resolution, and employability in an open, complex world.

However, to avoid the pitfalls of a proliferation of competing organizations and methodologies for assessing ESG standards, international institutions such as UNESCO, the Council of Europe, and OECD must impose a standard like PISA to ensure that data collection and analysis are as meaningful as possible.

The development of common transnational standards affirming the ideal of an open, cosmopolitan, democratic world founded on respect for fundamental freedoms is essential because of the challenges of sustainable development objectives, despite recurrent criticism from nationalist, cultural, and religious movements. Therefore, it is necessary to promote the development of global skills at the secondary level and in the context of lifelong learning for the benefit of all.

Chapter 4 – The multilingual advantage in the global contemporary workplace[166]

Mehdi Lazar

For 30 years, the world economy has been more global and multicultural than ever. In any given country, foreign-based companies operate daily, while overseas branches of the same companies are often present in various countries. The job market is consequently more global, multilingual, and multicultural, and the future workforce will need to be more linguistically and culturally heterogeneous.

In that context, bilingual and bicultural individuals with knowledge of one or more languages and their attendant cultures have a clear advantage since more jobs will require experience in international and cross-cultural areas.[167] On the other hand, we also know that half of the world's population speaks two or more languages, and there are many places where bilingualism or multilingualism is the norm, for example, in regions of Africa.[168] So, will half the world benefit from the new job opportunities created by a more global job market? Not exactly.

Being multilingual, multicultural, and multiliterate are not equivalent skills, and being multilingual is one of many conditions to be hired for any job. It does not replace a solid higher education. Still, it is becoming evident that linguistic and cultural fluency enhances one's "human capital" (the measure of the economic value of a person's skill set). Increasingly, with equal technical skills, a multilingual individual will be chosen over a monolingual person.

The main reason is that multilinguals display essential qualities and unique transversal competencies that are increasingly important

---

[166] This chapter's previous version was published in Language Magazine in 2018.
[167] Cere (2012).
[168] Grosjean (2010).

in a more internationally integrated job market. We can precisely identify four traits commonly shared by all multilingual and multicultural individuals that give a natural edge in the global marketplace: better focus and multitasking abilities, enhanced adaptability, increased cultural fluency, and more potential opportunities.

Focusing on a connected world

First, the cognitive advantages of being multilingual include increased mental flexibility and metalinguistic abilities, improved executive function, and better ability and willingness to learn a third language. The reason is that ideas come from a common source when using two or more languages. What Jim Cummins calls the standard underlying proficiency (CUP) model explains that proficiencies involving more cognitively demanding tasks (such as abstract thinking and problem-solving) are shared across languages.[169] The CUP provides the base for developing both the first language and the second or other languages. Consequently, any expansion of the CUP that takes place in one language will benefit the other languages. This theory explains why it becomes easier to learn additional languages and why individuals can function with two or more languages with relative ease.

Along with the CUP, research shows that information about both languages is activated in the brain even when a speaker only uses one language. In addition, because all languages are constantly activated in the brain, multilinguals must deactivate the language(s) that are not needed. By doing so, they enhance executive control functions (such as inhibition, working memory, and cognitive flexibility) and become better at focusing, multitasking, and selecting relevant information.

Researchers, like Ellen Bialystok, clearly show that bilingual or multilingual speakers have an advantage in language processing because they access linguistic information in their brains differently from monolingual speakers. They outperform monolingual speakers

---

[169] Cummins (1984); Cummins (2000).

in reaction times for language processing and produce relevant language in specific tasks. This is true for children, young adults, and older people who have demonstrated this "bilingual advantage." [170]

In an increasingly complex and connected world with an overwhelming number of distractions and masses of information, the ability to perform multiple tasks at once while remaining focused and selecting relevant information is an essential advantage of being multilingual.

Adaptability in an ambiguous world

Because all languages are constantly activated in the brain of a multilingual individual, multilinguals find themselves at various points on a situational continuum, which results in specific language modes.[171] The language mode is the state of activation of the multilingual languages and language-processing mechanisms at a given time. Multilingual individuals can be in a monolingual mode at one end of the language mode (in their first, second, or any additional language).

They then must choose and use the correct language and deactivate (or inhibit) the second or other one(s). At the other end of the continuum, multilinguals find themselves fully bilingual or multilingual, where they can code-switch or borrow between languages. So, in a sense, multilinguals must adapt to their situation. They use clues to select which language to speak, giving them more flexibility and the ability to read others. In multilingual and global workplaces, people navigate constantly on the continuum.

Multilingualism helps develop adaptability and social, emotional, and interpersonal skills. Indeed, multilinguals must be more aware of the listener's and others' needs and navigate and express various perspectives. In a world charged with ambiguity and global challenges, the capacity to understand and appreciate the viewpoints of others is an asset and can become a stepping stone to success.

---

[170] Bialystok et al. (2008); Bialystok et al. (2010).
[171] Grosjean (1998).

Cultural fluency in our global arena

Multilingualism also helps to build self-esteem and maintain a keen sense of identity while developing sensitivity toward other people and cultures. Multilinguals have direct access to two or more distinct cultures. From a sociocultural perspective, thanks to in-depth knowledge of languages, multilinguals have a better grasp of the cultural diversity in this world. They understand better that we are all unique individuals with different culturally defining backgrounds and that the world can be seen and described in diverse ways, through cultural lenses. Building on their knowledge of languages, they access distinct cultural repertoires, situate their cultural context, and better appreciate and navigate cultural differences.

Understanding cultures as "shared systems," including through their "hidden codes,"[172] gives multilingual and culturally fluent individuals the ability to communicate effectively with people from diverse backgrounds at home and abroad. Moving comfortably between cultures is essential for managing and leading people globally, building meaningful relationships with colleagues, and navigating increasingly diverse workplaces at home.

Cultural fluency, or intercultural competence, is the capability to relate and work effectively and appropriately across cultures—at home or abroad—based first on critical attitudes such as respect, openness, humility, and curiosity and then on skills like listening, observing, and evaluating.[173] By cultivating those attitudes, skills, linguistic abilities, and some knowledge of critical cultural elements, professionals can understand and value diverse perspectives, avoid preconceptions and misunderstandings, and enjoy better workplace relationships through effective and appropriate communication.

Most multilingual people are bi or multicultural or have a broad knowledge of distinct cultures and understand that cultural fluency is essential. In our globalized environment, people equipped to communicate with diverse groups and strong intercultural capacity have a tremendous advantage.

---

[172] Hall et al. (1990).
[173] Deardorff (2004).

More opportunities

Lastly, being multilingual can give a head start that is beneficial early in life and cumulative over time. Indeed, while language skills have always been a requirement in some fields, such as trade or diplomacy, nowadays, more traditional fields, organizations, and firms have a global reach. While research has shown that in the U.S., bilingual people often make less than monolingual people in similar jobs, the situation is changing rapidly. Being multilingual can give a head start in the competition for the best high schools and universities.[174]

Benjamin Voyer, professor at ESCP Business School, described in the French newspaper *Le Monde* the kind of profiles ESCP is looking for in the Bachelor's in Management Program: "What we are looking for are binational, trilingual profiles, but also good at math. Personalities who have lived experiences all over the world and did not want to be confined to a single country in higher education."

Being multilingual enhances people's human capital when the international competition for student recruitment is accelerating. Workplaces are more global, and employees proficient in multiple languages and quickly in multiple cultures have more opportunities. These opportunities will continue as we live in increasingly interconnected societies and workplaces.

In sum, in our global and ultra-competitive world, required personal and professional skills are more diverse and complex than ever. Communicating efficiently in many languages across distinct cultures has become necessary for many jobs. Multilinguals possess transversal competencies, such as taking different perspectives, ignoring irrelevant information, problem-solving, multitasking, and dealing with conflicting cues, which are and will be highly regarded in an increasingly integrated global work market. One can wonder if the saying "monolingualism is the illiteracy of the 21st century"[175] will not become a reality in the contemporary global workplace soon.

---

[174] Gándara (2014).
[175] Roberts et al. (2018).

PART 2.
Empowering students

Culture is a way of coping with the world
by defining it in detail.
– Malcolm Bradbury, *No, Not Bloomsbury*

Chapter 5 – Are U.S. college graduates culturally ready to work abroad? A survey study

Sergio Adrada-Rafael

In such a global world as the one where we live today, moving abroad to find better work opportunities and to experience a different culture and language is becoming the norm rather than the exception, which is valued by companies when these graduates return home and look for jobs (13, 15). College graduates aim to expand their horizons by immersing themselves in a new culture where they can also strengthen their linguistic and pragmatic skills (6, 8, 13, 15, 18). Numerous studies have investigated the benefits of studying abroad at the undergraduate level, pointing out how students return home with linguistic and cultural gains (7, 11) and have developed their pragmatic skills (18). Other studies have emphasized how learners' attitudes toward the language and the host country can play a differential role in their L2 development abroad (10). However, research is still limited on how college graduates who move abroad to work as teaching assistants might benefit from that experience and to what extent (4, 8). Some factors might explain how integrated these teaching assistants become in the host country. For example, some studies have examined how teaching assistants develop intercultural awareness and intercultural sensitivity abroad (3, 5, 9, 17, 19). Intercultural awareness and sensitivity would be related to learners' cognitive and behavioral abilities, respectively, and how these evolve. These would eventually lead to the formation of broader intercultural communication competence (5, 17). Other researchers consider intercultural sensitivity to be a transformational process, where individuals move from initial *denial* and *defense* stages (they believe there are no cultural differences or they see their world views as the right ones) to a final *adaptation* and *integration* stage, where learners embrace and enjoy the existing cultural differences (3, 5). Some studies have also shown how teaching abroad can positively affect the development of empathy and emotions toward understanding and appreciating others' cultures in different contexts (1, 2, 12, 14, 15, 16, 19, 20). Most of these studies have focused on Initial teacher education or pre-service courses but not temporary U.S. college graduates who move to Spain to work as teaching assistants (*auxiliares de conversación*, in Spanish). This chapter aims to explore how teaching assistants from the United States, who arrived in Spain to teach English in primary and secondary schools, perceive the linguistic and cultural challenges they have encountered during their time abroad. It also seeks to highlight how they have managed these situations and assess how culturally prepared they felt before their arrival in Spain.

Survey methodology: Exploring the experiences of English teaching assistants in Spain

Participants in this survey study were twelve recent college graduates from the U.S. who had completed their degrees at U.S. universities and were working as English teaching assistants at educational centers across Spain during the 2022-2023 academic year. The cities where they taught were spread throughout the country, including Madrid, Málaga, Elche, and Cuenca. Ten of them were teaching at the primary education level, and two of them at the secondary education level. Nine respondents started teaching as teaching assistants in September 2022, whereas the remaining three started teaching in September 2020, September 2021, and January 2023. Before arriving in Spain, they had all completed a Bachelor of Arts in various majors (Spanish, psychology, business, and other subjects). The number of years of formal study of Spanish ranged from two years in college to twenty years. Respondents' ages ranged between 22 and 26, and the average age was 23.33 years. Nine of them identified as females, and the remaining three as males.

The instrument employed to collect data for the present study was a survey designed and distributed using Google Forms. The survey consisted of 15 questions. Of these, 12 were open-ended, and 3 were Likert-scale-like. All questions were mandatory and had to be responded to so the teaching assistants could not skip any questions, which could affect the validity of the findings. The questions addressed both respondents' personal information (age, nationality, U.S. college where they studied, years of study of Spanish) and their cultural and linguistic attitudes and challenges faced while working in Spain as English teaching assistants. The latter included questions such as how confident they felt regarding their Spanish skills, how close they found their culture and the Spanish culture, or how they tried to overcome cultural or linguistic issues while living in Spain.

Once the survey was ready, it was sent to English teaching assistants in various Spanish cities via Google Forms. They were instructed to complete the survey and told their responses would be anonymous. They were also informed that completing it would take 15-20 minutes. Participants did not receive any rewards in exchange for participating in the study.

Exploring linguistic and cultural attitudes: Insights from English teaching assistants in Spain

In this section, a summary of the responses to the survey questions addressing linguistic and cultural attitudes will be laid out. Respondents were asked how confident they felt using their Spanish skills in Spain when they completed the survey in May-June 2023. Responses could range on a Likert scale from "not at all confident" to "very confident." Eight of the twelve *auxiliares de conversación* felt either confident (5) or very confident (3). Two of the remaining four were unsatisfied with their Spanish skills, and two were unconfident. These findings could be interpreted in light of the teaching assistants' degree of interaction with native speakers of Spanish during their time in Spain, as well as their previous study of the Spanish language in the US.

Teaching assistants were also asked how close they found their culture (US culture in this case) was to the Spanish culture where they were immersed. Their responses could range from "Not close at all" to "Very close." Half of them (6) responded that they were close (a three on a 1 to 5 Likert scale). Four believed they were not close, and one thought their culture and Spanish cultures were not close. Only one of the assistants responded that both countries are culturally close. From these responses, the overall picture shows that according to the teaching assistants, the U.S. and Spanish cultures do not seem similar.

A follow-up question asked the *auxiliares* for their impression regarding Spaniards' cultural habits. More specifically, they were asked whether Spaniards were homogeneous when comparing their cultural practices since assistants taught in different regions of Spain. Responses could range from "strongly disagree" to "strongly agree." Four of them responded that practices were similar, and four other assistants believed that their habits were not that similar, that is, heterogeneous. Three of the remaining four assistants found identical cultural practices, and one was very similar. Overall, it seems like there is less consensus when it comes to agreeing on Spaniards' homogeneity regarding their cultural practices.

The first open-ended question addressed how culturally prepared teaching assistants thought they were upon graduation and before arriving in Spain to start their journeys as teaching assistants. Responses showed a need for uniformity, as they differed in their degrees of cultural preparation. One of the teaching assistants mentioned that they "did not feel prepared at all, but it was easy to adjust once experiencing it." Other assistants, however, seemed to be a bit more prepared for their journey abroad. For instance, one said, "I felt somewhat prepared; nothing was too unexpected." Another assistant responded: "I wasn't entirely prepared for the lifestyle shift, but my open-mindedness and excitement of exploration made the adjustment smoother." That same assistant added that as time passed, they realized how their perspective and background changed even compared to fellow Americans. One more teaching assistant pointed out the fact of not being prepared for the Spanish culture: "I would say I was not very culturally prepared for the Spanish culture in particular, though I prepared to learn about and experience a new culture in general. Therefore, there was a bit of an adaptation and learning period, but one that I was ready for." Their response showed they were motivated and ready to learn about a new culture, but a specific adaptation to the Spanish culture was necessary. Two of the language assistants mentioned how having lived in Spain before as students helped them feel culturally prepared for this new experience: "Having studied in Madrid previously, I felt quite culturally prepared to move here to teach English."

"I believe that I was prepared for Spanish culture. Having spent time in Barcelona during my study abroad program, I had experience with the culture." Interestingly, an additional *auxiliar* also referred to having studied abroad in Spain, but in this case, to point out the existing cultural differences between cities: "After graduating, I was more culturally prepared than I would have been had I not studied in Barcelona for a semester. However, in a religious sense, Málaga is much more traditional than Barcelona, which was a shock factor during my first year here."

Finally, one of the assistants cited the influence of family friends and Spanish professors as the main reason for learning ahead of time about the cultural differences between the two countries: "I felt prepared because I had family friends and professors from Spain who had told me about the cultural differences. It was definitely very hard for me to adjust to mealtimes, though!"

A second open-ended question followed up on the first one and asked language assistants what they would have done differently in college to be more culturally acclimated when arriving in Spain. Once again, responses varied, with language assistants providing a variety of explanations of what they could have done differently during their college years to maximize their Spain-related cultural exposure. Two of the assistants referred to the importance of the media, such as watching Spanish shows or movies on Netflix or news in Spanish: "I would have watched more shows in Spanish (Castellano), I would have paid more attention to news from Spain, and I would practice speaking." One of them emphasized the importance of consuming Spanish-produced media not only for linguistic reasons but also to learn more about how people typically socialize: "Consuming more Spanish-based/produced media (movies, TV shows, books) would have made a difference. I wish I had started these habits before arriving in Spain because I have noticed that they are a great way to learn about how people interact and live their day-to-day lives."

Other assistants mentioned they would have taken more courses in Spanish if they had the opportunity to start college again to improve their Spanish proficiency and become more familiar with the peninsular Spanish dialect: "I would have taken more Spanish classes to improve my language skills." "Taken more Spanish classes focused on European Spanish specifically." Other assistants considered having chosen a different major or having reached out to other students who had studied abroad in Spain or directly to other teachers in Spain as critical factors to become more culturally prepared, as seen in their responses: "I would've spent more time defining my goals for the future and choosing a major more wisely"; "There were quite a few people from my college who studied in Spain, I could have made more of an effort to reach out and ask about their experiences."; "I would've reached out to more people already living in Spain in the field of education." Finally, one of the assistants wishes they had "traveled more beforehand" to be exposed to more cultures before traveling to Spain.

A third open-ended question inquired language assistants about the linguistic and cultural challenges faced in Spain and how they have overcome them. Responses showed various issues/topics teaching assistants had to deal with. Some referred to their difficulties in understanding the Spanish dialect in the region where they lived and how they got used to it by interacting with locals, as seen in the following responses: "Understanding the Andalusian accent has been a big challenge in Malaga. It was discouraging at times. Over time, I have become used to it"; "linguistically, learning the nuances and accents in the region I have been living in was another challenge. I tried to overcome this by practicing with locals"; "being placed in Andalucía, I knew that the accent in this region would be challenging, but I didn't realize how challenging it was... I have developed a greater understanding of Spanish, particularly the Andalusian accent, partly due to having a native Spanish speaker for a housemate"; "for some reason, the Andaluz accent was much harder for me to understand when a man was talking versus a woman." Language assistants also mentioned issues of linguistic diversity and race in a negative light in their responses as challenges to be overcome: "Growing up, my grandmother spoke to me in

Spanish so that I could understand and communicate in Spanish. However, the Spanish I speak is Latin American and is sometimes looked down on when speaking to Spanish people"; "ideas of race and diversity with patience and putting things into perspective." The latter response could allude to the observation that certain areas in Spain, particularly smaller towns, may exhibit limited diversity, particularly in terms of racial demographics.

Other responses referred to mealtimes, especially late dinners when compared to the U.S., stores being closed at noon due to "siesta" (nap time), and dealing with Spanish bureaucracy when applying for permits or other documents: "My main cultural challenges have come from the speed and consistency of the bureaucracy. I tried overcoming this with patience"; "my biggest challenges have been with the government offices in Spain. Applying for any permit or document feels like a guessing game. The best way to overcome bureaucratic problems is to act confidently and pretend you know what you are doing"; "pace of life, Spaniards appreciate their siesta time and don't value their work as much. Social life and care come first for them." A cultural reference to a slower and more social lifestyle compared to the U.S. can also be observed in this last response. Finally, one of the assistants perceived as a significant challenge the more colloquial Spanish used in Spain, in contrast with the academic Spanish they learned in college, as they had not had the opportunity to practice Spanish outside the classroom: "When I first arrived in Spain, I noticed that the Spanish I knew were, overall, somewhat formal and more suited for an academic setting. This was unsurprising given that I had little experience using the language outside of a classroom." This assistant added that they overcame this challenge by watching Spanish shows, communicating with their teachers, looking up unfamiliar words or expressions, and making notes of them.

The final survey question explored how their experiences as *auxiliares de conversación* compared to their cultural and linguistic experiences during any previous study abroad programs. Six of the twelve teaching assistants confirmed having studied abroad during college. Overall, all six *auxiliares* reported having vastly different experiences. When they studied abroad, they did not interact with locals often, and most administrative procedures (obtaining a visa and finding accommodation, among other things) were provided for them. As teaching assistants, they use Spanish more often and participate more in the target culture as they interact more with students and other Spanish teachers at their schools. Some responses summarizing the above points were: "My study abroad experience was very different from being an aux in that once arriving in Spain as an aux, I was completely on my own. I had only the other *auxiliares* to look to for help finding an apartment, opening a bank account, and applying for residency;" "it was completely different. The study abroad program provides lots of things for you (housing, visa, and more), whereas the auxiliar program does not;" "I only studied abroad for a term, barely used the Spanish language, and did not integrate with my community. As an *auxiliar*, I feel like I contribute to my neighborhood, interact with the people, and am more in touch with Spanish culture."

Insights from teaching assistants' experiences in Spain

The findings reported in the present manuscript have provided an overview of teaching assistants' linguistic and cultural experiences as they live and work in Spain. Most of them believe they could have been more culturally ready had they interacted more with Spanish speakers, taken more Spanish classes, or consumed more Spanish-produced media before they arrived in Spain. They have also found similar linguistic or cultural challenges, such as struggling to understand Spain's southern accent, colloquial forms that differ from the academic Spanish learned in the classroom, or getting used to different mealtimes or bureaucracy styles. For those who studied abroad, there is a general consensus that their experiences as teaching assistants have made them more independent and increased their interactions with native speakers and their cultures.

These findings can provide valuable insights for undergraduate students in the U.S. considering working as *auxiliares de conversación* in Spain after graduation. They can also be helpful for U.S. colleges and universities, especially for modern languages departments.

Recommendations can be offered based on the findings reported in this chapter. Modern language departments could connect with alumni who have experience teaching English in Spain and invite them to share their insights with students, either in person or remotely. This would provide students with a valuable opportunity to gain first-hand insights into what living and working abroad entails and how to navigate potential obstacles.

Additionally, modern language departments could collaborate closely with other offices on campus (e.g., Career Center, Office of Professional Development) to promote these teaching abroad programs upon graduation and to ensure that informational resources include cultural and linguistic tips to prepare students for the challenges they might encounter. Finally, language program directors and instructors could devote time in their classes to address linguistic or cultural issues related to living abroad. This would benefit the entire student community by helping them acclimatize faster to the host country.

Chapter 6 – Revitalizing for relevancy and representation: The revisioning of a multilingual and multicultural teacher education program

Joanna Greer Koch

The COVID-19 pandemic dramatically impacted the United States' educational landscape. Before the global pandemic, public schools in the United States faced significant teacher vacancies in multilingual and multicultural classrooms. However, the global pandemic "exacerbated a preexisting and long-standing shortage of teachers."[176] The U.S. Department of Education's Institute of Education Sciences (IES)—National Center for Education Statistics (NCES) reported that "nearly half (44 percent) of public schools currently report full- or part-time teaching vacancies...of public schools with at least one reported vacancy, 61 percent specifically identified the COVID-19 pandemic as a cause of increased teaching and non-teaching staff vacancies."[177] As a result, the United States' primary and secondary public schools have an immediate need to fill teacher vacancies in classrooms, which has resulted in non-instructional staff teaching in classrooms and impacting the overall school operations.

Moreover, there is a greater need for multilingual teachers throughout the country. Multilingual learners comprise about 10.3 percent, or 5.0 million, of the students in United States public schools. In response, federal, state, and local education agencies in the United States have taken steps to attract and retain multilingual teacher candidates and support teachers in meeting the learning needs of multilingual learners. However, the question remains: Will these efforts be enough?

Amid growing teacher vacancies in the U.S. since the global pandemic, education agencies have had to rethink, research, and

---
[176] Schmitt & deCourcy (2022).
[177] NCES (2022).

implement actionable steps to attract more prospective multilingual teacher candidates and retain existing multilingual teachers. Additionally, teacher preparation programs have had to re-evaluate their programmatic policies and procedures to ensure they attract and support multilingual teacher candidates in these roles while obtaining their initial teaching licenses. Therefore, this chapter will discuss the multilingual teacher shortage as it relates to defining it, explaining the impact of the pandemic on the shortage, and evaluating proposed solutions to the teacher shortage at multiple education levels. The chapter will highlight insights from scholarly literature, observations, and document analysis. The findings suggest successes and challenges in the educational agencies' proposed solutions. Addressing such achievements and challenges can revitalize teacher education programs to be more culturally relevant and representative of the multilingual society.

Teacher shortage: The who, what, & where

The first step in addressing the multilingual teacher shortage is to explain what a teacher shortage is, who these teachers are, and where the multilingual teacher shortage is occurring. The definition of teacher shortage is the "inability to fill vacancies at current wages with individuals qualified to teach in fields needed."[178] The National Center for Education Statistics (NCES) surveyed a sample of schools during the 2022-2023 school year about teacher absences. The NCES School Pulse Panel study collected data that revealed: "45% percent of public schools reported having one or more vacant teaching positions in October, and 53% percent of public schools reported in August feeling understaffed entering the 2022-2023 school year."[179]

When examining the demographics of teachers, most U.S. teachers are white, female, and monolingual. This highlights the need for more teacher education programs to attract and recruit multilingual individuals and people of color into the teaching profession to better meet the learning needs of students in

---

[178] Sutcher et al. (2016).
[179] NCES (2023b).

multilingual and multicultural classrooms. The U.S. Department of Education's National Center for Education Statistics (NCES) reported that 79.3% of public school teachers were white, non-Hispanic; 9.3% were Hispanic, regardless of race; 6.7% were Black or African American, non-Hispanic; 2.1% were Asian, non-Hispanic; 1.8% were of two or more races, non-Hispanic; 0.5% were American Indian/Alaska Native, non-Hispanic; and 0.2% were Native Hawaiian/Pacific Islander, non-Hispanic.[180] Based on this analysis, NCES proposed two crucial conclusions, including "teachers of given race/ethnicity were more often found in schools where their race/ethnicity matched a majority of the student body" and "at the same time, in schools where the majority of students were not White, the majority of teacher tended to be White."[181] This data shows that school districts and educator preparation programs are not recruiting or attracting many multilingual and multicultural teachers. School districts and educator preparation programs need to make more efforts to recruit and attract new multilingual teachers from various demographics, which will contribute to providing more qualified teachers to teach in multilingual and multicultural classrooms. Furthermore, stronger partnerships should occur between school districts, schools, and higher education institutions from the United States Historically Black Colleges and Universities, Hispanic Serving Institutions, Tribal Colleges and Universities, and community colleges to expand the teacher workforce and pipeline diversity.[182]

The global pandemic has led to a growing demand for qualified multilingual teachers in multilingual and multicultural classrooms.[183] Most teacher shortages are found in multilingual settings, with 6% of positions remaining unfilled.[184] According to U.S. Census records, the country is a multilingual nation, with immigrants from Mexico forming the largest group at 10.7 million, followed by individuals from India at 2.71 million, and those from China at 2.38 million.

---

[180] NCES (2020).
[181] Ibid.
[182] U.S. Department of Education (2022).
[183] Schmitt & deCourcy (2022).
[184] Wong (2023).

Additionally, schools in high-poverty and high-minority school districts report increasing teacher vacancies.[185] Although school districts had recruiting challenges before the pandemic, "shortages are much like school districts. They often begin and end at arbitrary lines that have more to do with privilege and zip code than the needs of children."[178] Therefore, another area where school districts and educator preparation programs need to make more effort is recruiting and attracting new multilingual teachers and teachers of color in special education, science, and math specialty areas.

Help wanted: The when and why

The second step in addressing the teacher shortage is to recognize when and why the teacher shortage continues to impact our schools. Since 1990-1991, the Department of Education has reported on teacher shortages by state and subject area in the "Teacher Shortage Areas (TSA)" report.[186] The ongoing shortages of multilingual and multicultural teachers can be attributed to factors such as modest salaries, low morale, frequent retirements, ongoing curriculum changes, and concerns about safety.[187] An opinion piece by Thomas Edsall in The New York Times explained that teachers are experiencing burnout due to "under-compensation" and "demoralization."[188] Concerning compensation, "wages are essentially unchanged from 2000 to 2020 after adjusting for inflation."[181] Also, teachers are not valued for what they have been hired to do: teach. Educators are required to do more work for less pay. They often have to take on other full-time or part-time jobs to pay for their living expenses. Therefore, another area that school districts and teacher education preparation programs should implement is providing a living wage to teachers, additional bonuses to multilingual professionals, and professional development. For instance, attracting multilingual teachers might occur if they receive additional compensation for their linguistic skills, which are seen as

---

[185] Turner & Cohen (2023).
[186] Schmitt & deCourcy (2022).
[187] Wong (2023).
[188] Edsall (2022).

an asset to any school system. Thus, if school systems offer a salary incentive for multilingualism, it could encourage more multilingual individuals to pursue degrees in education and consider careers in teaching.

Unfortunately, the "why" of a multilingual and multicultural teacher shortage is not new. Even though the COVID-19 global pandemic created unprecedented challenges that impacted teacher retention, schools have continuously seen a teacher shortage in multilingual and multicultural classrooms.[189] So, what efforts are being implemented in response to the teacher shortage? In 2022, the U.S. Department of Education's Secretary, Miguel Cardona, called on state and local education agencies and teacher education programs to address the teacher shortages.[190] Secretary Cardona's charge was in response to the COVID-19 pandemic, which amplified teacher shortages and caused educators to leave and retire.

Next steps: The how?

When Secretary Miguel Cardona called upon the national, state, and local education agencies to respond to the teacher shortage, he mentioned how the American Rescue Plan Elementary and Secondary School Emergency Relief Fund (ARP ESSER) could be used by state and local education agencies to recruit, train, and retain teachers, especially multilingual and multicultural teachers. In reflecting on Secretary Cardona's charge, three principal areas need continuous funding to help with the teacher shortage in the long term and ensure more multilingual teachers are in our multicultural schools.

Teacher residency and apprenticeship licensure programs

When the U.S. Department of Education issued funding from the American Rescue Plan Elementary and Secondary School Emergency Relief Fund (ARP ESSER), it provided $122 billion to state and local education agencies to recruit, train, and retain

---

[189] Wong (2023); U.S. Department of Education. (2000)
[190] NCES (2022)

teachers, including multilingual and multicultural teachers. With this funding support, school districts began exploring teacher residency programs, providing financial assistance to school employees—such as instructional assistants, paraprofessionals, and substitutes who are multilingual and come from diverse backgrounds—to become licensed teachers.[191]

Residential licensed teachers are full-time school employees enrolled in an accredited initial teaching licensure program. A rationale for the teacher residency program is that the participants are already invested in the school, connected to the students, established in their communities, and speak the communities' languages so that they would remain long-term as teachers.[192] The residential licensure opportunities have been working in communities with multilingual and multicultural communities since its implementation since a lot of the residential licensure teachers have families and need help traveling to other locations for licensure. Therefore, higher education institutions are redesigning their programs to be more attractive to residential licensure teachers, especially in multilingual and multicultural communities. For instance, the South Carolina Department of Education is working with higher education institutions to develop and recruit new educators of color and provide scholarships to promote a pathway toward training.[193]

Since residential licensure teachers are completing the initial teaching license while working full-time as a teacher, education preparation programs have to accommodate the teacher's full-time schedule. For instance, NC State University's Master of Arts in Teaching (MAT) Program redesigned its program to accommodate residential licensure teachers by offering 100% online courses to ensure teachers can work full-time and then take classes online during the evening hours. The NC State's MAT Program is also revitalizing one of its concentrations to reflect multilingual education curricula to better prepare its future teachers for the state's multilingual and multicultural society. North Carolina has

---

[191] U.S. Department of Education (2022).
[192] Wong (2023).
[193] U.S. Department of Education (2022).

approximately 9% of the total public-school population being identified as multilingual learners. This demonstrates a significant need for the state to teach multilingual pedagogies and attract multilingual teachers for those teaching jobs.[194]

It is becoming a trend in the higher education communities to provide accelerated pathways toward certifications by allowing teachers to receive an initial teacher license while getting paid for their full-time jobs.[195] If districts and higher education institutions collaborate to offer this customizable opportunity, more multilingual teachers will remain in the position long-term as they are invested in the school community. For instance, the Arizona Department of Education partnered with three state universities to support schools with recruitment, retention, and professional development with local communities.[196]

Another significant opportunity the school districts are implementing is teacher apprenticeships, which introduce high school students to the teaching profession by becoming paraprofessionals once they graduate. Then, the paraprofessionals can work towards a bachelor's degree to be certified to teach. Some states are referencing these programs as "Grow Your Own" programs. The strength of these programs is that the school districts can recruit teacher candidates from their community who are invested in the community, understand the community's needs, and provide more diversity within the teaching profession. For instance, the Tennessee Department of Education instituted a "Grow Your Own" program from the ARP ESSER grant to recruit, train, and support 650 future educators.[187] The challenge of the teacher apprenticeship program is increasing the interest of prospective teachers. Researchers have noted that "the interest in teaching has fallen among high school seniors and college freshmen to the lowest level in the last 50 years."[197] The main reasons for the lack of interest from high school students relate to teachers' salaries, fewer

---

[194] NC DPI (2022).
[195] Wong (2023).
[196] U.S. Department of Education (2022).
[197] Kraft & Lyon (2022).

opportunities for professional development, and a general sense of lack of morale from experienced teachers.

The teacher residency and apprenticeship licensure programs allow state and local education agencies to work with higher education institutions' educator preparation programs (EPPs) by customizing the curriculum and providing financial aid to reduce the cost of the EPPs and licensure examinations. Of course, the challenge of these programs is recruiting individuals to pursue teacher residency and apprenticeship licensure programs since teachers are not paid competitively, and some states barely provide a livable wage to teachers. However, the ARP ESSER funding did address the opportunity for state and local education agencies to provide more compensation to teachers.

Livable and competitive wage

Compared to other countries in the Organisation for Economic Co-operation and Development (OECD), the United States pays its teachers far less than 28 other OECD countries. In comparison, U.S. teachers work more hours per year than the teachers in the 28 other OECD countries.[198] The OECD countries are comprised of various countries worldwide, yet many are demographically smaller and less wealthy than the United States. Nevertheless, the United States needs to pay public-school teachers the compensation that teachers deserve. The global pandemic spotlighted teachers' salaries as more teachers left the profession to seek other employment opportunities with higher wages.[189]

One of the ARP ESSER funding objectives was to provide state and local education agencies with funds to recruit and retain educators by offering more livable and competitive wages. Teacher salaries are one of the reasons for a lack of interest and retainment of teachers, contributing to the teacher shortage. Therefore, the ARP ESSER funding allows states and local education agencies to provide more funding to new teachers' salaries, bonuses, and competitive pay opportunities. The major challenge of such financing is

---

[198] Schmitt & deCourcy (2022).

implementing continuous livable and competitive wages to retain educators. Rural communities struggle with providing livable and competitive wages due to teacher salaries being dependent on the local county tax system. With this reality, the federal and state governments must offer more equitable funding to ensure teachers are retained in rural and low-income communities, including multilingual learners who need multilingual teachers.

By providing more living and competitive wages to new teachers, more individuals will consider the apprenticeship and residency licensure programs. For instance, high school students, paraprofessionals, and instructional assistants are incentivized to pursue these teacher licensure opportunities. Another challenge in motivating individuals to pursue education preparation programs is the cost. Education preparation programs at higher education institutions can cost between $10,000-$29,000 because higher education costs have doubled due to inflation.[199] When you compare that with how much the new teacher makes, starting at $34,000-$40,000, it is understandable why individuals are not attracted to the profession.[200] Therefore, a significant challenge is continuously offering prospective teachers educational scholarships, stipends, and loan forgiveness opportunities to keep up with the cost of inflation.

Specific school districts are implementing the ARP ESSER funds to help address the under-compensation realities that most teachers face. For instance, Asheville City Schools in North Carolina provide bonuses of up to $3,000 to full-time employees.[201] Also, the Providence Public School District in Rhode Island is providing early signing bonuses to newly hired teachers and support staff.[192] However, school districts must attract new teachers in understaffed positions, including multilingual, special education, science, and math classrooms. International schools act as global educational hubs, facilitating cross-border learning and leveraging existing transnational networks to promote greater convergence.[202]

---

[199] Turner & Cohen (2023).
[200] NCES (2022).
[201] U.S. Department of Education (2022).
[202] Turner & Cohen (2023).

Retention and professional development

When the COVID-19 global pandemic occurred, many schools shut down, resulting in students losing weeks of valuable instruction time. Some teachers quit or retired before the students returned to school. As a result of the pandemic, "teachers' job satisfaction is at the lowest level in five decades."[203] The pandemic exacerbated teachers' stress, with schools closing, teaching days lost, learning how to teach online, and teaching with safety precautions. Teachers have felt "demoralized" by the system because the school districts did not recognize the extra requirements teachers had to deal with during the pandemic beyond just teaching the curriculum.

The ARP ESSER funding was implemented to help state and local districts think strategically about building up experienced teachers' morale to stay in the profession by providing more support staff, self-care/mental health days, professional development, and more time to plan instruction. For instance, the Pachogue-Medford school district in New York used the funding to hire permanent substitute teachers to help with classroom instruction when teachers needed self-care/mental health days or professional development. Also, the Puerto Rico Department of Education compensated the multilingual school staff to encourage retention. The Missouri Department of Elementary and Secondary Education used the ARP ESSER funding to strengthen its teacher mentoring program, implement surveys to determine working condition issues, and provide more social-emotional services for the teachers. Gaston County Schools in North Carolina is an example of a county that uses the ARP ESSER funding to provide additional support staff to schools that need additional classroom coverage.[204] Although school districts try to retain experienced and multilingual teachers, these successes must be more than a one-time effort. Providing opportunities for experienced teachers to have more support for multilingual staff in their classrooms, more self-care/mental health days, professional development, and flexible schedules to ensure

---

[203] Kraft & Lyon (2022).
[204] U.S. Department of Education (2022).

more time to plan and prepare for instruction should be the norm. A challenge is ensuring that these efforts are continuous, available for all teachers, and become the norm of a teacher's career.

Addressing multilingual teacher shortages

Although teacher shortages in multilingual and multicultural classrooms have existed for decades, the global pandemic intensified the issue, and unfortunately, multilingual students have been impacted. Multilingual students undoubtedly deserve professional multilingual teachers who have been trained in multilingual and culturally relevant pedagogies. Due to the shortage of qualified multilingual teachers, one of the objectives of the ARP ESSER funding is to ensure that more multilingual teacher preparation programs are available and funded. The ARP ESSER provides the funding to implement more teacher residency and apprenticeship licensure programs to attract and support multilingual individuals in becoming qualified teachers, contributing to more multicultural representation in the teaching field. Furthermore, livable and competitive wage opportunities and professional development will retain and reward multilingual teachers as professionals. However, the major challenge is ensuring that these funding opportunities continue and that legislators recognize the need to respond to the multilingual teacher shortage.[205] Without continuous funding, these action steps will end, the successes will diminish, and the "help wanted" sign will return in school districts nationwide. Therefore, it is critical that funding at all levels continue to ensure the training and support of multilingual teachers to prepare future multicultural citizens for the relevance of living in a multilingual society.

---

[205] Turner & Cohen (2023).

Chapter 7 – Educational projects of the Mission Laïque Française: Interview with Jean-Marc Merriaux

Gaspard Belhadj and Mehdi Lazar

This chapter is a transcript of a conversation with Jean-Marc Merriaux, General Director of the Mission Laïque Française (MLF). The MLF is an association promoting French culture and language in educational contexts. During this discussion, Gaspard Belhadj, the upper school student body president at the International School of Boston, and Mehdi Lazar asked Mr. Merriaux several essential questions. Their dialogue covered topics related to education, languages, culture, and the MLF and ISB's crucial roles in advancing these areas.

Could you give us an overview of the mission and objectives of the Mission Laïque Française?

The association was founded 120 years ago, in 1902, by Pierre Deschamps, an inspector from the national education system. Having had several teaching experiences abroad, he decided to promote a pedagogical model internationally based on multilingualism, interculturality, and secularism. The maxim of the association was to promote two cultures and two languages—meaning that it aimed to integrate the host country's culture and languages into its educational programs. Thus, schools typically teach in the local language, often English and French. This approach led to the second central pillar of the association: interculturality. It involved understanding and integrating into the local cultures without imposing a model but instead contributing to the cultural model of the host country.

Additionally, there was a significant focus on the Mediterranean, particularly in Lebanon. Deschamps believed that to establish a good French school, one must also be capable of establishing an excellent Arab school—an innovative idea at the time.

The third pillar, secularism, is a distinctly French concept that has been challenging to export. However, it is a vital principle upheld in our institutions. It represents absolute freedom of conscience, allowing individuals to believe or not believe.

Thus, over the past 120 years, we have tried to perpetuate these founding principles through a nonprofit model in the United States. As of today, we manage or support 108 schools worldwide, with varying levels of involvement ranging from complete management to pedagogical support, particularly emphasizing educational challenges and belonging to a network. This helps share best practices and support the projects of our network schools. The association has grown not only by operating its schools but also through partnerships and today. Our challenge is to strengthen these partnerships and animate this network.

Can you describe the international networks for each school?

Our educational approach emphasizes that each school retains its autonomy, meaning it can develop its model and approach for its students and educational community. While we might provide guidelines or strong principles important in an international environment, each school operates independently yet remains part of our supportive network. For instance, in Boston, schools are encouraged to maintain autonomy while still being part of our global network. This approach focuses on professional development, aiming to support each teacher throughout their professional journey and offering them ongoing training opportunities. We believe this reimagined vision of continuous education and professional development will enhance the excellence of our teachers and schools globally.

How does the MLF promote the French language and culture? What initiatives and programs have you implemented worldwide?

We primarily manage schools that comply with the French educational program, reinforcing the presence of the French language and culture, especially in non-Francophone countries. Beyond the primary educational mandates, we are also deeply involved in cultural and certification challenges. For instance, our schools engage in various cultural activities, like theatre and web radios, which strengthen the use of the French language and critical thinking skills. This is particularly evident in the United States, where the role of journalism as an independent power aligns with French cultural values like press freedom, a significant aspect of our educational and cultural promotion.

What challenges and opportunities do the MLF face in its efforts to promote the French language and culture?

One of the significant challenges extends beyond simply teaching French. We are focused on integrating scientific culture, which has been a significant part of French intellectual tradition but is often underemphasized compared to literature. For example, the solid mathematical tradition in France is not as widely recognized as it should be, despite our many successes in fields like the Fields Medal in mathematics. Thus, promoting scientific excellence and broader educational and cultural domains remains a critical objective.

In conclusion, could you discuss some innovative or unique initiatives the MLF is implementing or planning?

We are heavily focused on integrating technology into education, particularly the role of digital technologies and artificial intelligence. While we ensure that these technological advances do not overshadow education fundamentals, they are crucial for adapting to the continually changing educational landscape. We are also preparing for a training session in one of our schools in Dallas on the effective use of AI in education, emphasizing that while technology will enhance educational practices, it will not replace the traditional roles of teachers.

Finally, how does the MLF measure its success and the effectiveness of its programs?

Traditionally, our success was measured by our students' performance in examinations like the baccalaureate. However, we are moving towards a more continuous evaluation model that assesses not just academic achievement but also the quality of the learning environment and the pedagogical support provided to each student. This shift towards a more comprehensive approach to evaluation is crucial for adapting our educational practices to meet contemporary educational needs and challenges.

Chapter 8 – Multilingualism and neurodiversity in the contemporary world

Laurence Champomier

Multilingualism and neurodiversity, as emerging crucial dimensions in the professional landscape, bring significant benefits. Linguistic diversity enriches cultures and enhances communication, while neurodiversity underscores the natural variability in brain functions, fostering unique perspectives and innovative thinking. This convergence of elements profoundly influences interactions in the workplace, shaping how individuals interact, collaborate, and innovate within organizations. Education and the professional world are spheres where multilingualism and neurodiversity converge, influencing learning, communication, and skill development in schools and playing a crucial role in team dynamics in the professional world. This complex interaction raises fundamental questions about how these two dimensions are integrated, understood, and valued throughout educational and professional journeys.

Therefore, it is crucial to delve into how multilingualism and neurodiversity are considered and managed in the educational context. This exploration will not only shed light on the challenges but also reveal the opportunities that arise from this interaction. Understanding how these two dimensions influence individual development from school to transition into the professional world is critical to fostering educational success, professional training, and integration into the workplace.

In the first part, we will explore the complexity of these interactions both at school and in the professional environment, then identify the dynamics and challenges to determine the opportunities that promote an educational and professional environment that is inclusive and respectful of linguistic and neurological diversity.

Neurodiversity and multilingualism: The complexity of their interaction

The interaction between these two dimensions, which characterize our society's intrinsic diversity, is not simple. It is a complex interplay, often dynamic and subtle: while multilingualism enriches the palette of languages and cultures, neurodiversity underscores the natural variability of thought patterns. Understanding and navigating this complexity is challenging but holds immense potential for our educational and professional environments.

This complex interaction creates a field where nuances of communication, learning, and mutual understanding unfold uniquely: for example, linguistic versatility can lead to semantic subtleties, and cultural norms conveyed by each language in terms of communication can influence word choice, tone, and gestures. Some idiomatic expressions may be complex to translate literally and may vary from one language to another, creating misunderstandings; levels of politeness are expressed differently and can influence the dynamics of interpersonal relationships, cultural sensitivities on specific topics, emotional tones, all examples that are intensified when the dimension of neurodiversity is added among individuals learning or working together. Hence, we must deepen our understanding of the synergies between multilingualism and neurodiversity and their impact on personal and professional flourishing.

The development of multiple languages presents characteristics in individuals with neuro-functional atypicality. Remember that neurodiversity encompasses the natural diversity of brain functioning, including neurological conditions such as autism spectrum disorders, learning disabilities, and developmental disorders, among other cognitive differences. The educational and professional experience of multilingual and neuro-atypical individuals is often characterized by increased cognitive adaptability where linguistic variety combines with unconventional thought modes. Some studies suggest that multilingualism can benefit the cognitive development of individuals with these conditions.[206] For example, learning and using two languages can stimulate cognitive abilities, mental flexibility, and social communication.

Navigating the interplay of multilingualism and neurodiversity in educational contexts

The multilingualism-neurodiversity combination may present additional challenges that vary from person to person depending on their condition's severity and specific characteristics. Indeed, some individuals may encounter difficulties in verbal communication, understanding linguistic rules, or organizing ideas in two different languages due to sensory processing issues. Studies that have observed the effect of multilingualism on individuals diagnosed with ADHD (attention deficit hyperactivity disorder) show that this population can learn more than one language successfully.[207] Managing languages in the multilingual brain may involve competition and cooperation between different languages. Thus, the approach must be adapted to the individual needs of neuro-atypical multilingual learners by natural heritage who choose a multilingual education, considering their linguistic, cognitive, and social strengths and difficulties.[208]

At school, specialized and individualized support may be necessary to facilitate the learning and use of languages, such as speech therapy interventions or adaptations of teaching methods, as well as accommodations in the environment, tools, duration, and educational contexts. Whatever support is provided, an inclusive and personalized approach is essential to foster the flourishing and success of neuro-atypical individuals in their multilingual journey in school and later toward their professional transition. In the following paragraphs, we will observe the dynamics between neurodiversity and multilingualism at school and work in Europe and the United States.

---

[206] Durrleman (2021).
[207] Bialystok et al. (2016); Sorge et al. (2017).
[208] Paradis & Nicoladis (2007)

Neurodiversity and multilingualism in Europe

Europe is characterized by great linguistic diversity, with many countries where several languages are spoken and used daily. Thus, combining the two can represent challenges and opportunities for neuro-atypical individuals.[209] Accommodating neurological diversity in schools necessitates a range of flexible pedagogical approaches. This involves the collective effort of the entire educational team, including classroom teachers, specialized teachers, administration, and families. While multilingualism is often a family or geographic educational choice, many schools across different countries and regions are now promoting intercultural understanding and integrating linguistic diversity into their academic programs.

In the professional environment, some companies implement recruitment and human resource management policies that recognize the added value of neurodiversity and multilingualism within teams. For example, Auticon, a German-based IT consulting company whose employees are autistic, receives subsidies that reintegrate neurodiversity into the workplace. According to Lena Brosselin, this German-origin company has been applauded several times for its social enterprise model and inclusion initiatives by the Scottish government. In 2017, it won the UK Social Enterprise Award, which rewards establishments that contribute to society through their business model or positive social actions.[210] Another example is Franck Gillet, head of human resources at Renault Trucks, who explains how Renault Trucks has been committed to evolving its practices towards greater inclusion for years. This commitment was demonstrated through *Handi'Accord,* an agreement under which he recruited Bakay Fofana, a young autistic apprentice who was also selected for his bilingual French-English skills.[211]

Now more than ever, it is imperative to advocate for inclusive educational, linguistic, and social policies that recognize and actively support neurodiversity. It is crucial to understand that there is no one-

---

[209] Lequesne (2021).
[210] Social Enterprise UK. (2022).
[211] Renault Trucks (2006).

size-fits-all solution for integrating neuro-atypical individuals into a multilingual context. Creating inclusive environments fostering linguistic and social growth requires a personalized approach to acknowledging and embracing brain diversity. This approach should also address the unique linguistic needs of deaf individuals, posing the question: Can we identify the same structures and linguistic categories for sign and vocal languages for educational support and integration into professional life?

Neurodiversity and multilingualism in the United States

In her research, Bérengère Digard shows how understanding the interplay between social variations of multilingualism and autism could unveil new ways to support individuals on the autism spectrum.[212] In the United States, a vast country where linguistic diversity also exists due to immigration, multicultural communities, and the socio-linguistic history of the country, federal language policy enacts, adopts, or repeals language laws. The most significant issue was the Bilingual Education Act of 1965. Moreover, efforts have been made to support neurodiversity and promote the inclusion of neuro-atypical individuals, regardless of their native language or identity. These efforts manifest in inclusive educational policies, adapted teaching programs, specialized support services, and neurodiversity awareness initiatives. Initiatives begin with recognizing the linguistic rights of individuals and promoting respect for linguistic diversity in schools, workplaces, and society in general. They also include providing translation and interpretation services, ensuring access to educational resources in different languages, and valuing linguistic diversity as a cultural and intellectual asset.

However, concretely, observing the registration data of the *Boston public schools' dual language programs* obtained by the Hechinger report shows that neuro-atypical learners—who represent 22% of the student population—are significantly underrepresented in the district's seven bilingual programs. These students represent between 8 and 14% of enrollments in each of the five Spanish-English

---

[212] Digard (2020).

programs in the district. None are enrolled in the two-year Vietnamese-English program at Mather Elementary School. In the Haitian Creole-English program, so few students with an individualized learning plan are enrolled that the district cannot disclose the total without risking the students' privacy. Experts say this disparity is due to a lack of bilingual special education teachers. Still, it reflects whether neuro-atypical individuals can manage and thrive in multilingual education.[213]

Dynamics and challenges of the combination of multilingualism and specific needs

Starting from the accommodations and interventions implemented in the educational system, can we imagine a natural transition between school and the professional environment, allowing neuro-atypical individuals to manage their daily schedules and tasks effectively on the one hand and have access to professional development and continuous training adapted to their needs on the other?[214]

What solutions proposed at school are transferable to the professional environment?

For neuro-atypical multilingual learners with concentration or execution disorders, the solution at school is often to break tasks into mini-tasks, practice the ten-and-three suggested by Russel Barkley, and allow them to run or meditate for three minutes after a ten-minute task.[215] Barkley says that these learners know what needs to be done in one language or another; they just need help with execution and time management and can only complete a task by breaking it down (*multilayer* and *scaffolding*), all motivated by a final reward. This accommodation could be possible in the workplace provided that the multilingual and neuro-atypical employee, no longer having a personalized plan like at school, can be recognized

---

[213] Garcia Mathewson (2023).
[214] Barkley R.(2011).
[215] Higgins Averill & Rinaldi (2011).

as performing their tasks differently and can thus receive the granting of a breakdown of tasks to be accomplished into mini-goals over their day or week, as well as a staggered performance motivated by some form of retribution.

Moreover, studies show that one concentrates better and learns better in movement, which is more accurate for a hyperactive (ADHD) or kinesthetic person. More companies are prioritizing, just like at school, accommodations like dynamic seating, with fidgets or rollers, foot balloons, an air or ergonomic cushion, which allow movement. The focus is sometimes also on thermal and sensory comfort, i.e., considering the fact that neuro-atypical individuals have a brain that may induce hypersensitivity at the visual, auditory, olfactory, tactile, taste levels, avoiding garish or dull colors, cold-looking materials, unpleasant textures to the touch, visual distractors, bad smells, a noisy environment, too open, too straight-lined, with closed walls, without a relaxation corner. When several of these criteria are met, the range of recruitment possibilities increases and allows for the integration of as many diversities as possible within a team: cultural diversity, linguistic diversity, ethnic diversity, and neurodiversity.

What resources does the school have to promote successful inclusivity?

At school, directors of multilingual programs must establish close, rigorous, and structured collaboration between the team of multilingual class teachers and the special education team to support learners with an individualized plan developed after a standardized evaluation. This collaboration requires dedicating specific time for such activities in initial and continuing training calendars. It also involves planning monthly team meetings with clear objectives, evaluating them at the end of each period to measure the learners' progress, and then deciding whether to extend or modify the intervention based on these evaluations. A solution for the school would be to offer teachers of multilingual classes the opportunity to obtain accelerated training in special education in parallel with obtaining the bilingual authorization certificate (*CLAD & BCLAD* in California); this training could be initial or continuous.[216] However, is it materially realistic for a full-time teacher in a multilingual class to follow training in parallel with their work? Should these training courses instead be developed at a distance so that teachers interested in positions in multilingual classes do their training before being appointed to these positions? Or could a training system be designed with two teachers appointed to the same class who would alternate between the class and the training?

Can we envision reproducing this same scheme in the professional world by going through a period of transition and adaptation of the actors concerned? We will explore this possibility in the third part of this chapter.

From school to the workplace

What opportunities foster a multilingual educational environment for neuro-atypical individuals, and how can we envision their transfer and maintenance in the professional world? Several noteworthy educational initiatives in Europe and the United States include the adoption of International Initiatives (Senate Bill 41) by the Utah Senate in 2008. This initiative allocated funding for schools to implement two-language immersion programs, allowing students to learn English alongside Chinese, French, or Spanish. Governor Jon Huntsman Jr. (2005-2009) launched the *Governor's Language Summit* and the *Governor's World Language Council*, both aimed at creating a K-12 (from kindergarten to high school) linguistic roadmap for Utah. These decisions followed closely after the *No Child Left Behind Act* and aimed to open bilingualism to all by making it a part of the state's official educational program.[217] The Global California 2030 initiative shares the same goal of deploying bilingual programs in all public schools in the state.[218] Utah Governor Gary Herbert (2009-2021)

---

[216] Barkley (2011).
[217] Albrecht & Jokes (2003).
[218] Haworth Jacobs (2019).

stated, "These immersion programs add to Utah's appeal to the business world," and Senator Howard Stephenson (1992-2018) remarked, "It is a real advance in economic development for Utah that can have a population fluent in a multitude of foreign languages." The *Precodys Academy* in Europe, an alternative school without classes where everyone has their place concerning their individuality and differences, promises the same multilingualism objectives for all learners presenting neuro-atypical characteristics. English and sports have a significant place, and the founders' mission is benevolence, the use of innovative supports, and the organization of flexible classes with teachers who reassure and give confidence to learners who need it most.

However, what about the professional integration of neuro-atypical multilingual learners? Diversity in the workplace is an essential value to promote. It allows for integrating individuals with varied origins, cultures, experiences, and skills. By leveraging this diversity, companies can benefit from many advantages, such as creativity and innovation; different perspectives and ideas can lead to innovative solutions to company challenges. Innovative ideas and original concepts emerge by combining the skills of people from diverse backgrounds.

Additionally, collaborators are more motivated and involved in their work when comfortable in an environment that respects their linguistic or functional differences. This comfort often translates into improved overall productivity for the company. According to the Harvard Business Review, groups such as SAP, Hewlett Packard Enterprise, Microsoft, Willis Towers Watson, and Ford have launched programs conducive to neurodiversity. Other smaller companies highlight it to secure a competitive advantage. Rajesh Anandan, founder of Ultra Testing (software testing), for instance, asserts that with a staff composed of 75% employees with autism spectrum disorders, the startup has an edge in its field.

A school-to-work transition?

Are there programs to help neuro-atypical multilingual individuals feel valued in the workplace and succeed in the job market? Such support can include internships, mentoring programs, and accompanied learning. Employers can offer accommodations and additional personalized support to neuro-atypical and multilingual employees, including clear communication strategies, structured work environments, and professional development opportunities. For success, this process must be presented to the entire team and accompanied by an evaluation plan supported by a collection of information. This process could begin with a series of strategies aimed at building the employee's confidence, methods that would be followed by the implementation of adaptations, accommodations, and regulations of the daily routine, all supported by a regular collection of information that would show the value that multilingualism, differences in thinking, and diversity, in general, add to a team's performance. This awareness and training of the entire professional community on neurodiversity and the specific needs of neuro-atypical employees, as well as inclusion and effective communication, can contribute to creating an inclusive and respectful work environment. We will observe and illustrate the existing arrangements in Europe and the United States.

Multilingualism, neurodiversity, and professional integration in Europe

In France, the integration into the workforce of individuals presenting neuro-functional specificities known as ADHD is a topic that is increasingly garnering attention and benefiting from support measures. ADHD is recognized as a disability and is protected by the law of February 11, 2005, on equal rights and opportunities, participation, and citizenship of disabled persons. This recognition means that individuals with ADHD benefit from the same rights and protections as other disabled workers. Employers provide reasonable accommodations to enable individuals with ADHD to perform their jobs optimally. These accommodations may include adaptations to the work environment, flexible schedules, technical aids, and regular breaks.

One must then ask if these measures are tailored to each individual and established following individual contact to assess needs and define accommodations precisely and if this system is supported by regular follow-up and a collection of information aimed at its evaluation with adjustment as done in school.

Individuals with ADHD can benefit from specialized support and coaching, such as training to develop time management skills, organizational skills, and concentration techniques, which, added to their potential multilingual and multicultural skills, make the presence of these individuals foster listening, mutual respect, empathy, and add a significant amount of creativity within teams. Employers are encouraged to educate their staff about the reality of ADHD and the specific challenges those affected face. Can we also offer a tailored career path aimed at professional advancement? Could we implement special tools and personalized evaluations with predefined objectives to allow everyone to aspire to promotions or job changes? Let us take a closer look at what is being set up in the United States, using the example of California.

Multilingualism, neurodiversity, and professional integration in the United States

In a country as vast as the United States, it is essential to note that specific employment opportunities may vary depending on location and economic conditions. California, for example, with its diverse population and robust job market, can offer various work opportunities for multilingual and neuro-atypical individuals. Thanks to its thriving entrepreneurial ecosystem, multilingual and neuro-atypical individuals can leverage their unique skills, such as proficiency in multiple languages, creativity, and innovative thinking, to create businesses or offer specialized services in areas such as education, technology, translation, interpretation, language teaching, and multilingual customer service roles. The diversity of the California population creates a demand for professionals capable of effectively communicating with people of different linguistic backgrounds. Influenced by the famous example of the giant

Amazon and its AWS program, which continue to create equitable opportunities for neurodivergent talents from immigration and thus multilingual, many companies like Google, Apple, and Meta value neurodiversity and actively seek to create inclusive work environments. Individuals passionate about advocacy and helping others can find opportunities in non-profit organizations focused on disabilities, mental health, or neurodiversity. The Californian educational system offers employment opportunities for those interested in working with students with specific needs: special education teachers, paraprofessionals for atypical behavior-related needs, and roles where linguistic abilities and understanding of neurodiversity can be assets. Kipp Public School NorCal offers intentional coaching to its employees to fulfill its diversity and inclusion mission. They prioritize "that most of our staff and leaders represent the visible and invisible identities, perspectives, and experiences shared by our students and their families." It is also expected to see in job search engines, such as Indeed, a category labeled jobs for neuro-atypical or multilingual individuals, the goal being to promote positive reinforcement and positive discrimination, thus transforming what could be perceived as a weakness into a strength.

In conclusion, quickly adapting to changes is crucial in a constantly evolving world. The quote by Alexander Den Heijer, "When a flower doesn't bloom, you fix the environment in which it grows, not the flower," illustrates the fact that the responsibility for adaptation and inclusion is no longer that of the individual but that it is up to society and the workplace to celebrate diversities, transform them into assets, and prepare inclusion programs solidly, transparently, and measurably. Openness to neurological, linguistic, and cultural diversity, among others, allows a company to be more resilient in the face of challenges and new market trends. A team that embraces cultural, linguistic, gender, and sexual orientation diversity and brings together individuals with varied learning profiles and skill sets can better understand and meet a diverse audience's needs. Companies can gain competitiveness in an increasingly globalized market and strengthen a positive, attractive, and socially responsible brand image.

Chapter 9 – Dual-language programs in Southern Florida: A model for potential reforms to instruction for English language learners in Arizona, with implications for students' professional success

Michele Gerring

In 2000, Proposition 203, the English Language Education for Children in Public Schools Act, was passed in Arizona, limiting the extent to which teachers can allow the use of English Language Learner's native languages in public school classrooms beyond the students' first years of instruction. The use of students' native languages in instruction is called translanguaging.[219] Proposition 203 established the English-only model, Structured English Immersion, as the standard in Arizona, designating every student with a home language other than English as an English Language Learner. In Arizona, these home languages cannot be used to teach students in public schools, and these students are expected to spend one year receiving instruction separate from their native Anglophone classmates before joining mainstream classes.[220; 221; 222] From 2019 through 2025, Proposition 203 has faced significant criticism for being viewed as an impediment to the academic success of English Language Learners and for its perceived insensitivity to students' cultural backgrounds and emotional well-being. There are claims that

---

[219] More specifically, García, Johnson and Selzer (2017) define a translanguaging classroom as being the following: a space built collaboratively by the teacher and bilingual students as they use their different language practices to teach and learn in deeply creative and critical ways (p. 2).
[220] Gomez (2019).
[221] However, students often remain in instruction separate from their native Anglophone peers for years, and as a result, their grades in content areas often stay significantly lower than those of their native Anglophone classmates.
[222] Proposition 203 passed in 2000, with 63% of Arizonans supporting it. Heineke (2017), p. 25.

Proposition 203 discriminates against English Language Learners because, statistically, their status as native speakers of other languages puts them at a disadvantage even when graduating from high school.[223] Only 54% of English Language Learners graduated from high school in 2020, as opposed to the rate of the general population, 79% that year, according to the Arizona Department of Education, as cited in Gomez.[214]

Most English Language Learners in Arizona speak Spanish as their home language.[224] However, significant numbers of Arabic, Vietnamese, Somali, and Navajo speakers exist. This tendency is on par with contemporary trends in the US, where the population of Hispanics increased by 19% between 2010 and 2021, from 50.5 million to 62.5 million.[225] 80% of Arizona's English Language Learners are Latino.[214]

This chapter will examine evidence of the failure of the Structured English Immersion (SEI) model in Arizona in terms of its ability to facilitate the academic success of English Language Learners: empirically documented declines in these students' aptitudes in English under Proposition 203, as shown in a large-scale, quantitative research study by Mahoney et al.,[226] the fact that the SEI model does not employ the principles of Second Language Acquisition or facilitate students' attainment of Cognitive Academic Language Proficiency[227] Moreover, the SEI model in Arizona relies on erroneous conceptions of how people acquire languages, including the fallacious idea that young children acquire the finer nuances of language more quickly than older children and adults.[228]

The status quo that has existed since 2000 in Arizona can be contrasted sharply with the educational gains, translatable to the professional world, attained through dual-language programs in Southern Florida, an area with a strongly multilingual atmosphere. As of the 2019 U.S. Census, 22.5% of Florida's population, or 4.8

---

[223] Gomez (2021).
[224] Gomez (2019).
[225] Krogstad et al. (2022).
[226] Mahoney et al. (2022).
[227] Long & Adamson (2009).
[228] Combs (2012).

million, spoke Spanish at home. From 2013 through 2017, about 105,435 people above five in the U.S. spoke French at home, according to the U.S. Census Bureau American Community Survey.[229] There are over 300,000 Haitian-Creole speakers in Florida, according to the University of Central Florida's Department of Modern Languages and Literatures. Some school districts in Southern Florida have significantly higher populations of Spanish speakers than the national average, which is 10.4%. For example, in the Miami-Dade County Public Schools in 2023, 22.9% of students were English Language Learners. Spanish-English bilingualism is a prerequisite for many jobs in Miami-Dade County, opening doors to many professional opportunities in Florida.[230]

The number of bilingual schools in Southern Florida has been on the rise, and the success of bilingual education in this region could serve as a valuable example for legislators in Arizona, who are frequently encouraged by advocates for English Language Learners to reconsider Proposition 203. The success of bilingual education in Southern Florida is manifested by the success of the Coral Way Bilingual Program in Miami, as documented by Richardson.[231] A study done in five dual-language schools in Florida confirmed that English Language Learners enrolled in dual-language classes do better on achievement tests than English Language Learners in mainstream classes.[232] A study on the effect of a dual-language program at an elementary school in central Florida on English Language Learners' reading skills shows the same results.[233]

This chapter will explore how an analysis of dual-language and immersion programs in Southern Florida can inform potential reforms that could be made to programs for English Language Learners in public schools in Arizona, which is the only American

---

[229] Jaumont (2020).
[230] Fattal (2023).
[231] Richardson (1968).
[232] Reyes (2021).
[233] Black (2007).

state in which bilingual education and translanguaging are illegal.[234] This potential will be considered in light of the benefits that multilingualism has for students' professional prospects in the United States, particularly in the fields of government and social services, and this chapter will examine the implications that improvements in education for English Language Learners would have for Arizona students' success.

The disadvantages of the use of structured English immersion in Arizona concerning the academic success of English language learners

This section will examine research that shows that the SEI model used in Arizona and enforced by Proposition 203 does not facilitate optimal academic performance for English Language Learners. According to the Helios Educational Foundation, only 23% of Latino third-grade students in Arizona read proficiently, compared with the overall rate of 35% among third-graders.[235] Latinos account for only 25.5% of the student population at Arizona's three state universities, where Caucasian students represent 51% of the population.[236] While these statistics do not specifically show Proposition 203's flaws, they suggest that Arizona's educational system does not sufficiently support English Language Learners.

However, some studies directly reveal the limitations of Proposition 203. First, a large-scale, quantitative research study by Mahoney et al.[237] finds that Proposition 203 negatively impacts the learning of English Language Learners. They evaluated the consequences of Proposition 203 over 12 years to see whether the law meets the "third prong" of the legal case Castañeda vs. Pickard.[238]

---

[234] Bilingual education in public schools was made illegal in California in 1998, in Arizona in 2000, and in Massachusetts in 2002, ushering in an era in which the Structured English Immersion model was the standard in these three states. García & Wei (2014), p. 53. However, this law was overturned in California in 2016 and Massachusetts in 2017. Mitchell (2019).
[235] Helios Educational Foundation (2023).
[236] Ibid.
[237] Mahoney et al. (2022).
[238] Castañeda v. Pickard (1981).

The "three prongs" of Casteñada vs. Pickard refer to the criteria that programs for English Language Learners must meet to remain in effect legally: they must be founded on valid educational theory, they must be put into place using suitable resources, practices, and staffing, and they must meet specific standards showing their effectiveness.[239] Mahoney et al. tracked the progress of two groups,[240] one learning English as a new language but already knew Spanish, and the other, English-speaking students, most of whom knew only English, from 2002 through 2013. The differences in achievement between the groups became more dramatic between 2002 and 2013, showing that education for English Language Learners in Arizona has become less effective since Proposition 203. It was concluded that since the SEI model in effect in Arizona led to reductions in English Language Learners' achievement scores, thereby not meeting the third prong established in Casteñada vs. Pickard, Proposition 203 should be abolished.[228]

Second, the SEI paradigm espoused by Arizona since 2000 is not pedagogically sound because it fails to implement one of the critical principles of Second Language Acquisition by not implementing meaning-focused, communicative instruction and neglecting the development of students' Cognitive Academic Language Proficiency.[241] Long and Adamson's main complaint about Arizona's SEI program is that it strays away from a *focus on form*, meaning-focused communicative instruction, one of the main principles of Second Language Acquisition, which has been shown to yield the best results in language instruction. Instead, Arizona's SEI program focuses on language as an object or *form* in the plural sense of grammatical features.[242]

---

[239] Moore (2021). p.114-115.
[240] Mahoney et al. (2022).
[241] Long & Adamson (2012).
[242] Ibid. p. 43-44, describe the discrepancy between the *focus on forms* that Arizona's SEI programs use and the *focus on form* that is the modus operandi of Second Language Acquisition: One of the significant problems with Arizona's SEI approach is that by...focusing on language as object (grammar, vocabulary items, etc.), that of is focus on forms, not focus on form, it impedes children's access to the type of classroom linguistic

Additionally, Long & Adamson see Arizona's SEI paradigm as flawed because it does not provide instructional materials that include academic English or the concepts required to comprehend academic materials, both of which will be required for English Language Learners to use once they transition out of the separated first year of instruction and join mainstream classes.[243] They caution that robbing students of opportunities to use academic English or the concepts needed to work in academic classes is a disservice to English Language Learners because they will be ill-prepared to take classes with native-English-speaker classmates. Long & Adamson explain that acquiring Cognitive Academic Language Proficiency, the ability to use language employed in academia takes several years.[244]

Third, another aspect of Arizona's SEI model is that it incorrectly assumes that young children are significantly better at acquiring language at a sophisticated level than teenagers and adults.[245] More specifically, Combs writes that the underpinnings of the SEI model in Arizona are based on what she calls "folk theories" or "cultural models" of Second Language Acquisition.[246] The SEI model in Arizona uses a four-hour English language development model, in which English Language Learners are separated from their peers for four hours per day and receive instruction in English only. The *raison d'être* of this practice is the "time-on-task" principle, according to which English Language Learners will naturally improve their English by spending extended periods in English-only

---

environment they need...Focus on form, in contrast, involves meaning-focused communicative lessons during which students' attention is drawn to the language itself. Children and adult learners are much more likely to understand the meaning and function of a new (grammatical, lexical) item and remember it later when they have a felt need for it for whatever they are working on at the time and are more likely to be attending to the input.

[243] Ibid. p. 51.

[244] Long & Adamson refer to a 1981 study by J. Cummins, entitled, Age on arrival and immigrant second language learning in Canada: A reassessment, published in *Applied Linguistics*. Cummins found that immigrant students in Anglophone Canada need between 5 and 7 years to acquire vocabularies that are similar in quality to those of their native-English speaker classmates. Ibid. p. 53.

[245] Combs (2012).

[246] Ibid. p. 63.

instruction.[247] However, Combs points to the fact that Second Language Acquisition is much more complex than just the number of hours spent in the classroom and that it depends on how proficiency is defined, children's ability to read and write in their first language, the level of their parents' knowledge of the second language, and whether children receive first-language support at school.[248]

The effectiveness of dual-language programs in Southern Florida as a model for reforms to Arizona's educational policy on the use of translanguaging in public schools

Examining dual-language schools in Southern Florida can be very instructive as a model for reforming Arizona English Language Learners programs. Research supporting the academic benefits of dual-language education for English Language Learners (ELLs) in Florida includes Richardson's dissertation on the Coral Way Bilingual Program in Miami,[249] highlighting its success. Reyes' study[250] further demonstrates that achievement gaps between ELLs and native Anglophones are reduced more effectively in dual-language programs than in mainstream instruction. Additionally, due to dual-language program enrollment, Black's dissertation shows significant improvement in ELLs' reading skills.[251]

Dual-language education is highly developed in Southern Florida. The presence of the following programs in Southern Florida demonstrates this strong interest: Innovative dual-language programs, such as one in Haitian Creole and English at Rollins Green Elementary School in Boynton Beach, the first ever in Florida; high-performing dual-language schools, such as the International

---

[247] Ibid. p.72.
[248] Combs acknowledges research that young children acquire social aspects of language rapidly, with native or native-like accents, but insists on dispelling the myth that they are better at acquiring the nuances of language, in terms of syntax and lexical codes, than adults. Ibid. p. 73.
[249] Richardson (1968).
[250] Reyes (2021).
[251] Black (2007).

Studies Charter High School in Miami, rated the number one high school in Florida in 2015, and grants that Florida International University and the University of Central Florida have received, to prepare teachers to teach in dual-language programs.

Concerning examples of dual-language education programs that Arizona could eventually emulate for the academic and professional success of its students, it is essential to note the success of the Coral Way Bilingual K-8 Center in Miami, the first publicly-funded dual-language program in the US, and still one of the most successful dual-language programs in the US. Although there had been schools that taught students in German and Italian in the U.S. before the creation of Coral Way Elementary School's dual-language program in 1963, it was the first example of a program in the U.S. that educated both native English speakers and native speakers of another language (Spanish) in English and this other language, while simultaneously covering traditional academic subjects.[252]

The academic success of the Coral Way Bilingual K-8 Center has been well-noted throughout its history. Students at the school have earned high scores on standardized tests throughout its history, and in 2014, it was deemed the "School of the Year" by the Spanish Consulate. The positive results of this program in its first five years helped usher in the Bilingual Education Act of 1968, which created federal grants for school districts to create educational programs for children with limited proficiency in English.[253]

One of the documented sources of proof of the success of the Coral Way Bilingual Experiment, that is, the initial years of the dual-language program at Coral Way Elementary School, from 1963 through 1966, is a dissertation by Richardson.[254] She compares the performance of six groups of native Anglophone and native Hispanophone elementary school students, some of whom were enrolled in the Coral Way Bilingual Experiment and others not

---

[252] Cuban refugees and immigrants to Southern Florida founded Coral Way Elementary's dual-language program. Both native Anglophones and native Hispanophones take 40% of their content courses in Spanish and 60% in English. Reichard (2019).
[253] Ibid.
[254] Richardson (1968).

enrolled there, on the SAT and the Cooperative Inter-American Test.[255] Richardson's dissertation confirmed the hypotheses of the school district that students in the bilingual program would have scored at least as well as students not enrolled in the bilingual program and that both Hispanophones and Anglophones improved their scores in English and Spanish from year to year.[256; 257]

Furthermore, another study on dual-language programs in Florida, conducted in 2021 by Reyes, is worth considering. Reyes was motivated to conduct this study because significant discrepancies in achievement exist between English Language Learners and non-English Language Learners in Florida, from kindergarten through high school.[258] Her study focused on the academic achievement discrepancies between English and non-English Learners enrolled in third grade at five elementary schools in Central Florida. The ACCESS test evaluated dual-language acquisition and reading proficiency using the iReady Diagnostic 2 Tool.[259] Reyes' findings confirmed that for English Language Learners, enrollment in dual-language instruction saw more significant increases in reading proficiency in English than English Language Learners experienced in mainstream instruction. Thus, being enrolled in dual-language programs helps English language learners reduce the discrepancies in their achievement levels compared with native speakers of English.[260; 261]

---

[255] Coady (2020). p. 90-91.
[256] Ibid. p. 90-93.
[257] Richardson surmised that the Hispanophone students may have done better in English than the Anglophones did in Spanish because of the intrinsic incentive that they had to acquire English at a high level as residents of a city where English was the dominant language. Coady (2020), p. 94.
[258] Reyes (2021). p. 1.
[259] Ibid. p. 4-5.
[260] Ibid. p. 18-19.
[261] Reyes posits that mainstream instruction classes, which concentrate mostly on the syntax of language and forms of language, do not facilitate the development of comprehension needed for the development of academic language in the content area, as opposed to dual-language instruction, which does encourage the cultivation of understanding of concepts that are key in both the first and second languages. Ibid. p. 19.

Third, another study that reinforces the idea of the effectiveness of dual-language programs on the development of English Language Learners' literacy is a study by Black,[262] who evaluated the progress of the reading skills of English Language Learners in an elementary school in central Florida. The study subjects were in grades 1 through 5, and Black used qualitative methods to examine work samples and conduct observations and interviews. Black identified ten factors that affect the process of Second Language Acquisition for English Language Learners enrolled in dual-language programs: validation of culture and language, the necessity of a comfortable learning environment, the transfer of reading skills from the native to the second language, the incorporation of literature within the reading block, additional linguistic support across the content area, the development of thinking skills, strategies supporting English Speakers of Other Languages, creative activities integrated within literacy instruction, language arts in both languages and the imbalance of instruction in the native and first languages. All factors except for the imbalance of instructional time in the native and second languages facilitated the development of reading skills; this factor alone stymied it. Black concludes from her study that the students' participation in a dual-language program facilitates their reading progress.[263]

Advocating for dual-language programs: A call to reevaluate Arizona's Proposition 203 and embrace bilingual education

In conclusion, an examination of the drawbacks of Arizona's Proposition 203, banning the use of English Language Learners' native languages in public school instruction, and an analysis of the improvements in their academic performance when they are enrolled in dual-language programs, sheds light on the fact that it would be in the best interest for legislators in Arizona to abolish Proposition 203 and, at the very least, to allow translanguaging in public schools, and ideally, to create dual-language programs of their own. This is the

---

[262] Black (2007).
[263] Ibid. p. ii-ix.

reason that educational professionals determine educational policy best. The legal case Casteñada vs. Pickard has not been overturned.[264] Thus, there is still a precedent in educational programs for English Language Learners. These programs must still be based on sound educational theory, implemented using appropriate practices, staffing, and resources, and meeting specific effectiveness standards.[265] Indeed, Mahoney et al. disproved the pedagogical effectiveness of Arizona's SEI model.[266] Long, Adamson, and Combs pointed out how its underpinnings contradict the principles of Second Language Acquisition, which scholars and practitioners widely accepted in the fields of bilingual and multilingual education as top-of-the-line.[267] Moreover, research by Richardson, Reyes, and Black demonstrates the effectiveness of dual-language programs on the academic performance of English Language Learners.[268]

With the United States becoming increasingly diverse, and with the link between academic success and professional success being inextricably linked for many occupations, educators must have at their disposal the ability to facilitate their student learning to the utmost that it is possible, thus the importance of allowing educators in Arizona to establish dual-language programs. In the United States as a whole, bilingualism has many economic advantages. Specifically, 9 out of 10 employers need employees who are fluent in languages other than English, 56% claim that this need will only intensify in the next five years, 47% say that they need bilingual candidates for the domestic market alone, one in three employers who need bilingual candidates say that they do not have enough of them, and one in four employers lost some business because they did not have enough bilingual candidates.[269; 270]

---

[264] Castañeda v. Pickard (1981).
[265] Moore (2021), p. 114-115.
[266] Mahoney et al. (2022).
[267] Long & Adamson (2009); Combs (2012).
[268] Richardson (1968); Reyes (2021); Black (2007).
[269] ACTFL (2019) interviewed 1,200 employers in the U.S. to assess the extent of these needs.
[270] New American Economy (2017) reports that between 2010 and 2015, the need for bilingual workers in the U.S. increased by more than double, with

Just as English Language Learners and native Anglophones alike enrolled in dual-language programs in Florida see their career prospects strengthened due to their bilingualism, biculturalism, and bilateralism, Arizona's students, both English Language Learners and native Anglophones would also find it to their advantage to have more opportunities to achieve high levels of proficiency in both Spanish and English.

Several statistics show the burgeoning need for bilingual employees in Florida. For example, the number of online job postings for bilingual candidates more than doubled between 2010, when there were 7,565 in Florida, and 2015, when there were 18,116, according to New American Economy. Some metropolitan areas in Florida had triple increases in online job advertisements for bilingual people.[271]

Statistics also show a strong need for bilingual candidates in Arizona's economy. Abolishing Proposition 203 and creating dual-language and immersion programs would greatly benefit English Language Learners' employment prospects. New American Economy reports that in 2015, 4% of job advertisements in Arizona asked for bilingual candidates, although only 2% of working-age adults in Arizona are bilingual.[272] Between 2010 and 2015, online employment advertisements for bilingual candidates increased by 60.3%, while the need for Spanish-speaking candidates increased from 5,873 to 11,990 positions.[273]

240,000 such postings in 2010, and 630,000 in 2015. For jobs in Spanish, the number of job advertisements asking for fluency in Spanish rose by 150% (New American Economy, 2017a). Additionally, Agirdag (2013) found that bilingual young adults in the U.S. make between $2,000 and $3,300 more at the start of their careers than people who grew up with limited proficiency in a second language but whose primary language is English. Furthermore, Rumbaut (2014) found that the adult children of immigrants in Southern California who became fully bilingual were more apt to finish their high school degrees and, after graduation, to hold more prestigious jobs and make more money than the adult children of immigrants who spoke only English, or who had limited bilingualism.
[271] New American Economy (2016b).
[272] New American Economy (2017b).
[273] Ibid.

The importance of facilitating the professional success of Latino students in Arizona by striking down Proposition 203 and establishing dual-language and immersion schools is accentuated by the projection that Latino students are expected to account for more than 50% of Arizona's population by 2026, according to the Helios Education Foundation.[274] Indeed, it would be an asset to Arizona economically to raise the bar of its competitiveness with other states, such as California, Utah, Texas, North Carolina, New York, Florida, Washington, Minnesota, and New Mexico, by allowing for the creation of dual-language and immersion schools, especially since there are now about 3,600 dual-language and immersion programs in the United States, as of 2021.[275] Indeed, the dramatic increase in dual language and immersion programs between 2006 and 2021 has been deemed a "dual language revolution."[276] Arizona would do well to orient its steps according to the needs of the future, which are increasingly bilingual, for the academic, economic, and professional success of all of their students by pursuing the route that many teachers, administrators, and parents in states such as Florida have followed, in making dual-language programs an essential part of their educational offerings.[277]

---

[274] Helios Education Foundation (2023). What we do. Arizona.
[275] American Councils for International Education (2021).
[276] Henderson & Palmer (2021), p. 10.
[277] I would like to extend my thanks to Regina Mazzurco González, M.S.W., B.A., Spanish, for making me aware of the issue of Proposition 203 and the use of the Structured English Immersion (SEI) model in Arizona.

PART 3.
Empowering organizations

Learning another language involves learning different words for the same things and another way of thinking.
– Flora Lewis, The New York Times (1978)

Chapter 10 – Navigating the benefits and challenges of multilingualism and cultural fluency in Silicon Valley: Myths and reality

Isabelle Finger

From an early age, I have been accustomed to deciphering new cultural references, adapting to unwritten rules, and being an outsider. I never feel entirely at home, and I have always loved it! I have been exposed to various cultures and languages after living and working in Switzerland, France, Germany, Slovakia, and the United States. As a Leadership and Career Strategy Coach in Silicon Valley,[278] I have helped dozens of foreign-born professionals build careers and lives in the world's largest technology hub.

This chapter is based on my observations, discussions, and experiences with immigrants from around the world, who are often highly educated and work in the tech or professional service industries. It is common for them to speak more than two languages. They usually learn English as a foreign language in school or later in life. Although this population does not represent immigrants' entire

---

[278] The name "Silicon Valley" was coined in the 1970s to describe the south part of the San Francisco Bay Area where the leaders of the silicon transistors industry had their headquarters. While this industry lost its predominance over time, it created the foundations for the tech industry to flourish and develop. Technically, Silicon Valley covers the counties of Santa Clara, San Mateo, and part of the counties of Alameda and Santa Cruz. Officially, San Francisco is not part of Silicon Valley. However, "Silicon Valley" is not only a location, but also a specific culture. With the development of a large tech ecosystem in the city of San Francisco after 2000's, the terms started being confusing. Locally, people prefer to speak from the "San Francisco Bay Area" and "Silicon Valley" is barely used. Internationally, the term keeps its aura of legend and describes indeed the whole tech hub rather than a specific geographic area.

experience in Silicon Valley,[279] it illustrates the difficulties people face when adapting to a new culture. Additionally, Silicon Valley has an exciting environment since it is very international and firmly rooted in American culture.

California and the San Francisco Bay Area have enjoyed a worldwide reputation as dreamland since the Golden Rush (1848-1855) for many good reasons: spectacular natural beauty, excellent climate, abundant opportunities to become rich and famous, and progressive and open-minded culture. The initial impression of the picture may seem accurate, but upon closer examination, contradictions emerge, illustrating the complexity of reality. This complexity underscores the necessity for concerted efforts to adapt and thrive in such an environment.

Foreign-born in Silicon Valley – a quick look at the demographics

39% of the three million people in Silicon Valley are foreign-born, three times higher than the U.S. level (13%). Those foreign-born are more educated than the national average, with 52% having at least a bachelor's degree (US average: 32%). They also have a higher income than the rest of the country ($138,100 vs. $67,300).[280] They benefit from a robust social status in the community. In the technology sector, 69% of the workers are foreign-born—with India and China accounting for 39% (25% and 14% respectively)—while people born in the United States only account for 31%. A specific sub-group of the immigrants working in technology in Silicon Valley are the entrepreneurs who founded some of the giants in the industry like Elon Musk (Tesla and SpaceX), Apoorva Mehta (Instacart), or Andrey Khusid and Oleg Shardin (Miro), to name a few.

In everyday life, such immigrants can find international schools where their children can be educated in their native language

---

[279] Many immigrants in Silicon Valley are working for low wages jobs and are far away from the same level of social status and stability, especially among the population from Latin America and Asia. 21% of the immigrant workforce is not fluent in English and 18% of the immigrant population of Santa Clara is undocumented.
[280] Joint Venture Silicon Valley (2022).

(especially if they come from France, Germany, China, or Russia), and they can quickly meet and network with many of their compatriots, leveraging the presence of consulates, national chambers of commerce and start-up accelerators. As a result, many think they can rely on their national communities and that their integration will be easier in such an open, tolerant, and diverse ecosystem. They believe individual strengths and hard work trump social origins and cultural differences. While this is more likely to happen in Silicon Valley than in many other places in the United States, many immigrants are still surprised in their first year by how much they still need to learn and adapt to the American culture and way of life.

Silicon Valley, a specific culture anchored in the American culture

Silicon Valley has specific codes, etiquette, and communication methods that are essential in how people behave to grasp opportunities. In her book *The Culture Map: Breaking Through the Invisible Barriers of Global Business*,[281] INSEAD Professor Erin Meyer defines eight key dimensions[282] and places countries on a continuum for each. Misunderstandings happen when there is a gap between people's preferences from distinct cultures. According to this framework, the United States uses assertive low-context communication, developing trust based on tasks performed and strongly preferring application-first discussions. They are placed more in the middle of the scale for feedback style, decision-making

---

[281] Meyer (2014).
[282] Communicating: are people evolving in a low or a high context environment? Evaluating: do people prefer direct or indirect feedback? Persuading: do people convince others using principles or applications first? Leading: do people value more egalitarian or hierarchical power structures? Deciding: do groups tend to make their decisions in a consensual or top-down way? Trusting: do people develop their trust in each other based on tasks or relationships? Disagreeing: Do people adopt a more confrontational or more avoiding attitude toward conflicts? Scheduling: do people have a linear or flexible perception of time?

process, and conflict management. Finally, they have some preferences for an egalitarian leadership style.

These trends are still prevalent in Silicon Valley and are even more pronounced than the national average. On the Communication scale, local Venture Capitalists require investment pitch presentations to be done in a clear, simple, explicit, and short way. The standard advice for entrepreneurs is to communicate at the language level equivalent to that of an 8th-grade student. Complicated language is considered, at best, as a lack of respect for your interlocutor's precious time and mental space and, at worst, as a way to mislead them about the product's value. On the direct vs indirect feedback, foreign-born are often surprised not to get a much more direct and precise assessment of their work. To convince people from Silicon Valley, you should not only adopt an application-first approach—but you also must be "data-driven." In terms of the decision-making process, Silicon Valley has built flat organizational structures aligned with an individualist vision of society and an admiration for analytical capabilities. Since anyone can theoretically innovate and bring the next big idea, the communication lines are open, and anyone is invited to share their ideas and opinions in meetings. At the same time, getting a product to market and being willing to fail quickly and learn fosters top-down decisions. Companies often discuss "disagree and commit" to balance both approaches. In terms of earning trust, Silicon Valley firms advocate for performance reviews and meritocracy, investing millions of dollars in highly sophisticated systems and processes to ensure everyone is treated based on their performance and outcomes rather than on subjective criteria. Therefore, it might look like foreign-born people are well equipped to succeed, as the culture of Silicon Valley values individual skills over relationships.

Challenges faced by foreign-born in Silicon Valley: Silicon Valley's culture of ambiguities for foreign-born

Numerous discussions with local foreign-born have consistently highlighted four significant challenges. First, many foreign-born find it difficult to develop trust in the system, and some feel that the game is "rigged." The main reasons mentioned by immigrants are the "soft" approach to conflict and feedback, the contradiction between the claimed meritocracy and the actual biases at play, and the real impact of relationships on an individual's professional success. The constant need to recalibrate the messages of fellow Americans remains a challenge and a burden, even after years in the region. Among Europeans, the frequent use of hyperbolic terms like "awesome" or "amazing" is often a topic of humor. The French, for instance, might point out that "not bad" is often the highest praise from a French manager, while Germans and Dutch might suggest that not receiving criticism is already a positive sign. The gap between the claimed meritocracy and the actual impact of biases toward certain minorities has come under increasing scrutiny within companies and the media. Consequently, foreign-born individuals often question how they are perceived and rewarded by others.

Furthermore, reconciling the vocal emphasis on individual skills and the fundamental role played by relationships remains a challenge. In a job market where people stay, on average, less than two years in the same job, personal and long-term relationships are theoretically less crucial, at least within the same company. However, the reality is slightly different. To succeed anywhere in Silicon Valley, you need social credibility to bring people around to your point of view and get them on board. Many backdoor conversations happen outside of offices.[283]

Second, many immigrants also feel a lack of confidence. Besides the fact that many of the people you encounter here are from prestigious universities or are working in the largest technology companies in the world, the way people tell their stories on LinkedIn or other social media can feel impressive, complex to assess, and even more challenging to adopt and replicate.

Third, many local companies are unfamiliar with foreign companies and universities, making immigrants' experiences and qualifications less recognized than their counterparts in their home countries. This can lead to profound disappointment when

---

[283] Mundi (2017).

immigrants realize that their efforts and the social prestige they previously enjoyed have vanished.

Fourth, the technology industry has created many new jobs and become inundated with titles for those jobs. This makes the landscape difficult to read for newcomers and requires a deep understanding of the context of the different companies.

All of this and the frequent resulting imposter syndrome make the crucial activity of networking a challenging one for foreign-born. It can feel like the chicken and egg issue where you need a network to get your first job. Still, you cannot get a network if you do not have many resources to offer—especially in an environment that is very dynamic and where people have a lot of ideas and ambitions.

Career Impact

A foreign-born's first Silicon Valley job is often one to two steps more junior than they would have accepted in their country of origin, especially for women, non-Europeans, and people who did not study in the United States. It can take years to catch up on the career trajectory, particularly for manager positions. For instance, among computers and information systems managers working in Silicon Valley, 41,8% are born in the United States, 32% are naturalized citizens, and only 26.1% are non-citizens. In comparison, they represent respectively 29.4%, 28.5%, and 42.2% of the total workers in IT roles.[284]

For professionals in services-oriented roles like Sales, Marketing, or Customer Services, companies hire foreign-born people to manage their businesses and operations in foreign countries. While this can be a valid steppingstone, and many immigrants are motivated to keep a working relationship with their country of origin, the risk is keeping that scope longer and needing help accessing more extensive responsibilities.

In my interviews, nobody cared that I had worked for Google in Russia for over five years, leading a team of 5 people. The only job I could get was an individual contributor role focused on

---

[52] Otoiu & Titan (2017).

Russian clients. Even if I grew my portfolio very successfully, Russia never became a key market for my company, and I did not have the same chances to be promoted as my colleagues working with larger markets. Getting access to US-based clients was almost impossible for me. I had to change company to break that system. – Business Development Manager, Tech Company

For software engineers, data analysts, data scientists, and other IT roles, foreign-born people avoid mentioning their language skills altogether.

In Germany, I was working on automated speech recognition projects. Here, my first job was as an hourly paid contractor. It took me two years to get a full-time position, even if I was clearly overqualified. Nobody ever mentioned me being fluent in German and Italian. I quickly stopped speaking about it as it felt out of the scope of my job anyway. – Computer Linguist, PhD, Tech Company

As a result, many immigrants are tempted to focus their time on their communities. This tactic can work in specific cases—mostly when the community is large enough, at least within a particular scope, has many people in influential positions, and is willing to help immigrants. However, many communities do not fit this description. In that case, spending much time with compatriots can be a two-edged sword. While the presence and companionship of people from their own culture provide a much-needed space for genuine interactions and well-being, there is a risk of focusing too much on this comfortable environment. As time flies, building a professional network becomes even more challenging.

Strategies for a better use of foreign-born skills in the Silicon Valley job market

Despite the wave of layoffs in the tech industry, the "talent war" for qualified workers remains intense.[285] Long-term data suggest that talent will continue to be scarce in the future. By 2030, the country is projected to face a shortage of 2.5 million STEM jobs, increasing the

---

[285] Smith (2023).

demand for international students, particularly from China and India.[286] In this context, it is crucial to fully leverage the skills and experience of foreign-born individuals. How can this be achieved?

While Silicon Valley claims to value flexibility, adaptability, and the capability to learn, neither companies nor foreign-born individuals connect the experience of speaking different languages and having spent time in other countries with a higher likelihood of developing solid and soft cognitive skills. So far, research on the cognitive impact of speaking other languages points out that multilingualism is correlated with better-developed executive functions of the brain, defined as a solid capacity to plan, display self-control, and stay focused. Multilingual people solve complex problems more creatively, leveraging their habits of expressing similar thoughts in different languages.

Decision-making is also positively impacted. When multilingual people use a language other than their native language, they benefit from emotional and cognitive distance and tend to make more rational decisions.[287] Another example is the capability to learn and adapt as an adult. Language learning trains the brain to learn new skills and concepts faster. This list of examples strongly correlates with the World Economic Forum's list of the top soft skills in demand in the job market.[288]

Therefore, it seems essential to increase research and awareness about the holistic impact of multilingualism on professional competencies and ensure that companies have the knowledge and tools to incorporate it adequately into their hiring processes. Additionally, organizations should better understand foreign credentials and higher education institutions. Finally, investing in inclusive company cultures that account for country of origin on top of other criteria like gender or ethnicity also has the potential for higher retention and better performance of the foreign-born workforce.

---

[286] Holon (2023).
[287] Keysar et al. (2012).
[288] Masterson (2023).

On the employees' side, three strategies show reliable results if implemented consistently and with patience. First, foreign-born should advocate for their cognitive and soft skills rather than taking them for granted. This requires finding examples where such skills were at play in previous experiences. This strategy is essential not only in the hiring process but also on an ongoing basis to build a reputation and work toward future opportunities. Second, foreign-born people should invest time and effort in learning and reflecting on American and Silicon Valley cultures. Erin Meyer's book is a great starting point. Helena Seo, from Korea, also offers an exciting example of transforming her Korean habits into strengths in her work.[289]

> Because English is a second language, the reality is that I will never be as eloquent or inspiring with my words as native speakers. Realizing this helped me become a doer with a strong bias toward action. (...) In Korean, there is a concept called "noon-chi." It's almost impossible to find the exact equivalent in English, but the best possible translation is probably "tact." It's the skill of reading between the lines and acting sensibly based on a tactful interpretation of the situation. This is the virtue I was taught in Korea. It's the sixth sense that enables you to read people's emotional states and relate to them. When noon-chi is combined with empathy, authenticity, and self-awareness, you can lead teams with high emotional intelligence.
> – Helena Seo, Doordash, 2020

Third, foreign-born people should speak more about their experience in their countries of origin in a way that connects an aspect of their culture to its meaning for them. Rachel Arnett, Assistant Professor of Management at Wharton, calls this interaction "rich cultural-identity expression."[290] When people at work can go over the superficial small talk over the weather or some national food specialties, inclusiveness is increased, and foreign-born workers can feel more connected with their colleagues as it fosters mutual respect, trust, and the likelihood of being included in meaningful projects.

---

[289] Sea (2020).
[290] Arnett (2023).

However, foreign-born workers should avoid contentious topics that could alienate trust and empathy.

To conclude, Silicon Valley illustrates the ambiguity multilingual and multicultural people face. While those characteristics are reputed to be vital assets in the job market, the structure of Silicon Valley's economy makes them less desirable. It is not enough for job seekers to master a language other than English; the question is how to leverage this asset meaningfully to prosper. While long-term trends in demand for qualified professionals might favor foreign-born professionals, cultural changes and adaptation are slow, and foreign-born people will continue facing the mentioned challenges for some time.

The example of Silicon Valley is fascinating as it could be a window into what more parts of the world could look like if we continue to see highly educated professionals gathering in tech and finance hubs. How will the local cultures resist and adapt? How can different minorities benefit from the same game rules and improve collaboration? Further research about the microcosmos of Silicon Valley might help better understand the experience of multilingual people living far away from their countries of origin and in helping craft inclusive work and life environments.

Chapter 11 – The four dimensions of global leadership

Mehdi Lazar

Since Peter Drucker famously stated that "culture eats strategy for breakfast," it has become evident that managing corporate culture is essential for organizational success. Since the acceleration of globalization, many organizations have also sought leaders who can seamlessly navigate different countries and cultures, undertake expatriate assignments, comprehend diverse markets, and manage multicultural teams.[291] This is particularly true since Globalization 4.0, the rapid spread of digital technologies, and the Fourth Industrial Revolution. Consequently, nowadays, one can say that culture also eats leadership from breakfast.

Culture is "the collective programming of the mind which distinguishes the members of one category of people from another."[292] It is central to all human beings. Since people drive business, all organizational activities, from leadership to decision-making, are influenced by culture. While globalization does lead to a certain degree of cultural convergence, where behaviors become more similar, unique beliefs and value systems still exist globally. Global leaders must simultaneously deal with cultural convergence and divergence and understand and anticipate these patterns.

In this context, finding leaders able to skillfully and thoughtfully negotiate different cultures is critical for successful organizations. Global leaders are highly efficient professionals who skillfully navigate the international arena and bring value to businesses and organizations worldwide. The global nature of their reach characterizes them. They build cross-cultural relationships and blend the qualities of traditional leaders – such as the ability to influence individuals and groups toward achieving goals - with a global

---

[291] Brimm (2019).
[292] Hofstede (2011).

perspective. Global leaders focus heavily on cultural and intercultural dimensions of their work to enhance business effectiveness through coordination and cooperation among employees and between staff and external business actors with different cultural norms and expectations.

Developing a global mindset is essential for leaders dealing with various countries and cultures and diverse teams of professionals. This mindset helps them understand others' behaviors and learn to identify their cultural values and biases. Doing so can be achieved through specialized training and the development of culturally appropriate interpersonal skills. This ability to navigate and negotiate cross-cultural differences is indeed paramount when leading global teams. Teams, defined as small groups of individuals working together to achieve a joint mission, require high levels of coordination, communication, consensus, and collaboration. Research on organizational behavior identifies common traits in high-performing teams, including a shared mission understood by all, team members' accountability and clearly defined tasks, shared values and rules, effective communication, trust, and a sense of belonging among team members. Global teams are culturally and logistically complex; leading them requires a specific skill set and mindset.

This chapter explores the four essential dimensions of successful global leadership by delving into four key dimensions: Fostering a Global Mindset, Developing Intercultural Competence, Learning Intercultural Leadership, and Embracing Cross-cultural Management. By examining these areas, the chapter seeks to provide readers with a comprehensive understanding of how global leaders can effectively navigate and thrive in diverse cultural environments.

Fostering a Global Mindset

Most of us previously worked in local organizations, interacting with colleagues and clients who were culturally similar and often in the same building or country. This context facilitated communication and decision-making tremendously, and international business was limited in scope and reach. However, as companies expand internationally and grow more diverse at home, teams become more global, and employees become geographically dispersed, leading to diverse communication styles and decision-making processes. The once cohesive corporate culture can start to fragment, resulting in miscommunication and eroded trust, particularly between the head office and regional units. Not addressing these issues may undermine the qualities contributing to a company's success.[293]

Companies must, hence, be operationally prepared to achieve their full international potential. For that, leaders must instill a global mindset in their corporate culture and daily operations and grow their global mindset. Leaders' global mindset has been essential to the business conversation for two decades. It involves certain traits such as knowledge about various cultures, political and economic systems worldwide, a deep understanding of one's global industry, enthusiasm about diversity, and eagerness to challenge oneself. Global leaders cope and thrive in uncomfortable environments and are adept at building trusting relationships with diverse individuals by demonstrating respect, empathy, and active listening skills.[294] Global leaders often possess extensive international experience, are multilingual, and can leverage global professional networks. However, their defining trait is their ability to create value by guiding their organizations to embrace a global perspective.[295] Jack Welch said it a few years ago when he declared, "The Jack Welch of the Future cannot be like me. I spent my entire career in the United States. The next head of General Electric will be somebody who spent time in Mumbai, Hong Kong, and Buenos Aires. We must send our best and brightest overseas and ensure they have training that will allow them to be the global leaders who will make GE flourish in the future."[296]

Although challenging, several strategies exist to transform an organization for global growth and to develop one's global mindset.

---

[293] Meyer (2015).
[294] Javidan (2010).
[295] Cabrera & Unruh (2013).
[296] Black et al. (1999), p. 20.

First, leaders must focus on all employees' mindsets, encouraging them to design products and processes for multiple markets from the start. Codifying this global philosophy into company culture and branding the initiative internally is critical so that everyone, leaders and all employees alike, can develop a global mentality. For instance, designating global "ambassadors" on various teams can further support this effort. In addition, fostering a global mindset in global leaders involves several strategic approaches.

Linda Brimm's work on the Global Cosmopolitan Mindset provides valuable insights into developing a global mindset. In her book, "The Global Cosmopolitan Mindset: Lessons from the New Global Leaders," Brimm builds on previous work highlighting the importance of embracing change.[297] Furthermore, understanding the life dilemmas and opportunities implicit in navigating the rapidly changing global environment.[298] Brimm invites leaders to follow concrete strategies to be more globally minded, such as embracing cultural diversity by participating in cross-cultural training programs and international assignments, working in companies that promote the acquisition of global competencies through continuous professional development programs, connecting with organizations that facilitate global networking opportunities, or attending international conferences and building relationships with global peers, and implementing global leadership practices by adopting inclusive leadership styles and fostering a culture of collaboration across borders. By integrating these strategies, leaders can grow their global mindset and become more capable of navigating the complexities of the global business environment.

However, this is only part of the equation.[299] Cultural differences in leadership styles can lead to misunderstandings in a global context. For instance, Americans view themselves as egalitarian and the Japanese as hierarchical. However, Japanese managers find American bosses confusing because they make decisions autocratically despite their egalitarian appearance. This

---

[297] Brimm (2015).
[298] Brimm (2018).
[299] Kelly (2019).

contradiction makes it difficult for Japanese managers to adapt. Such issues are shared globally, as managers and leaders often need help distinguishing between authority and decision-making styles, leading to challenges in adapting leadership approaches across cultures.[300] Leaders often prioritize expanding their foreign market share by adding languages, opening new offices, and supporting new currencies. To be highly effective, they also need to develop their intercultural competence.

Developing Intercultural Competence

In business, we often discuss cultural fluency, which refers to understanding different cultures, including their values, norms, and communication styles. It involves navigating and interacting effectively with people from diverse cultural backgrounds. Cultural fluency is often considered a necessity in business nowadays and is undoubtedly a must for global leaders.[301] However, I encourage leaders to go further and develop intercultural competence, defined as "the capability to shift one's cultural perspective and appropriately adapt behavior to cultural differences and commonalities."[302] In other words, intercultural competence is communicating and behaving appropriately in intercultural situations. It is more active than cultural fluency and encompasses knowledge, attitudes, and skills that enable effective interaction across cultures.

Intercultural competence is essential as a global leader, as misunderstandings can arise in interactions between individuals and organizations from diverse cultural backgrounds.[303] In addition, while culture was once seen as a barrier to interaction and a source of friction, it is now also viewed as a resource for organizational learning and competitive advantage. Companies that effectively utilize their multicultural workforce can better meet diverse client needs and accelerate knowledge transfer. Diverse teams also have

---

[300] Meyer (2017).
[301] Meyer (2016).
[302] Hammer (2015).
[303] Aureli (2020).

cultural diversity and can enhance organizational outcomes. Diverse teams bring a wide range of information, ideas, and perspectives, fostering creativity. However, conflicting norms and differing assumptions among team members can hinder their creative potential. If leaders fail to recognize and address these issues, cultural diversity might impede a team's creative performance. Thus, global leaders aim to use intercultural competence to identify cultural characteristics, make comparisons, and provide insights on managing cross-cultural interactions to avoid conflicts and benefit from cultural differences.

Darla Deardorff states that intercultural competence encompasses essential knowledge, attitudes, and skills. These attitudes include respect, openness, and curiosity. The knowledge components include cultural self-awareness, deep cultural knowledge, and sociolinguistic awareness. Finally, the necessary skills are listening, observing, evaluating, analyzing, interpreting, and relating.[304] Mastering those competencies contributes to a leader's achieving effective and appropriate communication and behavior in intercultural contexts. Developing intercultural competence requires rigorous and active experiential training, such as sensitivity training, simulations, or living and working abroad experiences.[305]

Some methods also exist to develop intercultural competence in individuals in general, which can apply to global leaders. Being proactive in this area is critical. Fostering self-improvement and a growth mindset[306] is essential for global leaders. For instance, Darla Deardorff's story circle method[307] can help develop intercultural competence for global leaders by fostering a deeper understanding and appreciation of diverse cultural perspectives. Through structured storytelling and active listening, leaders can engage in meaningful dialogues that promote self-awareness, empathy, and cultural humility. This process can help leaders recognize and bridge cultural

---

[304] Deardorff (2006b); Deardorff (2009).
[305] Black & Mendenhall (1989).
[306] Brimm (2015).
[307] Deardorff (2020).

differences, improving their ability to navigate complex global environments and build more inclusive, collaborative teams.

Moreover, self-reflectiveness is essential. Because of one's inherent blind spots, seeking external expertise is essential to assess one's (inter)cultural competence accurately.[308] The Intercultural Development Inventory (IDI) is a reliable tool that offers a developmental model that measures someone's competence and provides a roadmap for improvement. IDI is used worldwide, is offered in eighteen languages, and provides an external perspective and guide to help leaders focus on onboarding strategies, team motivation, and understanding cultural influences on behavior.

Finally, global leaders must consider leadership and management distinct yet complementary functions. Both are essential for success in today's world of business. As John P. Kotter wrote in his 2001 article,[309] management is about handling complexity, while leadership, on the other hand, is about navigating change. Global leaders need to consider this dichotomy and apply it to their contexts: a focus on people—through intercultural leadership—and processes—with cultural management—will help them be successful in the 21st century.

Learning Intercultural Leadership

As a global leader, leading change requires communicating efficiently across cultural barriers, which is challenging in very different cultural contexts. In defining "culture," one is bound to encounter many nuances.[310] Some definitions focus more on socializing processes: "Culture is everything we learn from the moment we are born." Other definitions seem to belong more to the realm of ontology: "Culture is the way in which human beings give meaning to life, and the challenge of 'being': how we deal with the passage of time, the relationships between human beings, and the relationship of human beings with their physical environment."

---

[308] Hyun & Conant (2019).
[309] Kotter (2001).
[310] Clark (2008).

Others focus on the external/functional representation of a culture's dominating norms and values, as in "culture is a system of norms, values, and beliefs that identifies a social group."

Much literature has been written over the last two decades on the impact of cultural differences on organizations and teams. Some authors' work has focused on identifying, based on dominant cultural patterns, the cultural variables that can most affect team behavior and performance. Cultural behavior models have been shaped based on the influence of certain variables, such as "power distance," "individualism vs. collectivism," "masculinity versus femininity," and "long-term vs. short-term focus." One of Hofstede's seminal work conclusions is that cultural values shape personal behavior, and these, in turn, shape organizational culture, affecting all an organization's actions and operations.[311] Understanding and negotiating how cultural values shape organizational culture is essential for a global leader. Global leaders are encouraged to adopt a framework that identifies cultural variables based on dominant cultural patterns and use it to impact team behavior and performance significantly.

Erin Meyer's Culture Map[312] offers such a framework designed to help navigate cross-cultural communication in business. Meyer identifies eight dimensions where cultural differences can lead to misunderstandings: Low-context vs. high-context communication, direct negative feedback vs. indirect negative feedback, principles-first vs. applications-first persuasion, egalitarian vs. hierarchical leadership, consensual vs. top-down decision-making, task-based vs. relationship-based trust, confrontational vs. avoids confrontation, and linear-time vs. flexible-time approach to scheduling. These scales help managers and leaders understand and bridge cultural gaps to improve communication and collaboration across diverse teams. This model can be used in conjunction with Diana Clark's two-step process to increase the efficiency of global teams.[313] Clark recommends establishing a team diversity chart by completing a

---

[311] Hofstede (1980).
[312] Meyer (2016).
[313] Clark (2008).

cultural diversity questionnaire. This questionnaire helps the team collaboratively explore cultural variables, which can be based on Erin Meyer's Culture Map, for instance. Team members share what cultural variables are similar and those that differ, analyzing their potential impact on team performance. This step is critical to realizing the potential impact of cultural variables on the team's social capital and performance. This step helps the group build on shared values, manage differences, anticipate misunderstandings, and leverage diverse mindsets for innovation and problem-solving.

Secondly, the group assesses the team members' need to balance between processes and integration during their collaborative work. In other words, this step aims to determine if the team and the global leader should focus more on processes or integration of team members, knowing that the right balance is highly subjective and depends mainly on the experiences, cultures, and expectations of team members.[314] A self-assessment questionnaire gauges critical criteria, allowing the team to refocus at crucial moments of the year, if necessary. This approach helps teams understand cultural differences, organize effectively, communicate to achieve results, and balance process and integration focus. Moreover, the team can collectively propose critical actions and recommendations for a team charter to find an optimal balance between focusing on effective work processes and emphasizing integration and diversity.

Finally, global leaders should promote their attitudes by leading by example. For a global leader, having oneself or team members focus on mutual learning is highly beneficial. Global teammates who engage in mutual learning share risks and adapt to norms, absorbing cultural knowledge through listening and observation. Trust, built on common interests, fosters a shared responsibility for bridging cultural gaps, leading to more comfortable and effective collaboration. Global leaders are indeed intercultural leaders; they understand that building trust in a remote team requires clear communication, consistent reliability, and genuine connections.

Regular check-ins, transparent goal-setting, and timely feedback are essential. Utilizing video calls to foster personal interactions

---

[314] Ibid.

fosters trust and engagement while encouraging group members to share openly during routines, which can help reduce the gap created by physical distance. Intercultural leaders know that showing empathy by understanding individual challenges and offering support is also crucial. Celebrating achievements and recognizing efforts helps build a positive team culture. For global leaders, establishing these practices creates a foundation of trust, even without face-to-face interactions. Consistency in communication, expectations, and feedback helps team members understand their roles and responsibilities clearly, reducing ambiguity and fostering trust. When global leaders are consistent, they create a stable environment where team members feel secure and confident, ensuring that the team functions smoothly and effectively despite the physical distance. In a sense, intercultural leaders are also cross-cultural managers who understand what it takes to navigate the complexity of leading intercultural and international teams.

Embracing Cross-cultural management

As mentioned, dealing with the complexity of international operations and intercultural teams requires a global leader to be an efficient cross-cultural manager. Unlike an intercultural leader focusing on people from diverse backgrounds, a cross-cultural manager emphasizes the processes necessary to manage global teams efficiently.

Managing global teams involves navigating myriad complexities, including distance, time zones, language barriers, cultural differences, and conflicting organizational processes. Effective communication and negotiation skills, a common language, and cultural sensitivity are essential to managing these complexities and building social capital. The processes involved in managing global teams must be meticulously designed to ensure seamless coordination and integration across diverse geographical locations. This includes establishing clear communication protocols, standardized workflows, and robust conflict resolution mechanisms to address any issues arising from cultural misunderstandings or misaligned expectations.

The global leader / cross-cultural manager focuses on group effectiveness in this context,[315] specifically, how groups achieve their outcomes. Leaders rely heavily on communication technologies when dealing with global virtual teams with members from different nationalities and cultures working together across geographical distances to achieve a common goal. These teams may vary in lifespan from a few hours to indefinite periods and can be part of a single organization or multiple organizations working on a joint project. The processes governing these teams must be adaptable to the dynamic nature of virtual collaboration, ensuring that technological tools effectively provide a sense of mutual commitment to organizational goals, enabling global teams to maintain efficiency and respond to the ever-changing environment characterized by cultural and logistical complexity.

Global teams, especially those spread across several time zones, require global leaders to implement fair processes to ensure equity and inclusivity. For instance, it is crucial to rotate meeting times so that it is not always the same individuals who have to take calls early in the morning or late at night, regardless of their proximity to the headquarters or group size. This approach helps to distribute the inconvenience evenly and fosters a sense of fairness among team members. Additionally, opportunities for exciting projects and promotions should be accessible to everyone on the team, not just those closer to decision-makers. This ensures that all team members feel valued and motivated, which is essential for maintaining high levels of engagement and productivity.

Finally, preventing conflicts is essential in global teams. Global leaders should be able to learn and implement strategies to keep disagreements from escalating into conflicts, ensuring smoother interactions within global teams. For instance, training in conflict resolution techniques can equip team members with the skills to navigate disagreements more constructively and help when conflicts arise. Similarly, regular check-ins can be helpful to address any issues

---

[315] Thomas & Peterson (2017).

before they escalate. These strategies enhance rapport, camaraderie, and optimal team performance in a globalized work environment.

Conclusion

In this chapter, I have covered four critical dimensions of successful global leadership. Some strategies are not new and might seem obvious to many, but they are often neglected. Some are more forward-looking and can provide new ideas to aspiring and practicing global leaders. In any case, learning global leadership and cross-cultural adaptability requires patience, practice, and perseverance. Innovative and forward-thinking leaders and companies recognize this and adapt their approaches accordingly.

Following the recommendations in this chapter can help leaders engage in learning journeys that can help them better grasp the nuances of various cultural approaches, empowering them to make better decisions in cross-cultural interactions. Ultimately, businesses are made of teams of people, and understanding how to work with professionals from various backgrounds is an asset in our globalized economy. For instance, during performance reviews with a French employee, one might initially explain their approach and ask them to adapt. However, in a subsequent meeting, one might find it more effective to adjust their leadership style to the employee's cultural norms.

The key takeaway is that being a successful leader in one's culture does not guarantee global success. A global leader needs a versatile approach to motivate and engage people worldwide. It is crucial to be knowledgeable and flexible enough to choose the most effective leadership style for each cultural context and decide when to adapt to achieve the desired results.

Finally, being a global leader is more than financial success or access to more senior positions. Global leaders are also citizens of the world. With high intercultural competence and a leadership mindset, global leaders understand the impact of their actions, take accountability, and act with the greater good in mind.

Chapter 12 – Could international schools be the incubators for culturally competent organizations?

Françoise Bougaeff

"It takes a glocal village to raise culturally fluent multilingual professionals."

While it is difficult to provide a satisfactory definition of an international school, we know that, for the past 20 years, they have been disparately flourishing across the globe, ranging from traditional pragmatic types inherited from the postwar era to newer types arising from a competitive education market. The population and expectations of international schools have shifted and increased with globalization and marketization, leading to a vision of international education to prepare the children of a mobile and non-mobile upper-middle class to enter a high professional position that will contribute to a desired social and cultural status.[316] Today, a broadly agreed-upon definition of what makes an international school is an educational institution that promotes international education by adhering to a curriculum from a country other than the one where the school is located that caters to both local students who seek a more global education and students who are not nationals of the host country.

Since the Organization for Economic Co-operation and Development (OECD) created the first Program for International Student Assessment (PISA) report in 2000, the rise of benchmarking practices at the international level has motivated active research and assessment of the quality of educational systems and institutions in different global and local contexts. There is no one-size-fits-all education model nor worldwide education policymaking. Therefore, it is a balancing act for international educators to reconcile a global narrative created and spread by international agencies through their curricula and practices while remaining rooted in local communities

---

[316] Schippling (2018).

and realities to stay relevant in everchanging professional settings that require a global intercultural mindset and a connection to the people and markets they encompass.

The École Internationale de Genève, founded in 1924, is the first school to incorporate 'international' in its title. It primarily catered to the children of diplomats and employees from international organizations. Post-World War II, international schools saw a significant rise, driven by normative and pragmatic motives. The normative aspect aimed to foster an intercultural dialogue for better international understanding and global peace, while the pragmatic aspect was a response to the growing international migration of highly qualified employees in global companies since the 1950s who sought quality education for their children.

Many international schooling definitions and typologies have been proposed in the past century, but all have shown the limits of a normative approach. Philosophically, the *raison d'être* of international education, however, can be approached from two directions that are not mutually exclusive: a "top-down" approach considers addressing global and national needs, and a "bottom-up" approach, the development of the individual.[317] The 'top-down' approach addresses global and international issues and aims to create a better world. In contrast, the 'bottom-up' approach, which concentrates on individual development from an emotional and behavioral perspective, offers a more personal and nuanced understanding of international education.

In both directions, the acquisition and embodiment of interpersonal skills and intrapersonal awareness are at the heart of the mission of international education[295] through a built-in "international mindedness" and a pedagogy towards "intercultural literacy," students acquire the knowledge, behaviors, and understanding to negotiate intercultural meaning-making daily.[318]

To delve into a crucial aspect of fostering international mindedness in educational settings, we first explore the foundational role of curricula in shaping students' global perspectives and examine

---

[317] James (2005).
[318] Heyward (2002).

the importance of a well-designed curriculum that embraces diversity, promotes intercultural understanding, and encourages critical thinking on global issues. Then, we investigate the outcomes of an internationally minded education and reflect upon how students develop a rich and valuable cultural capital that equips them to navigate the complexities and expectations of an interconnected world. Lastly, we address international schools' unique challenges in balancing global perspectives with local contexts and explore approaches for international schools to effectively blend global awareness with regional relevance, allowing them to become genuinely "glocal" institutions. This chapter thoroughly explores the multifaceted journey towards international mindedness in education, aiming for transferability and embodiment in the workplace.

Building international mindedness through adequate curricula

Beyond the academic content of any school, there are a series of components that make the "ethos" of the education it means to provide, which should be found in the environment it builds for and around its students. The Greek word "character" is commonly used to describe the guiding beliefs and values that characterize a community and will appeal to its members' ethics and personal principles. "International mindedness" is the term that has been coined and promoted to describe the specific ethos – with its underpinning rationale, aims, and values – that international schools should live by.

To be "internationally minded," one must first be aware of the "global" nature of things and develop "global mindedness," i.e., a form of acute awareness of global concerns that are not attached to any nation. In short, "global mindedness" describes the scope and the extent of the area in which any subject will be relevant. "International mindedness," however, relies on a keen sense of identity and recognition that differences between people are starting points for new alliances to tackle global challenges together. For example, the concern for climate change and the destruction of the icecap, which does not belong to any nation, is an example of global-mindedness. However, the cooperative and collaborative political actions taken to slow its destruction and prevent further damage rely on international mindedness.[319] Thinking globally is undoubtedly a mindset everyone who is not living under a rock in the 21st century has acquired. However, international education equips students with skills and attitudes geared towards agency, not just awareness.

Nevertheless, those terms can appear both biased and misleading. Biased, because only the most privileged can afford to be globally minded, one must be reassured about their daily subsistence to broaden the scope of their concerns. This is misleading because problems such as racial conflict or even environmental damage are issues that also need to be addressed nationally or even at a smaller level. It highlights that having an international mindset cannot be exclusive to reasoning at a local level. As stated in UNESCO's 2014 report *Global Citizenship Education: Preparing Learners for the Challenges of the 21st Century*, the articulation of the global with the local is at the heart of the notion of education for global citizenship that entails connections between the regional and the global and a curriculum that will prepare students to understand and engage with global issues in a spirit of openness to difference. What pedagogical principles should such an education provide to develop the skills of "intercultural literacy" and reach international mindedness?

Heyward's model includes "the understandings, competencies, attitudes, language proficiencies, participation and identities necessary for successful cross-cultural engagement"[320] to develop students' intercultural literacy skills, which can be divided into intercultural understanding, competence, and communication.

Intercultural understanding is awareness, understanding, and appreciation of one's own and other cultures. It implies openness towards and respect for diverse cultures. Even though such a notion might seem elusive and challenging to assess, the Intercultural Sensitivity Scale (ISS) created by Chen and Starosta has proven efficient at measuring intercultural sensitivity. This scale is a 24-item questionnaire aimed at measuring intercultural sensitivity. While it has the subjectivity bias of any self-evaluation tool, it builds a

---

[319] James (2005).
[320] Heyward (2002). p.10.

conceptual framework around intercultural understanding and appreciation using five factors based on its statements: intercultural engagement, respect for cultural differences, interaction confidence, interaction enjoyment, and interaction attentiveness.[321]

Intercultural competence can be taught across subjects as part of a school's mission through a pedagogy based on inquiry and critical thinking designed to help students understand different worldviews and examine and respect them. It also encourages interaction with local communities and cultures as part of the curriculum to develop intercultural competence. The next level is an internalized personal frame of reference-based worldviews and a deep sense of empathy that can lead to intercultural competence in how one behaves and communicates with others.[322] Making an intercultural individual comes first from an internalized comprehension and a set of attitudes—based on respect, openness, curiosity, and discovery—knowledge and skills that can be used externally by having ad hoc cultural and sociolinguistic behaviors.

Intercultural communication, from a teaching and learning perspective, is typically embedded in an academic subject such as foreign languages or social studies. However, the degree to which subjects such as foreign languages and social studies are intercultural depends on the orientation of the curriculum and the pedagogy used to deliver it. A critical feature of any international school is its foreign language curriculum. It is a keystone of intercultural understanding and communication. No language is neutral; therefore, exposing students to various texts and representations of a culture may allow them to develop their critical understanding of the cultural aspects of language and their representations.

Interestingly, many international schools have native speakers teaching foreign languages. It is a way to guarantee some extent of "tandem learning" to enhance linguistic and intercultural understanding between the teacher and their students. However, it might also be a way to continue the dangerous archetype of the native speaker as the linguistic and cultural model and target of language

---

[321] Chen & Starosta (2000).
[322] Deardorff (2006b).

learning, what Adrian Holliday called native-speakerism. The native speaker archetype could tend to reinforce cultural stereotypes while ignoring the diversity present in the infinite number of speakers who use the dominant language of their region with different accents and varying proficiency levels.[323] Indeed, it can be objected that creating a divide between native and non-native speakers is counterproductive in our globalized world, and even more to produce a global education.

The output: A valuable and international cultural capital

International education represents a new form of power in a globalized world because it provides an "international capital" that gives its students the means to be comfortable engaging in global arenas.[324] In many countries, there is a stratification between students attending national and international schools. Indeed, national education systems worldwide have made cosmopolitanism part of their school curricula. In that national setting, students acquire alleged cosmopolitanism by learning foreign languages and other aspects of the intercultural competence woven into history, civics, and other subjects with their co-nationals, not with "foreigners."[325] In contrast, students who attend international schools are likely to acquire cosmopolitanism as cultural capital, both experientially and empirically. Spending a significant part of their developmental years outside their parents' or local culture, these internationally educated "third culture kids" become adept at navigating multicultural settings due to their heightened awareness of the global sociocultural landscape.[326] Their global perspective, adaptability, multilingual abilities, and diverse worldviews make them valuable assets for any professional organization.

According to Bourdieu, singular competence represents cultural power as "both dispositions of openness to people and cultures different than one's own as well as the competencies required to enact

---

[323] Holliday (2006).
[324] Resnik (2018).
[325] Igarashi & Saito (2014).
[326] Weenink (2007).

such openness with ease."³²⁷ As we approach the notion of cultural capital applied to international schooling in a globalized world, we can split it into the three traditional Bourdieuan categories used to describe any form of cultural capital and encompass a variety of elements symbolizing the arbitrary resources perceived by socio-professional actors:

First, the embodied state of the Bordieuan social habitus refers to how individuals perceive the social world around them and react to it.³²⁸ In that sense, the intercultural literacy they acquire in an international school, based on the intercultural understanding, competence, and communication described earlier, would ingrain the individuals with the skills and dispositions to navigate the global arenas successfully. For an international school, the intercultural curriculum and the foreign languages program are the symbolic vectors of the cultural capital they implant in their students. Linguistic capital is significant, and proficiency in English is not negotiable for any school to claim to offer an international education, whether it delivers its curriculum in that language or not. The value of English as the universal lingua franca reach automatically provides high status and exchange value in the market economy.³²⁹ However, even in English-speaking countries, acquiring proficiency in one foreign language is an integral part of the perceived linguistic capital because it allows one to communicate efficiently with more people and can provide an opportunity to become a more mobile global citizen. Research also shows that aside from the linguistic benefit, the experience of learning a new language positively influences the metacognitive awareness of young, multilingual children in terms of their willingness to communicate.³³⁰ The accumulation of cultural capital in the embodied state, i.e., in the form of culture (the German *Bildung*), presupposes a process of embodiment and incorporation that implies a labor of assimilation requiring the learner to invest time

---

³²⁷ Resnik (2018).
³²⁸ Bourdieu (1986).
³²⁹ Resnik (2018).
³³⁰ Le Pichon et al. (2013).

and effort personally. Like the acquisition of muscle mass, it must be done firsthand through proper training and cannot be delegated.

Second, the objectified state of cultural capital is only relevant if its properties are defined in their relationship with its embodied form, as they constitute their materialized embodiment.[331] In the educational context, cultural capital is objectified in material objects or media, characterized by their symbolic way of showing embodied capital. Even if this objectified capital is not materially transmissible, its holders can obtain proof of their skills, practical experience, and attitudes in the traditional Bourdieuan way. The most apparent objectified form of international schooling is all the physical and material objects or media produced individually or collectively. They can be awards and prizes from interculturally relevant competitions, especially if won during a language contest, a Model U.N. simulation, or some other competition requiring some of the attitudes, knowledge, and skills on which intercultural competence is built. They can also take the form of videos and photos of participation at an event or trip, or even more so, an international exchange or volunteer experience to show how embodied global citizenship is. Many companies specializing in organizing volunteering opportunities partner up with schools to help them make it part of their curriculum to take their students outside of the classroom to use their acquired skills. Those real-life experiences can also make a perfect topic for an entry essay to apply to university or a scholarship.

Finally, the institutionalized state of cultural capital encompasses all the education credentials that legally and socially recognize the qualifications of their bearer and confer their validity. Academic qualification is independent of the individual bearing it, but it materializes cultural competence. One of the characteristics of the institutionalized state of cultural capital is that it has relative autonomy regarding the individual bearing it, even regarding the nature of the cultural capital they effectively possess. It is not proof of the embodied state but instead institutes cultural capital by what Bourdieu calls the "collective performative magic of institutional

---

[331] Bourdieu (1986).

acts."³³² The simple holding of some academic qualifications secures the belief of cultural competence and imposes an institutional recognition of the cultural capital possessed by any given individual bearing them.³⁰⁹ Academic qualifications also make it possible to compare their holders and exchange them (by substituting one for another in succession). Additionally, it makes it possible to establish "conversion rates" between cultural capital and economic capital by guaranteeing the monetary value of a given academic capital.³⁰⁹ This conversion of cultural capital into economic capital is likely, combined with the neoliberal marketization of education and the increasing demand for school choice, one of the main factors of the international schooling explosion.

The multiscale dilemma of international schools: How to be "glocal"

Our global village has transitioned from a world organized in nation-states, putting the national community and its values at the center, to a world organized in different domains.³³³ This shift has led to two different perceptions of cosmopolitanism reflected in the missions of the many international schools that blossomed in the post-WWII world order:

- Cosmopolitanism is a normative ideal for worldwide institutionalized world culture and a human rights discourse that takes humanity rather than nationality as a primary frame of reference.
- Cosmopolitanism is an empirical phenomenon that integrates the flows of foreign people and cultures and "localizes" everyday practices beyond national borders by expanding their horizons.³³⁴

Conversely, national education policies and school curricula define students as members and actors of their nation: "Education has always been the peaceful weapon in the nation state's struggle to

---

[332] Bourdieu (1986).
[333] Mangez et al. (2017).
[334] Igarashi & Saito (2014).

create and maintain its identity."[335] However, the focus has shifted today, and education has "become less concerned with national identity and more concerned with economic performance in an internationally competitive market."[336] Education systems worldwide have legitimized cosmopolitanism, taking humanity, rather than nationality, as the primary frame of reference and promoting international education to function globally and participate in a global economy.[337]

International schools serve as transnational education hubs, facilitating cross-border learning processes and leveraging existing transnational connections to foster further convergence. By interacting with national systems, they produce a frontier zone and a new institutional form that is only partially national and international.[338] They then represent distinct forms of global embeddedness in the national territory, i.e., a distinct spatiality embedded in the national.[339]

World-wide education actors like OECD and UNESCO have played a significant role in this phenomenon. By propagating models and policies, they do not support the unification of systems but instead encourage a dynamic relationship between them. They do so by relaying neo-liberal rhetoric that promotes the commodification of education and greater autonomy for schools. In this way, they are more likely to encourage, rather than hinder, the initiatives of organizational networks that create, support, or affiliate with schools that differ from the national school system of the country. The rise of independent schools with an international mission also consolidates the importance of networks, as most of them are affiliated with one or with many. These networks encourage the emergence of entrepreneurs within the various school systems, giving them logistical and rhetorical support and making them ferments of a fragmentation that operates along two axes, one linked to social stratification and the other to the differentiation of educational

---

[335] Green, cited by Walker (2000).
[336] Walker (2000).
[337] Igarashi & Saito (2014).
[338] Sassen (2000).
[339] Resnik (2012), citing Sassen (2003).

models and projects.³⁴⁰ Similarly, national and international education systems do not converge toward a singular international education model; it is quite the opposite: like governments and businesses, they enhance their influence by being different, not similar.³⁴¹

Global-local dynamics in education: The role of international schools

It is difficult to grasp a school's global-to-local ratio. The motive for integrating global curricula and putting intercultural fluency at the core of their educational mission has yet to be openly communicated in national schools. However, it is proudly affirmed and constantly further developed in international schools. Often independent organizations, whether they are non-profit or not, are significant actors in local education markets, which plays a considerable role in their acute pedagogical watch: when different schools are situated within policy and physical infrastructures that allow them to compete for a shared pool of potential students it is determining for them to stay perceptive, responsive, and sensitive to the global challenges.

International schools' strategic planning benchmarks their strengths and weaknesses within the macro-environmental domain of the national and international policies, the imperatives of the professional world, and the micro-environmental domain of the local challenges faced by the specific populations and population niches for whom the school can provide an extra value. By staying attuned both globally and locally to the ever-changing environment their students stem from and are bound to be in after their education, the international schools operate as complex systems that consistently adjust their throughput to build the skillset their students need to engage in diverse organizations they will join as adults successfully.

With a rich diversity inherently built into the DNA of their social fabric, international schools' dedication to cultural fluency is at the core of their mission, curricula, and the experiential learning

---

³⁴⁰ Ibid.
³⁴¹ Steiner-Khamsi (2015).

opportunities they craft. By doing so, they equip their students to inquire critically about the world, respectfully engage in it with others constructively and empathetically, and safely face personal and professional challenges by using their informed judgment to make responsible decisions.

A culturally competent work organization acknowledges the significance of cultural diversity and weaves it throughout its operations, from managing its team to interacting with customers. Culturally competent organizations, nurtured in international schools, excel in managing the intricacies of global markets and engaging with diverse customer bases.

To remain efficient and relevant, such businesses must effectively navigate global markets, foster innovation, attract and retain top talent, and build a loyal and diverse customer base. To do so, what do they need at the end of the day? Visionary and strategic thinkers who can understand the global market dynamics and foresee future trends to devise accurate strategies. Inclusive and empathetic leaders and employees who foster an inclusive culture create an environment where everyone feels valued and respected. Adaptive and Innovative people who are flexible can adapt to changing scenarios, cultural shifts, and market demands and are willing to experiment and take calculated risks to stay ahead in competitive markets. Ethical and responsible individuals who prioritize ethical practices and corporate social responsibility through a commitment to fair and sustainable business operations.

Undeniably, international schools serve as vital incubators that prepare future professionals for success in culturally competent organizations. These institutions equip students with a comprehensive suite of tools, including linguistic proficiency and intercultural understanding, for fostering inclusivity, driving innovation, and developing adaptable communication skills. By instilling the necessary attitudes and skills, international schools enable businesses to transform their concepts into sustainable and practical strategies, ensuring their ideas are not just visionary but also actionable and relevant, both locally and globally.

Chapter 13 – Multilingualism and cultural fluency within multinational corporations operating in Francophone Africa: Implications for French-language programs

Steven J. Sacco and Megan Diercks

The editors of this much-needed volume declared in their call for papers that multilingualism is attaining a new supremacy in global business and global affairs. "The number of multilingual individuals worldwide is increasing, and the view of multilingualism is changing rapidly in the professional world."[342] Research confirms the accuracy of their statement in their description and power of multilingual workplaces, which is known in global business research circles as *Multilingual Franca*.[343] Despite the dominance of English, most workplaces worldwide, according to *Multilingual Franca* researchers, are inherently multilingual.

The rise in multilingualism is encouraging news for French-language students and educators. In an article by Ashreena Kaur, CEOs were surveyed about the most important languages for success in global business, and French was ranked second, ahead of both Spanish and German. The CEOs, all multilingual, also stated that multilingual professional proficiency will:

- Make you stand out,
- Make you a better communicator and, thus, a better manager and leader,
- Help you impress more clients,
- Boost your career trajectory.

"The climb to the C-suite is crowded, competitive, and merciless. You need every edge you can get—and according to the decades of experience of senior executives who have seen what it takes to get to

---

[342] CALEC (2023).
[343] Feely & Harzing (2003); Lønsmann (2014); Janssens & Steyaert (2014); Angouri (2014); Sacco (2017, 2019, 2022). Lüdi et al. (2016).

the top, knowing the best languages to learn for business is one of them."³⁴⁴

In support of Kaur, DeBoer reports that French is one of the fastest-growing languages in the world.³⁴⁵ DeBoer cites three reasons we listed in our U.S. Department of Education grant proposal designed to create a seamless K-16 multidisciplinary Francophone African curriculum.³⁴⁶ They include:

- A "population explosion" in Francophone Africa is expected to continue into the coming decades.
- A population that already includes more than three times the number of French speakers compared to Francophone Europe.
- The number of French speakers is projected to reach 800 million by 2050.

We agree with his assessment that "where population growth happens, economic importance tends to follow." Our future graduates, equipped with French skills, cultural fluency, and global business principles, face a promising future within the global economy, especially within companies in Francophone Africa.

Despite the veracity of the editors' two declarations, multilingualism in global business continues to face a significant challenge within professional workplaces worldwide: The "Englishnization" movement. The "Englishnization" movement has negatively impacted multilingualism within multinational corporations for the last decade and a half. At the head of the Englishnization movement is Hiroshi Mikitani, the founder of Rakuten, a Japanese competitor to eBay and Amazon. In his last years of managing this new consumer giant, Mikitani declared an end to multilingualism in his home offices and affiliates worldwide. Included in this mandate was the original home of Rakuten in Japan. Mikitani gave his 7,100 employees two years to achieve professional proficiency in English or face demotion or dismissal.³⁴⁷ In other

---

[344] Kaur (2023).
[345] DeBoer (2023).
[346] Diercks and Sacco (2023).
[347] Pfanner & Martin (2015).

words, Mikitani expected Japanese managers to work in English even with their Japanese counterparts at their home offices and facilities in Japan. The English-only movement automatically placed Rakuten's Japanese workers at a disadvantage vis-à-vis Rakuten's American or British colleagues for promotions and salary increases. Japanese managers and workers were forced to create or rebut proposals in their second language, while their American and English counterparts had the advantage of working in their native language. Honda's president, Takanobu Ito, dismissed Mikitani's movement as "stupid."[348] Mikitani could have mandated professional fluency through a score of 800 on the TOEIC (Test of English for International Communication) without eliminating multilingualism within the corporation.[349]

Supporting the Englishnization movement, a parallel movement known as Business English as a lingua franca (BELF), a field of research clustered within business schools worldwide, has professed that multilingualism threatens productivity. BELF researchers point to a Tower of Babel for corporations that allow multiple languages to flow in the workplace. BELF researchers have announced, after two decades of worldwide research, that English is the language of global business. BELF researchers neglected to add Africa, which comprises 16.2% of the global economy (and growing), in their workplace language research studies for unknown reasons. One can only wonder why Africa was not included in their studies.

BELF declarations of English as the global language of business can be summed up in two bold statements:

- "The role of English as the international business lingua franca is now beyond dispute."[350]
- "Ready or not, English is now the global language of business."[351]

Neeley said, "By mandating English, Rakuten was prepared to join the approximately 52 percent of multinational companies that had

---

[348] Wohlsen (2013).
[349] Ibid.
[350] Gerritsen & Nickerson (2009), p.180.
[351] Neeley (2012).

adopted a language different from their originating country to meet global expansion and business needs better."[352] Audi, IBM, Microsoft, Nestle, and Samsung were listed among the corporations.

Rebutting the Englishnization myth

The senior author, a consultant and visiting professor at the *Institut National Polytechnique Félix Houphouët-Boigny* (INP-HB) in Côte d'Ivoire and a Fulbright-Hays *chef de mission* in Cameroon, decided to test the BELF claims in a series of four empirical studies.[353] He conducted the studies because the English-only claims ran counter to his experience with U.S.-based multinational corporations such as General Electric (GE) and Cargill, where he consulted with company representatives in French and English. In discussions with company officials and INP-HB alums, both admitted to working in English and French. Francophone Africans work in French with coworkers and in English with monolingual senior managers or during global videoconferences.

In the first three studies, 212 Francophone African engineers, agronomists, and logisticians representing 135 multinational corporations (MNCs) operating in Francophone Africa participated in surveys. Many participated in follow-up interviews to reveal more about their use of English and French in their workplaces. For the sake of brevity, here are the results of the four studies:

- All 135 multinational corporations are multilingual, although 85% usually mandate only English in their workplaces.
- French was the primary language used in over half of the corporations.
- Among logistics and supply chain experts, French was used 72.2% during the workday compared to 27.8% for English.

---

[352] Neeley (2017).
[353] Sacco (2019); Sacco & Ohin-Traoré (2022); Sacco & De Koffi (2022); Church-Morel et al. (2023).

- Francophone Africans work in French with coworkers, suppliers, and customers and in English with monolingual senior managers and non-French-speaking customers.
- Unexpectedly, French was the dominant workplace language in multinational corporations such as General Electric, Yara International (a Norwegian MNC), MTN (a South African MNC), and Olam (headquartered in Singapore).
- In Mauritania, Senegal, and Tunisia, French and African languages (Wolof, Derja, Hassaniya) dueled for first place in the workplace—ahead of English, which placed third in some multinational corporations.
- Unlike Rakuten, Francophone Africans communicate with each other in their native language or French ("I use Wolof with the Senegalese members of my team so they feel more at ease and so that I'll be better integrated and accepted by them.")

With apologies to Neeley's "ready-or-not" stance, English is *not* the global language of business—at least not on the world's second-largest continent. The four studies also strongly suggest that Gerritsen and Nickerson's "now-beyond-dispute" pronouncement is *in dispute*.

Creating a seamless interdisciplinary Francophone African curriculum for K-16 educators and students

Despite the evidence that French plays a significant role in workplace language use in Francophone Africa, multilingual proficiency in French and English is insufficient for our students. Cultural fluency is as essential, if not more so. Our students' knowledge of Francophone African cultures, history, economic and political systems, literature, cinema, and storytelling falls behind their understanding of France, Quebec, or France's French-speaking cousins worldwide. Africa is the world's second-largest continent, with a population of 1.2 billion people, and its economic activity accounts for 16.2% of the global economy.[354] With birth rates twice that of other African countries, economists predict that the number of French-speaking Africans in 21 of Africa's 54 countries will surpass 800 million by 2050.[355] The need for French-speaking professionals in global business, philanthropy, diplomacy, education, and the military has never been more significant as the French language blankets the African continent from Morocco to Madagascar and Senegal to Djibouti.

For this reason, the AATF is seeking grant funding through the U.S. Department of Education and the Coca-Cola Foundation to design and develop a program entitled "Creating a Seamless Interdisciplinary Francophone African Curriculum for K-16 Educators & Students." The project, when completed, is intended to provide a seamless K-16 curriculum accessible for free on the AATF's website to both AATF and non-AATF members. As a result of this curriculum project, the AATF also seeks funding from the Fulbright-Hays Group Projects Abroad Program to provide K-16 French-language educators with free instructional month-long workshops during the summer of 2024 in a Francophone African country.

The proposed program is multi-dimensional. Subject matter will include a comprehensive study of language, culture, history, geography, economic and political systems, international development, literature, art, music, dance, social justice, cooking, and storytelling. Print mediums, such as books, newspapers, and literary works, will only serve as one source of information. To provide first-hand information, the AATF curriculum development team will interview village elders, storytellers, women beekeepers, farmers, green energy entrepreneurs, professors, economists, politicians, NGO directors, and clergy, among others, to provide educators and learners with a well-rounded analysis of Francophone Africa. The AATF's long-term, post-grant goals concerning Francophone Africa are to assist AATF members in (1) launching additional online intercultural exchanges, (2) establishing study-

---

[354] BBC News (2019).
[355] BBC News (2019).

abroad programs in Côte d'Ivoire, Senegal, Cameroon, Morocco, and Tunisia, (3) encouraging joint research and faculty exchange, (4) facilitating student exchange, and (5) continuing to address critical educational issues such as women empowerment, sustainability, and social justice.

The AATF proposes to package these subject matter areas into distinct curricular units for use at all levels of instruction. Inserting AATF-developed Francophone African materials into existing K-8 dual-language immersion (DLI) curricula nationwide is a natural fit. DLI curricula are holistic and comprehensive, including social studies, language, literature, music, art, and science. The AATF team will publish sample units on storytelling, short stories, poetry, geography, history, language differences, science, and cultures and customs through its website. When available, DLI teachers can invite African community members to share realia and activities such as drumming, puppet making, and games with DLI students. The AATF-developed Francophone African can only strengthen the DLI mission of developing well-rounded, globally aware, and creative problem solvers who desire "to care for and serve others."[356]

At the high school level, a veteran French teacher best expresses the use of the multidisciplinary Francophone African units:

> More than ever, high school students need to be enticed by course content that is approachable, relatable, and linked to shared experiences. To that end, studying oral traditions in Côte d'Ivoire will allow us to document better, compare, and discuss linguistic and cultural trends in literature, music, and perhaps even media. As an illustrative example, an AP French unit on Identity and the Quest for Self might incorporate materials about the role of love and relationships in adolescence: An Ivorian storyteller's oral account and a French hip hop artist's song would be examined and compared. Personal examples from contemporary American music could be added for a multicultural and intergenerational perspective.[357]

---

[356] Albert Einstein Academies, p. 1.
[357] Toomey (2024).

At the postsecondary level, they will comprise a significant minor, a certificate program, and instructional tracks in Francophone African Studies. They include (1) engineering and environmental sciences, (2) global business, economics, and entrepreneurship, (3) literature and cinema, (4) music, dance, and poetry, (5) international relations and development, and (6) global security and military sciences. The curricular structures, from tracks to majors, are designed to attract French majors and business, economics, engineering, and political science majors. The modules and materials will be customized for our graduates to meet the current and future geopolitical, socioeconomic, and military needs of the United States in Africa as it competes in a heated continental rivalry with China and Russia. Multidisciplinary programs such as San Diego State University's International Business Program, which combines language and business as double majors, or the University of Rhode Island's International Engineering Program, which combines language and engineering as double majors, could serve as models for AATF-member institutions.

AATF curriculum developers will design and develop customized pedagogical packages (goals, lesson plans, comprehension checks, language-building activities, task-based activities, and outcome assessments) to accompany our modules and materials for use in elementary dual-language immersion programs, middle schools, high schools, and post-secondary programs in community colleges, colleges, and universities. To illustrate the look of a sample multi-disciplinary track, here is one designed to attract K-12 students enrolled in Junior Reserve Officers' Training Corps (JROTC) and college students enrolled in ROTC.

The Global Security and Military Sciences Module (designed for ROTC and JROTC students)

1. Francophone African geography, history, economics, social, and political structures
2. An overview of AFRICOM, its mission, and its opponents in Francophone Africa accompanied by testimonials by U.S. and anti-U.S. military personnel
3. Identification of present and future security challenges for the region

4. An overview of related cultural issues such as gender, religion, and social justice
5. Articles in French about military activities in Francophone Africa
6. Five to ten storytelling episodes focusing on the cultures of Francophone Africa
7. Excerpts of literary works (novels, short stories, poetry) focusing on the cultures of Francophone Africa
8. Five to ten relevant films

Advancing Francophone Africa studies: A multifaceted approach

To promote multilingualism and cultural fluency in professional settings, the AATF will develop curricular modules and materials focusing on Francophone Africa with two goals: (1) to educate current French-language students better and (2) to attract new French-language students majoring in engineering, international relations, development, economics, entrepreneurship, global business, and environmental and military sciences.

The proposed curriculum development team comprises the top curriculum French language developers in the U.S. Most team members have won teaching awards and are in high demand for in-service training with districts in all 50 states. Many have published popular textbooks worldwide, and several have won research awards. The two team leaders, both Americans, have lived and worked in many of the countries in Francophone Africa, while the third team leader was born in Burkina Faso and raised in Côte d'Ivoire. All have extensive networks leading to invited lectures and interviews with village chieftains, political figures, academic leaders, storytellers, women entrepreneurs, green energy gurus, NGO directors, and U.S. military personnel headquartered in AFRICOM. The team's experience and professionalism, along with the AATF's extensive reach to teachers and professors in all 50 states, will help to ensure the production and dissemination of the project's learning outcomes.

The proposed project will thoroughly study Francophone Africa's cultures, histories, economics, political structures, social justice issues, and environmental problems and solutions. Three years of Zoom contact with Francophone Africans of numerous professions (NGO directors, politicians, economists, clergy, farmers, storytellers, and village elders, among many others) will enrich the curriculum development team. Complementing first-hand contact, team members will pull back Francophone Africa's cultural curtain through the study of literature, cinema, poetry, music, dance, and storytelling. The proposed project is designed to enrich French-language programs from French dual-language immersion schools to junior high schools, high schools, colleges, and universities. The development of interdisciplinary modules and materials is designed to expand the study of French, attract students outside of humanities, and prepare them for potential careers (engineering, international development, global business, economics, and more) connecting to Francophone Africa. Eminent French-language scholar and AATF and JNCL/NCLS member Karen Sorenson reminds us that "Language is 'soft diplomacy.'" Learning to communicate respectfully in the target language and culture is the ripple in the diplomatic stream. The proposed project will develop thousands of "ripples" in the African stream, which, over time, will enhance relations between the U.S. and African nations and peoples.

Chapter 14 – Prospects and challenges of incorporating multilingualism and multiculturalism into the higher education system in Bangladesh: A case study

Md. Zubair K. Khan

Multilingualism and *multiculturalism* are interconnected concepts that usually exist like two sides of a coin. In other words, there is a proximity between language and culture in any society, which Sapir's literature rightly articulates as "language does not exist apart from culture, that is, from the socially inherited assemblage of practices and beliefs that determines the texture of our lives."[358]

Every day, we communicate with people from other cultures at various times, such as in the classroom, during workplace meetings, while having diplomatic conversations for international collaborations, or as tourists. Globalization and technological advancement have transformed the world into a global village, where people from diverse cultural backgrounds interact using languages different from their native ones. Knowledge of different languages has boosted an individual's cultural awareness and competency. It increases empathy for people of other cultures with different values and mindsets, rituals and traditions, and ways of communication.[359] In that sense, all the nation-states on the globe are de facto multilingual, subject to a variant that may persist to the point that multilingualism is accepted and practiced by local inhabitants and in terms of other socio-cultural factors within their territory.[360]

Over the last two decades, higher education in Bangladesh has integrated multilingualism and multiculturalism through the process known as Internationalization at Home (IaH). In other words, the blending and integrating of various cultures and languages into Bangladesh's traditional norms primarily happened through the

---

[358] Sapir (1985).
[359] Drobot (2022).
[360] Chen (2010).

rapid growth of private universities in the country's higher education sector.³⁶¹ Yuto Kitamura, an Associate Professor of International Development at Nagoya University, Japan, believes that the expeditious expansion of the private sector in Bangladesh's higher education during the last two decades has engendered a healthy learning environment in Bangladesh, and this would undoubtedly gratify social demands and surge cultural plurality for the people of Bangladesh.³⁶²

The following part of this discussion will explain how distinct cultural practices penetrated Bangladeshi culture in conflux with other languages. For a practical analysis, one university, Chittagong Independent University (CIU), has been considered an exemplary institution to highlight how multilingualism and cultural diversification have intervened in Bangladesh's higher education through its IaH processes.

Multilingualism & multiculturalism: Understanding & nexus

Multilingualism and multiculturalism are complex, vibrant, and thought-provoking phenomena that have been extensively explored and discussed. Despite the vast research and intellectual debate devoted to understanding how a multilingual and multicultural society is formed, scholars have yet to reach a consensus on defining these concepts. This lack of agreement stems from the fact that the definitions of multilingualism and multiculturalism can vary widely among different communities, influenced by their unique ideologies, histories, beliefs, and cultural backgrounds.

In general, multilingualism is defined as 'the presence of several languages in one country, community, or city' or 'the ability of an individual to maintain communication through languages other than his/her mother tongue.' King articulated multilingualism as 'the presence in a geographical area, large or small, of more than one 'variety of language,' i.e., the mode of speaking of a social group whether it is formally recognized as a language or not; in such an

---

[361] Kabir & Chowdhury (2021).
[362] Kitamura (2015).

area individuals may be monolingual, speaking only their variety.'[363] Cenoz and Gorter defined 'multilingualism' as 'the ability of societies, institutions, groups, and individuals to engage regularly with more than one language in their daily lives.'[364] Multilingualism can be differentiated from another homogeneous term, plurilingualism, in that multilingualism indicates the presence of multiple languages in a language ecology. In contrast, plurilingualism refers to an individual's ability to speak two or more languages.[365]

Multiculturalism is, on the other hand, another thought-provoking and perplexing term that has multiple geographical exegesis. From a philosophical perspective, it refers to "the existence of difference and uneven power relations among populations regarding racial, ethnic, religious, geographical distinctions and other cultural markers that deviate from dominant, often racialized, 'norms.'"[366] Multiculturalism from a geographer's context denotes circumstances beyond formal efforts to illustrate and incorporate cultural dissimilitude, drawing attention to how the margins of intersectional identities are encountered, reinforced, and renegotiated through everyday life.

One of the unique characteristics of culture is that it constantly changes its traditions, values, and mindsets to respond to its members' needs. In that sense, one accepted social practices or attitudes fifty years back may be considered obsolete today. Thus, multiculturalism may be, in its simplest form, explained as a system of beliefs and behaviors that recognizes and respects the presence of all diverse groups in an organization or society, acknowledges and values their sociocultural differences, and encourages and enables their continued contribution within an inclusive cultural context which empowers all within the organization or society.[367]

There is an implicit affinity between language and culture, based on the understanding that language is a key to a society's cultural past

---

[363] King (2018).
[364] Cenoz & Gorter (2023).
[365] Jhingran (2019).
[366] Clayton (2020).
[367] Rosado (1996).

and understanding of 'social reality.'[368] From that perspective, multilingualism can be regarded as an inseparable subset of multiculturalism, just as language is part of any culture.

Policy initiatives to achieve multilingualism and multiculturalism in higher education in Bangladesh

With the advancement of communication technology, availability of internet resources, increased cross-border job opportunities, and fast-forwarding demand for quality education, most developing countries have taken several initiatives to achieve at-home internationalization to meet global needs.[369] Bangladesh is one of the pioneering countries within the South Asian region that has taken several initiatives to institutionalize multilingualism and multiculturalism into the higher education system through incorporating Internationalization at Home (IaH) initiatives over the last two decades. These initiatives include- modification and internationalization of academic curriculum and syllabus, determination of English language as a compulsory learning medium for almost all post-secondary degree programs, enhancement of cross-border mobility facility for students, modernization of learning facilities, proliferation of online exchange programs and service-learning initiatives in cooperation with organizations and provide special facilities to underprivileged groups of people such as Rohingya and aboriginal people located in the hillside areas.

Correspondingly, the government of Bangladesh has created education opportunities for 1.2 million students annually by establishing more than 160 tertiary-level educational institutions throughout the nation during the last two decades.[370] A University Grant Commission report has also revealed that private universities in Bangladesh are taking a leading role in institutionalizing IaH

---

[368] Stanlaw et al. (2018).
[369] Zolfaghari et al. (2009).
[370] Bangladesh Education Statistics (2021).

initiatives compared to those of IaH initiatives institutionalized by public universities.[371]

Case study: Multilingualism and multiculturalism initiatives at Chittagong Independent University

Internationalization at Home (IaH) is one of the most frequently discussed and overly addressed issues in the present global education paradigm in general and tertiary-level higher education in Bangladesh in particular. Several eminent educationists throughout the globe have attempted to expound the notion of IaH from divergent perspectives and have drawn precise fine lines from other frequently interchangeable words, such as globalization, educational enlightenment, and modernization.[372] For instance, Beelen and Jones defined Internationalization at Home (IaH) as "the purposeful integration of international and intercultural dimensions into the formal and informal curriculum for all students within domestic learning environments."[373]

The Chittagong Independent University (CIU) is one of Bangladesh's unique and leading private universities. It was founded in 1999 in Chittagong district as a branch campus of the Independent University of Chittagong (IUB). Since its establishment, the CIU has been consistently proven as one of Bangladesh's leading higher education institutions. It is one of the most emerging and promising universities within the Asian region, and it has deeply embedded and institutionalized the IaH on campus. The CIU is also working progressively towards reaching its goals by enhancing cross-border connections, organizing cultural exchange programs, developing international standard academic curriculums, facilitating modern technologies in and out of the classroom, and so on.

A tripartite internationalization approach has been ingrained in the CIU's policy by giving specific concentration on the enhancement of (i) structural, (ii) opportunity, and (iii) engagement

---

[371] University Grant Commission (UGC) report. (2017).
[372] Lies (2023); Lies (2022); Altbach et al. (2010).
[373] Beelen and Jones (2015).

of both students and teachers in leveraging the IaH. These approaches have further incited CIU to achieve five overarching IaH goals, which are:

1. Increase financing for enhancing domestic research and international research collaboration overseas.
2. Maintain academic advancement in research and teaching while patronaging the mobility of researchers, educators, and students.
3. Integrate teaching and course materials in line with modern internationalism and European unity.
4. Promote and patronage the growth of adaptable communication and linguistic abilities (predominantly English) among students besides their native language.
5. Create and foster a knowledge-sharing platform on cultural and scientific advancements with other parts of the globe.

Other distinctive IaH initiatives taken by CIU include:

CIU's Collaborations with Other Top Universities Abroad: The CIU has maintained solid collaborative academic connections with numerous world-class universities from various parts of the world, including North America, Europe, Australia, and Asia regions, although the university curriculums are developed by following the North American style. The CIU works closely with these international institutions in various international forums, such as organizing student and faculty exchange programs, collaborative research and short course programs, joint international conferences and academic seminars, cultural exchange programs, intellectual discourse programs, and other academic programs.

The objective of CIU's global partnerships with renowned academic and other institutions across the globe is to ensure better opportunities for students, faculties, and staff to gain diverse knowledge, build cross-border relations that can be beneficial in the future, introduce students with diverse cultures, practices, and so on. These initiatives would create opportunities for both institutions to bring advancement in academia and science, which is one of the mottos of IaH.

CIU's Institutional Excellence Initiatives: It is indubitable that assuring academic quality is not a trend or fashion of an institution; instead, it has become an essential component for the internationalization of higher education nationally and internationally. The CIU also believes that the IaH and institutional quality are inseparable and uncompromising at all dialectical levels when discussing collaboration and academic progress. To that end, CIU has launched several programs to achieve academic excellence:

- <u>The Institute of Governance, Development, and International Studies (IGDIS, est. 2017)</u>: In collaboration with Seoul National University Asia Center (SNUAC), South Korea, the primary objective of IGDIS is to research local and national governance issues in Bangladesh, as well as other development issues at local, national, regional, and international levels and the contemporary international affairs. Under this institutional banner, eight international seminars, two webinars, one international faculty exchange program, and four academic publications have been conducted till today.
- <u>The Institutional Quality Assurance Cell (IQAC, est. 2016)</u>: The IQAC was formulated at CIU to institutionalize and uphold the quality of education by advancing its curriculum and the learning environment. IQAC's mission and vision are to progressively escalate the quality culture in academia and pursue educational advancement through self-assessment and responsive exertion, striving to create resourceful, ethical, and visionary graduates. Undoubtedly, establishing IQAC is one of the effective ways for CIU to institutionalize the IaH by assuring and guaranteeing its quality of education.
- <u>Center for Excellence in Teaching and Learning (CETL)</u>: It is undeniable that a set of competent, skillful, and professional personnel is crucial for achieving institutional IaH. Keeping this in mind, the CIU has set up the CETL as an opportunity platform for all faculty, staff, and students to improve their professional, managerial, and intellectual

development by organizing programs, workshops, and seminars. The CETL has also conducted several workshops during the last few years to help students and staff improve their professional and learning skills by inviting national and international experts. Two other learning centers such as the Center for Entrepreneurship, Innovation, and Sustainable Development (CEISD) and the English Language Centre (ELC), have been established in the CIU as non-credited, extra-curricular learning platforms to improve student's entrepreneurship, interpersonal skills, linguistic proficiency, and cultural development.

CIU's Initiatives Towards Student's Interpersonal & Cultural Development: Cultural diversity, interpersonal development, and curriculum-based academic learning are vital to students' success. Understanding unfamiliar cultures and recognizing similarities with them help students develop a tremendous respect for diverse customs and practices. This awareness not only enhances their leadership skills but also aids in building international networks. CIU has launched several faculty-oriented and unified cultural clubs to achieve this goal. Further, engagement in faculty-controlled club activities (like in CIU Marketing Club, CIU English Debate Club, Creative Writing Club, and CIU-Law School Debating & Mooting Club) helps students enhance their mental growth and creativity, achieve leadership skills, boost their self-confidence, and thus help them better prepare for the real-life challenges, besides academic developments.

Challenges & policy recommendation

Based on the CIU mentioned above's curriculum-related and extra-curriculum-oriented mechanisms and initiatives and considering its persistent endeavor for academic excellence throughout the last 23 years of its academic journey, it is pertinent to say that the CIU is one of the few universities in Bangladesh that has successfully institutionalized the Internationalization at Home. However, throughout this IaH journey, CIU also has gone through many obstacles and challenges. Some of these are:

- The funding opportunity is the biggest challenge for most postsecondary higher education institutions behind institutionalizing IaH in Bangladesh. Even though public institutions receive government subsidies and funding, private universities are deprived of government funding and thus depend on students' tuition or personal donations. It is challenging for CIU to manage external funds to initiate academic advancement programs. Hence, the government should finance all universities, irrespective of whether they are private or public institutions, to overcome this challenge. This is also practiced in many developed countries, like Germany and Finland.
- Unstable and uncontrolled campus student political engagements are another crucial challenge Bangladesh's higher education industry faces. Given the political landscape of the past decade, there have been numerous instances where universities were compelled to suspend academic classes, halt regular activities, and evacuate hostels due to internal political unrest. Although this has happened primarily in public universities, it also has a far-reaching impact on private universities regarding institutional security and traveling. To overcome this obstacle, the government must adopt policies to free all tertiary academic institutions from political interference and disturbance.
- The availability of more grants and scholarships from both government and non-government sources could be a game-changer for students in Bangladesh. By providing special consideration for bright but financially disadvantaged students, we can create a more equitable and promising future for higher education in the country.
- Lack of job satisfaction and motivation among faculties are two other essential weaknesses of the higher education institutions in Bangladesh. Some contributing factors include a lack of research and academic training facilities, the absence of a staff development program, a heavy teaching load, and an unclear recruitment and promotion system. Even though CIU is

concerned about these issues and is taking necessary policy initiatives to overcome these problems.
- The future of higher education in Bangladesh is global. The CIU should take more initiatives to build cross-border partnerships and collaborations with international institutions regarding staff and student mobility. We can genuinely internationalize higher education at home by fostering more joint research projects and joint curriculum development initiatives.

Embracing internationalization: Advancing multilingualism and multiculturalism in higher education

Undeniably, in this twenty-first century, the internationalization of higher education is one of the most concerned and widely discussed issues in the higher education paradigm due to globalization and the advancement of information and communication technology worldwide. It is also one of the most influential and practical ways of institutionalizing multilingualism and multiculturalism within a campus. Despite several shortcomings, the CIU has successfully institutionalized the IaH through its curriculum advancement, cross-border collaborative research initiatives, and other activities.

Chapter 15 – Understanding the shortage of French-language teachers in Canada

Hélène Leone

The coexistence of Canada's two official languages, English and French, has dramatically influenced its history. Together with Indigenous languages, these languages reflect the country's history, diversity, and inclusive society.[374] English and French are recognized in the legal statutes, including the Constitution of Canada of 1867 and 1982, the Official Languages Act of 1969, and the Charter of Rights and Freedom enacted in 1982. They are granted equal status, rights, and privileges in all services provided by Parliament and the federal government of Canada, thereby promoting linguistic duality and safeguarding language rights for Canadian citizens belonging to the English- or French-speaking minority in a province or territory.

English and French, as Canada's two official languages, are recognized in sections 16 to 23 of the Canadian Charter of Rights and Freedoms, preserving and promoting the two official languages, granting minority-language educational rights for English-speaking children in the province of Quebec and French-speaking children who reside in a province where French is the linguistic minority of the province.[375] While education in Canada falls under provincial and territorial jurisdictions, Canada's federal government is committed to providing support, including partial funding, for minority-official- language education and second-language instruction across the country.[376]

With a population of 35 million, the 2021 Canadian census revealed that 75.5% of respondents identified English as their official language at home, 30% reported knowledge of French, and 12.7% claimed a native language other than English or French. Despite

---

[374] Government of Canada (2018).
[375] Canadian Charter of Rights and Freedom (1982).
[376] Council of Ministers of Education, Canada (2001).

French being the official language spoken at home for 21.4% of Canadians, only 18% identified as bilingual.[377] Notably, approximately 84% of those identifying as Francophones reside in Quebec, with one million Francophones living outside of Quebec and 1.1 million Anglophones living in Quebec.[378]

Minority-language education and second-language instruction in Canada

Canada operates under a federal system comprising ten provinces and three territories. Governmental authority is shared between the federal government and the provinces and territories. The British North America Act of 1867, now called the Constitution Act, designated education as a provincial and territorial responsibility, leading each jurisdiction to establish its department or ministry of education. Each province and territory "set up unique educational structures and institutions reflecting each region's diverse historical and cultural heritage, with the authority to delegate power to local school boards, commissions, or other recognized agencies."[379] As of June 2021, eight provinces and territories have integrated early childhood learning and development into their education systems, while others maintain separate departments or ministries for elementary-secondary education and postsecondary education, adult learning, and skills training.[380] In 2022, Statistics Canada reported 270 minority-official-language schools in Quebec and 750 minority-official-language schools in other parts of Canada. There are approximately 2,106 French-as-a-second-language primary and secondary schools,[381] 75 French-language colleges, and 30 French-language universities, with the majority in Quebec.[382]

Although not required, most provinces and territories have mandatory French-language programs for students in kindergarten to

---

[377] Statistics Canada (2024).
[378] Canadian Heritage (2018).
[379] Council of Ministers of Education, Canada (2001). p. 5.
[380] Council of Ministers of Canada, Canada (2024).
[381] Gaumont (2023).
[382] Canadian Heritage (2018).

grade 12. Four programs are available: Core French, Intensive French, French Immersion, and the Francophone program. Each program is designed to achieve different language proficiency outcomes, with mandatory instruction periods, curriculum, rationale, conceptual framework, and learning standards.[383] Core French, also known as basic French, was first introduced in the early 1960s when there was a growing recognition of the importance of bilingualism and the equal status of English and French in Canada. The program is offered through an English-language school board, following a curriculum emphasizing oral communication and providing students with basic French skills relevant to everyday life.[384] Core French is introduced in the intermediate and middle school program, grades 5 to 8, and is taught as a separate subject, one to three hours per week. The Intensive French program is optional for grades 6 and 7 students. The program is similar to Core French; however, the Intensive French program aims to accelerate language acquisition by increasing instructional time and providing an intensive period of French language instruction within a brief time frame. Some school districts may provide up to 80% instructional time in French for grades 6 and 7.[385]

An English-language school board may also offer the French Immersion program. Originating in Quebec in 1965, the program was initiated by anglophone parents who felt their children were not achieving sufficient French language proficiency in the Core French program. The 1963 UNESCO report Foreign Languages in Primary Education inspired the French Immersion program. The program took a controversial approach, with only one teacher speaking French to anglophone students.[386] Known as a 'language bath,' this method involved daily immersion without using the student's first language (L1).[387] The goal was not to 'teach' the language but to immerse students in real-life linguistic situations. In 2021, Statistics Canada reported that one in six children, close to 700,000, were

---

[383] Leone (2024).
[384] Arnett & Mady (2017).
[385] Ibid.
[386] Jezer-Morton (2020).
[387] Stern (1963).

enrolled in French immersion in Canada outside Quebec.[388] Today, the French immersion program is available to students in kindergarten to grade 12; students receive instruction in French for at least 50% of their instructional time, covering both language studies and other subjects. French immersion programs allow students to be in an immersive bilingual context, developing the language skills to communicate orally and in writing *en français* and acquire 'functional bilingualism.'[389] The implementation and delivery of the French immersion program "must parallel the regular English program in structure and content, as per the curriculum requirements and education program order."[390] Students are expected to speak French in the classroom. However, communication between the school and family is usually in English.

By section 23 of the Charter of Rights and Freedom enacted in 1982, the Francophone program is offered through the French-language school board, le Conseil Scolaire Francophone (CSF). All subject areas are taught in French, except for English Language Arts. The program aims to ensure all students develop bilingual fluency in French and English, including advanced literacy and numeracy skills and core competencies. It enables them to communicate and interact effectively, orally and in writing, asserting their cultural identity as francophone students in a minority context.[391] More than 180,000 students attend the Francophone program offered at 700 primary and secondary schools through the French-language school board.[392]

Factors contributing to the shortage of qualified French-language teachers

In 2019, the Office of the Commissioner of Official Languages released a report outlining four factors contributing to the shortage of French-language teachers in Canada:

---

[388] Statistics Canada (2024).
[389] Government of British Columbia (2022).
[390] Ibid.
[391] Ibid.
[392] Fédération nationale des conseils scolaires francophones (2019).

1) Insufficient teacher training and professional development opportunities in French, leading to positions being filled by teachers who may lack language proficiency, linguistic competency, and cultural fluency;
2) The reluctance of teachers to accept positions in remote and isolated communities due to the high cost of housing and the need to relocate;
3) Systemic challenges in recruiting and retaining French-language teachers due to poor working conditions, low salaries, and competition from other educational institutions and community organizations;
4) A lack of support from school leadership and administration leading to a shortage of pedagogical resources and classroom spaces dedicated to minority official-language programs and second-language instruction.[393]

The French-language teacher shortage was worsened during the COVID-19 pandemic as French-language instruction was given priority to students in physical classrooms over those opting for remote or virtual learning.[394] Some school boards were said to have abandoned French-language instruction and provided students with self-directed computer programs. Consequently, school boards began seeking individuals proficient in French to tutor online, even though some lacked professional certification as classroom teachers. Alternatively, English-speaking teachers were temporarily assigned to classrooms.[395]

Language proficiency, linguistic competency, and cultural fluency

The terms proficiency, competency, and fluency are frequently used interchangeably, yet they carry distinct meanings. While all three describe a level of ability, proficiency pertains to the skill level attained to perform a task; competency relates to the unconscious

---

[393] Office of the Commissioner of Official Languages (2019).
[394] Alphonso (2020).
[395] Ibid.

knowledge, understanding, and behavior required to complete a task authentically; and fluency refers to the ease, flow, and accuracy with which a task is performed. Chomsky made a fundamental distinction between linguistic competency, referring to the speaker-hearer's knowledge of the language, and language proficiency, the performance and use of a language in real-world situations.[396] This can be extended further to Saussure's distinction between langue, the internalized organizing principles of a language's vocabulary, grammar, and sound system shared by a linguistic community, and parole, the oral and written utterances and acts produced by a speaker.[397] Fluency in a language requires an authentic level of accuracy and the ability to adapt to different contexts and linguistic interactions without hesitation, interruption, or difficulty.

The concept of fluency extends to cultural fluency, also called intercultural competence. Cultural fluency is navigating and interacting within different contexts, adapting one's behavior to diverse cultural norms, values, beliefs, and social and linguistic practices. Being culturally fluent requires more than knowledge of the 'other;' it requires "an understanding of the environment in which the culturally fluent contact is taking place […] one must move through the cultural shock and the skills of communication with a critical knowledge of the dominant culture."[398] The term culture shock was first introduced in the 1960s and refers to the four stages one might experience when encountering a new culture, environment, and situation.[399] The first stage is the honeymoon or contact phase, the initial excitement and enthusiasm of the new experience. The regression stage begins as differences become apparent, leading to potential misunderstandings, confusion, and frustration. During the adjustment phase, one may feel isolated, rejected, or undervalued. Finally, in the recovery phase, where cultural differences are accepted, one functions effectively within the second culture.[400]

---

[396] Chomsky (1965).
[397] Saussure (1966).
[398] Leitch (2017), p. 403.
[399] Oberg (1960).
[400] Leitch (2017); Oberg (1960).

When culture is integrated into language teaching and learning, students acquire the tools to communicate in a new language and develop the skills and understanding to navigate different contexts and linguistic interactions.[401] Language acquisition goes beyond grammar and vocabulary for individuals; it involves understanding the cultural nuances interwoven within the language.[402] To communicate effectively, learners must explore the various cultural elements of the language they are learning.[403] To be functionally bilingual means using both languages in various contexts, social interactions, and real-world situations. It requires understanding both languages' linguistic and cultural nuances, switching between languages effortlessly, and adapting language use according to the situation and the speaker-hearers involved.[404]

Teacher training

In Canada, all teachers must hold a minimum Bachelor of Education degree to obtain their teaching license. This is called a Certificate of Qualification (COQ) in British Columbia. Due to the shortage of French-language teachers, ministries of education may authorize school boards to hire non-certified teachers, granting temporary teaching permits and letters of approval.[405]

Increasing enrolment in faculties of education and teacher training programs would seem to be an evident and effective solution to addressing the shortage of French-language teachers in Canada. However, in 2023, the Association Canadienne des Professionnels en Immersion (ACPI) reported that some faculties of education and teacher training programs limit the number of students admitted into their French-language programs despite Canada's shortage of teachers. Limiting enrollment often results from a need for more funding and financial support, a lack of administrative infrastructure, and a shortage of French-speaking university faculty and course

---

[401] Hossain (2024).
[402] Ibid.
[403] Kramsch (1993).
[404] Office of the Commissioner of Official Languages (2019).
[405] Gaumont (2023).

instructors. Consequently, program courses are shared between various departments or faculties, creating redundancies within courses and gaps in the curriculum. This fragmentation can render these programs ineffective and deemed inadequate, deterring prospective students.[406]

The challenges for teacher training and recruiting future French language teachers are significant, especially in provinces where French is a linguistic minority community. Few English-dominant post-secondary institutions offer courses in French on how to teach specific academic subject areas like mathematics, the sciences, humanities, and the arts. Faculty and course instructors may speak French in class, but academic materials, including master syllabuses and online modules, are in English. This is often the result of the faculty and course instructors' language proficiency and linguistic competency, the lack of funding for authentic materials in French, and the translation of master syllabuses and equivalent course materials already available in English. It is important to note that efforts have been made to add courses in French relevant to Indigenous perspectives, equity, diversity, inclusion, and anti-racist pedagogies.

Recruitment, retention, and relocation

In 2023, the Canadian Teachers' Federation drew attention to Canada's nationwide teacher recruitment and retention crisis. It was argued that the main issue was a shortage of teachers and inadequate working conditions.[407] Substandard and poor working conditions include 1) oversized classrooms, 2) inadequate support and lack of resources for students with special needs, 3) the increase of psychological and physical violence in schools, and 4) the decrease in student enrolment in teacher education programs. These factors have led to daily staff shortages and unqualified teachers being placed in the classrooms. In 2024, the Ontario Ministry of Education reported that more than a quarter of their public schools face staff

---

[406] Ibid.
[407] Canadian Teachers' Federation (2021).

shortages daily. As a result, school administrators and principals spend more time finding emergency replacements, dealing with scheduling, and covering classes themselves rather than completing their other administrative and educational duties.[408]

Recruiting and retaining teachers for schools in remote and isolated areas also presents several challenges, often discouraging teachers from relocating and staying in these regions for the long term. These communities typically have a small population, resulting in a limited pool of qualified teacher candidates. Remote and isolated areas often lack adequate transportation options, amenities, affordable housing, and desirable living conditions, reducing the appeal to prospective teachers. Teachers in these regions may also experience isolation from family and support networks and face cultural and community differences, impacting their ability to integrate into the local community and feel supported in their new environment. They may also face heavier workloads, including multi-graded classrooms, and have limited time and access to support staff, professional development, pedagogical resources, learning materials, and Internet access. Teachers living in regions where French is a minority language find it difficult to speak, hear, and read French. They feel isolated and far from French-speaking communities, impacting teacher motivation and students' engagement with French-language learning.

Shortage, supply, and demand

Over the past two decades, there has been a 40% increase in demand for French immersion programs and second-language instruction across Canada, with an annual growth rate of +5% per year in larger urban areas.[409] In 2021, the Association Canadienne des Professionnels de l'Immersion estimated that the shortage of French-language teachers will persist until 2031. The study reported an estimated shortage of 1,000 to 1,400 French-language teachers, affecting 51% of rural and 40% of urban schools. Additionally, of the

---

[408] Naccarato (2024).
[409] Merchant (2023).

10,630 English-language schools in Canada that offer French language programs, one-third have reported a shortage of French-language teachers, leading to an estimated shortage of 7,000 to 8,000 teachers, affecting 36% of these schools.[410]

The need for qualified French-language teachers has created disparities in the quality of the delivery and implementation of French-language programs, particularly evident in rural and isolated regions and Western provinces.[411] The shortage has also led to issues related to equity, access, and development of French-language programs nationwide. Consequently, some school boards have resorted to intentionally restricting enrolment in French-language programs by imposing "artificial roadblocks like enrolment caps and lotteries, preventing some children from accessing these programs."[412] The shortage of certified and qualified French-language teachers has also created a highly competitive recruitment process, with employers having to negotiate against "another program (French or English as a first language), another province, the private system, or another business sector."[413]

Tackling the French language teacher shortage in Canada: Challenges and solutions

The practical implementation and delivery of French minority-official language education and second-language instruction in Canada depend on the availability and quality of instruction, teaching, and learning. However, a shortage of qualified French-language teachers has resulted in larger class sizes, less personalized learning, and lower quality of instruction. Although Canada's federal government is committed to supporting minority-official language education and second-language instruction, significant disparities persist, particularly in remote, isolated areas and provinces where French is the linguistic minority.[414] Students enrolled in French-

---

[410] Association Canadienne des professionnels de l'immersion (2021).
[411] Government of Canada (2018).
[412] House of Commons (2018).
[413] Gaumont (2023).
[414] House of Commons (2018).

language programs often lack opportunities to practice and speak French outside their classroom, limiting their ability to develop language proficiency, linguistic competency, and cultural fluency in French. It becomes a domino effect; high school students graduating from French-language programs do not always have the French language skills required to become future French language teachers who can effectively deliver an educational program *en Français*.

The shortage of French language teachers is also due to the inability of education faculties and teacher training programs to meet the supply, needs, and demands of school boards across the country, particularly in provinces where French is a linguistic minority. Consequently, school boards may hire teachers without adequate French language skills or professional certification or recruit teachers from other provinces and French-speaking countries. School boards struggle to attract qualified candidates, limiting access to French-language programs for some students.

In 2018, the federal government of Canada released the 2018-2023 Action Plan for Official Languages to commemorate the 50th anniversary of the Official Languages Act. The plan aims to increase the national bilingualism rate from 18% to 20% by 2036.[415] To achieve this goal, Canada must raise the bilingualism rate of English speakers outside of Quebec from 6.8% to 9%. However, there is a concerning decline in the number of students graduating from teacher education programs specializing in French education. Moreover, due to varying sub-standard working conditions in education, there is a highly competitive market for French-language speakers with a high level of fluency in other professional sectors, including government, business, and translation services. This has led to fewer individuals pursuing careers in education. Addressing the shortage of French language teachers will require policymakers, educational leaders, and stakeholders to work together to attract individuals to the teaching profession and ensure French minority-language and second-language instruction in Canada.

---

[415] Government of Canada (2018).

PART 4.
Empowering citizens

Technology will never replace great teachers, but technology in the hands of great teachers is transformational.
— George Couros, *The Innovator's Mindset*

Chapter 16 – Multilingualism in the age of artificial intelligence

Pascal Vallet

Delving deeper into the philosophical underpinnings of Ludwig Wittgenstein's contemplation on language, we encounter a paradigm that challenges our conventional understanding of communication and comprehension. Wittgenstein's proposition, "If a lion could talk, we could not understand him," transcends the mechanics of linguistic exchange to probe the essence of meaning itself. This statement illuminates the profound interconnection between language and the forms of life—how language is inextricably tied to the activities, practices, and, indeed, the very fabric of our existence. It suggests that language comprehension is not merely about syntax or semantics but is deeply rooted in its speakers' shared experiences and life forms.

From this perspective, language reflects a community's unique way of being. Our words are imbued with our community's collective experiences, values, and understandings. They carry the weight of our cultural heritage, the nuances of our social interactions, and the depth of our perceptions. When Wittgenstein posits the incomprehensibility of a speaking lion, he points to the vast chasm that cultural and experiential differences can create in understanding. This chasm challenges the translation process, which seeks to bridge disparate worlds through language.

The advent of AI in translation introduces a new dimension to this challenge. With its algorithms and neural networks, AI offers remarkable capabilities in processing and translating languages at a speed and scale previously unimagined. However, as we ponder the intersection of language, culture, and AI, we are led to inquire further: How can AI be designed to account for the cultural sensitivities and experiential depths integral to human language? Can technology fully comprehend the human condition well enough to translate words, meanings, contexts, and cultures with fidelity and respect? This question opens a vast field of exploration, challenging us to envision a future where AI can genuinely understand the lion's speech—not just the sounds it makes but the profound cultural and existential contexts that give those sounds meaning.

The influence of language on thought

Language is not merely a tool for communication but a profound influencer of thought, shaping how we perceive and interact with the world. The ability to convey complex ideas through sound modulation is a uniquely human trait, allowing us to transmit knowledge and ideas across vast expanses of space and time. Our cognitive processes are notably influenced by the language we use.

The magic of language lies in its ability to form thoughts out of air vibrations, a process so ordinary yet extraordinary. The spoken word transforms into a vehicle for idea transmission, enabling the creation of thoughts as whimsical as a "jellyfish waltzing in a library while thinking about quantum mechanics."[416] This capability underscores the importance of language in human evolution and societal development. Moreover, the diversity of languages—approximately 7,000 spoken globally—presents a kaleidoscope through which we view the world. Each language offers a distinct lens with its unique sounds, vocabulary, and structure. The question of whether our language shapes our thought processes is an age-old debate, and scientific studies continue to provide new insights into this discussion.

Languages vary in how they categorize and perceive numbers, colors, grammatical gender, and more, affecting our ability to perform tasks, perceive colors, and associate characteristics with objects. These variations illustrate the language's role in shaping our perception and categorization of the world. Moreover, how languages frame events can influence memory, attention, and even moral judgments. The distinction between "He broke the vase" in English and "The vase broke" in a language like Spanish can affect the allocation of blame and punishment. This insight into the

---

[416] Boroditsky (2018).

linguistic framing of events reveals the profound impact of language on social interactions and legal systems, highlighting the broader societal implications of linguistic differences.

The diversity of languages reflects the human mind's flexibility and ingenuity. Each language represents a unique cognitive universe, offering diverse ways to solve problems, categorize the world, and express emotions. One compelling example comes from the Aboriginal Kuuk Thaayorre people of Australia, who use cardinal directions instead of relative directions like left and right. This linguistic feature requires them to remain constantly oriented to the cardinal points, a skill that significantly differs from the spatial cognition of those who use languages like English. Such examples suggest language influences how we navigate the world and organize and understand space and time. The Kuuk Thaayorre's conceptualization of time, unanchored from the body and aligned with the landscape's cardinal directions, illustrates how language can impact our temporal perception. This contrasts languages that structure time linearly or according to the speaker's orientation, highlighting the solid cognitive effects of linguistic differences.

The perception of time: Navigating cultural nuances in translation

More broadly, the concept of time, deeply ingrained in the fabric of societies, displays striking differences across cultural landscapes. These differences reflect not only on the perception of time but also on its management, social behavior, and even on the fundamental values within cultures.

Cultural differences in time perception can be broadly categorized into Polychronic (P-time) and Monochronic (M-time). In polychronic cultures, time is perceived as more fluid and flexible. Multiple tasks are often handled simultaneously, and interruptions are seen as a natural part of life. Relationships and interactions take precedence over strict adherence to schedules. This approach to time is common in Latin American, African, and Arab cultures, emphasizing people and relationships rather than on a strict schedule. Contrastingly, monochronic cultures value a linear approach to time, focusing on scheduling, punctuality, and the sequential completion of tasks. Time is compartmentalized and managed carefully, with a strong emphasis on deadlines and schedules. This perspective is prevalent in countries like Germany, Switzerland, and the United States, where time is often equated with money, and efficiency is paramount. For instance, in Germany and Japan, there is a strong emphasis on punctuality and adhering to schedules. These cultures are known for their tight timekeeping, reflecting a monochronic view where time is a resource that should be used wisely.

On the other hand, countries like Brazil and France tend to perceive time more flexibly. Adjustments to schedules and delays are standard, as the focus is on the event rather than strictly adhering to predetermined times. The Balinese finally have little interest in keeping accurate track of linear time, as Americans and many Western cultures do. "Time is money" is an alien concept to them.

Interestingly, the Balinese have no word for "time" as a concept of duration, and the modern notion of time was introduced first by the colonial Dutch when they erected a public bell tower in the center of Denpasar. "The purpose of traditional Balinese calendars is not to chronologically track human events but to organize time to delineate the ritual behavior necessary to preserve cosmic order. It is the quality, not the quantity of time, which is important. Do not tell a Balinese which day he is in, but tell him what sort of day he is in."[417]

Navigating these cultural differences requires awareness and adaptation, especially in global teams where perceptions of time can lead to misunderstandings and frustrations. For teams working across cultures with different perceptions, for example, on the concept of time, adopting best practices like setting milestones for flexible cultures or maintaining punctuality and deadline awareness in linear time-preferred cultures can enhance collaboration and understanding. Understanding and respecting these diverse temporal orientations is crucial in fostering effective intercultural communication and cooperation. It underscores the importance of cultural sensitivity in our increasingly globalized world, where

---

[417] Couteau & Breguet (2014).

navigating cultural differences in time perception is beneficial and necessary.

Integrating the concept of time into our examination of language and thought underscores a fundamental truth: the way we perceive and manage time is a vivid reflection of cultural identity and values. This realization brings to light the challenges inherent in translating words and the essence of cultural expressions and temporal concepts. If the idea of time varies so profoundly from one culture to another, translating discussions related to time could yield vastly different meanings for the recipient, especially if the translator needs more awareness of these cultural nuances.

As we delve into the age of AI, the journey of language translation is not solely focused on bridging linguistic divides but also profoundly involves grappling with cultural nuances. This task goes beyond the technical to embrace the profoundly human aspect of understanding the rich tapestry of human cultures. The challenge lies in developing AI technologies that are linguistically adept and culturally sensitive, capable of capturing the nuanced layers of meaning without compromising the integrity of our diverse cultural identities, thereby enriching our global communications and interactions.

Linguistic relativity and complexity of translation

The translation domain extends beyond the mere conversion of words from one language into another; it involves the intricate process of transferring meanings, cultural nuances, and conceptual frameworks across linguistic boundaries. The complexities of translation are illuminated by the Sapir-Whorf hypothesis (Linguistic relativity), which posits that the structure of a language influences its speakers' worldview and cognition. The hypothesis underscores the profound challenge of translation in the face of linguistic relativity and determinism, which is particularly important when considering the capabilities and limitations of AI in this endeavor.

- Language-value non-equivalence
  The study by Liu Yang and Luo Shan highlights the significant hurdles in translation arising from the non-equivalence of language value between Chinese and American cultures. This disparity, viewed through the lens of the Sapir-Whorf Hypothesis, illustrates how cultural values and language characteristics are deeply intertwined, posing a formidable challenge for translators striving to convey the full depth of meaning from one culture to another. The non-equivalence issue underscores the necessity for human or AI translators to profoundly understand both source and target cultures to achieve accurate and meaningful translations.[418]

- Linguistic relativity and determinism
  Gene Van Troyer's exploration of the Sapir-Whorf Hypothesis sheds light on the complexity of translation due to linguistic relativity and determinism. The idea that language shapes our perception of the world suggests that individuals who speak different languages may experience and understand their environments differently. This variance in perception complicates the translation process, challenging the translator to bridge linguistic gaps and divergent worldviews.[419]

- Multilingual awareness
  Pavlenko's emphasis on multilingual awareness highlights the importance of understanding and navigating the multifaceted implications of Whorf's ideas in translation. Recognizing arguments lost in translation underscores the crucial need for translators to be deeply aware of the linguistic and cultural subtleties inherent in both the source and target languages, an area where AI capabilities have yet to fully mature.[420]

---

[418] Yang & Shan (2022).
[419] van Troyer (1994).
[420] Pavlenko (2016).

- Lexical variation's impact
  The work of Taofeek Olanrewaju Alabi on lexical variation between English and Ogu languages exemplifies the impact of cultural understanding in translation and language teaching. The study illustrates how differences in greeting and food terms can affect the learning and translation processes, highlighting the role of cultural nuances in achieving effective communication and understanding between languages.[421]

- Translation complexity
  J. Katz's discussion on the empiricist assumption regarding the correspondence between thought and language presents a unique challenge in capturing linguistically neutral meanings across cultures. This complexity in translation emphasizes the difficulty of finding equivalences for culturally specific concepts. This task requires linguistic skills and a deep understanding of the cultural contexts that shape language use.[422]

- Cultural decoding, recoding, encoding
  Davood Mashhadi Heidar and colleagues address the complexity of translation in light of the Sapir-Whorf Hypothesis by suggesting that translation involves a process of cultural decoding, recoding, and encoding. This perspective highlights the intricate dance of understanding and conveying words and the cultural and conceptual frameworks they inhabit. The process demands cultural insight and cognitive flexibility that challenges AI's replicating capabilities.[423]

The collective insights from these studies reveal the daunting challenge of translation in the context of linguistic relativity. The process is not merely linguistic but deeply cultural, requiring an understanding of the subtle ways in which language shapes thought

---

[421] Alabi et al. (2022).
[422] Katz (2006).
[423] Heidar et al. (2012).

and perception. As we consider the role of AI in translation, it becomes evident that while AI can offer remarkable capabilities in processing languages, its ability to navigate the complex terrain of cultural nuances and conceptual frameworks needs to be questioned. The challenge, therefore, is not just technological but also philosophical, calling for a nuanced approach to translation that respects the depth and diversity of human language and thought. In this light, the quest for effective translation is a journey toward deeper cultural understanding and empathy, underscoring the importance of human insight in bridging the worlds between languages.

SYSTRAN's odyssey: Early machine translation and the quest for cultural context

Before 2000, research on SYSTRAN, one of the pioneering machine translation systems, highlighted its benefits and limitations, with some insights relevant to linguistic relativity. SYSTRAN was notable for improving accessibility to information across languages and facilitating international communication, particularly within the European Commission.[424] Its early adoption and technical innovation highlighted the potential of machine translation in supporting multilingual documentation and communication efforts.[425]

However, SYSTRAN faced limitations in capturing the nuances of cultural and contextual elements inherent in language. This issue is closely aligned with the challenges posed by linguistic relativity, which suggests that the structure of a language affects its speakers' worldview and cognition. The system needed help understanding and translating idiomatic expressions, slang, and culturally specific references, highlighting the complexity of language beyond mere word-to-word translation. The necessity for significant post-editing by human translators to imbue translations with cultural sensitivity underscored the system's limitations and the intricate relationship between language, thought, and culture—a relationship that

---

[424] Senez (1994).
[425] Pigott (1992).

SYSTRAN and similar machine translation systems could not fully navigate.

These early explorations into machine translation with systems like SYSTRAN laid the groundwork for understanding the complex interplay between language, culture, and technology. They prefigured the ongoing challenges in AI translation to account for linguistic relativity. They emphasized the need for advancements beyond literal translation to encompass the deeper cultural and conceptual frameworks that shape human language and thought.

Given the complexities identified in early machine translation systems like SYSTRAN, a pertinent inquiry emerges: To what extent can advancements in Artificial Intelligence contribute to overcoming machine translation's inherent limitations in capturing the intricate interplay between language, culture, and cognition? This question invites a comprehensive evaluation of AI-driven approaches in machine translation, focusing on their ability to integrate deeper cultural insights and contextual understanding into the translation process, thereby aligning more closely with the multifaceted nature of human language and thought as proposed by the Sapir-Whorf hypothesis.

Artificial intelligence and translation in 2024

As we delve into AI's capabilities in language and translation, we are prompted to reconsider how AI translates and the depth of understanding it can achieve. Beyond the mechanics of language lies the intricate theory of linguistic relativity.

The integration of AI in translation, through advancements in Natural Language Processing (NLP), Machine Learning (ML), and Natural Language Understanding (NLU), has transformed the approach to overcoming linguistic barriers. Denis Vaz's exploration of AI applications in computational linguistics, along with the research by Cheng et al. on context-based AI translation, provides a compelling overview of AI's capabilities and future potential in this field.

AI's evolving proficiency in NLP enables it to understand and process human language in a previously unattainable way. This involves translating words and identifying and interpreting idiomatic expressions, slang, and cultural references, crucial for accurate and meaningful translations. ML algorithms further enhance this capability by learning from vast datasets, improving the AI's performance over time through exposure to various linguistic patterns and nuances.

NLU stands as a critical component in this technological triad, granting AI systems the ability to grasp the intent and sentiment behind words, thus facilitating translations that are not merely literal but contextually and culturally informed. This is where the research by Cheng et al. becomes particularly relevant. Their study on ChatGPT's context-based translation illustrates how AI can surpass traditional translation tools by incorporating domain-specific knowledge and contextual understanding, thereby providing translations more aligned with human communication's nuances.

The advancements highlighted in this research demonstrate AI's ability to bridge cultural and linguistic divides effectively. By leveraging the contextual and cultural insights that Natural Language Processing (NLP), Machine Learning (ML), and Natural Language Understanding (NLU) offer, AI translation tools are moving toward a future where translations are not just about conveying information but about fostering understanding and connection across diverse linguistic landscapes.

However, the journey continues. The research also points towards the challenges that lie ahead, including the need for further improvement in AI's ability to handle the complexity of human languages, the ethical considerations surrounding AI translations, and the importance of ensuring that these technologies remain accessible and beneficial to all.

The integration of AI in translation, as detailed by Denis Vaz and Cheng et al., highlights the remarkable progress made and lights the path toward a future where communication barriers are significantly reduced. Through continuous advancements in NLP, ML, and NLU, AI is set to redefine the bounds of linguistic understanding, making the world a smaller, more connected place.

Grasping the lion's speech

The insights from examining AI's application in translation and the concept of linguistic relativity underscore its pivotal role in overcoming language and cultural barriers and enhancing global communication. This advancement surpasses simple literal translation and incorporates essential cultural nuances, facilitating more precise and sensitive international engagements. Such progress in AI-driven translation technologies promises to significantly improve interactions among global enterprises, emphasizing the importance of continued efforts in innovation and cultural comprehension within AI development for a more interconnected world.

However, this reliance on technological solutions introduces a nuanced challenge: the diminishing incentive to learn foreign languages and engage directly with other cultures. While AI facilitates communication accuracy, it inadvertently risks diluting the rich, immersive experience of language learning and cultural exchange. The depth of understanding and the appreciation gained from learning a language and its cultural context are irreplaceable. They foster empathy, enhance cognitive flexibility, and deepen our connection to the world's diverse tapestry of cultures.

Moreover, by bypassing the effort to learn foreign languages, we risk missing the profound personal and professional growth opportunities with language proficiency. Learning a language is more than acquiring a tool for communication; it is an exercise in opening one's mind to diverse ways of thinking, living, and interacting. It is a direct pathway to understanding the "other," appreciating the subtleties of cultural differences, and navigating the complexities of international relations with nuance and sensitivity.

Therefore, while we embrace AI's capabilities to make international collaboration more seamless and practical, it is imperative to maintain a balance. We must leverage AI to supplement, not replace, our efforts to learn and understand the languages and cultures of our global partners. This balanced approach ensures we know the intrinsic value of linguistic diversity and cultural exchange. It encourages us to continue exploring, learning, and appreciating the vast richness of the world's cultures, thereby enriching our personal and professional lives.

As we circle back to Wittgenstein's philosophical musings on language and understanding, we are reminded of the essence of proper communication: the ability to share and comprehend experiences beyond the constraints of our language and culture. AI-assisted translation, grounded in an understanding of linguistic relativity, offers a bridge to this understanding. However, the journey to fully grasp the "lion's speech" requires us to tread beyond technological aids, embracing the challenge of learning and experiencing the world through the eyes of its diverse inhabitants. In doing so, we enrich our understanding of others and deepen our appreciation for the intricate mosaic of human existence.

Chapter 17 – Empowering youth to shape the digital narrative of the African continent: WikiAfrica Education's experience

*Dina Rosa Agyemang, Fatou Alhya Diagne,
Tobechukwu Precious Friday, Elena Korzhenevich, Marta Sachy.*

In the professional world, the progress of globalization holds significant importance for various reasons, along with the ability to speak multiple languages and cultural fluency. In the labor market, multilingual individuals are essential for communication and collaboration. It contributes to promoting diversity and inclusion in companies and organizations. Linguistic and Cultural diversity can bring a variety of perspectives and innovative approaches. A specific focus may be on Africa when addressing multilingualism and cultural diversity. This continent is known for over 2,000 spoken languages and countless culturally rooted traditions within the same country.

Children learn the local language as their first language in the family context and their initial educational environment. This primary language is often the local language used in informal and familial interactions that develop at a regional and community level. Subsequently, during their education, they acquire a second European language, such as English or French, commonly intended as "ex-colonial" languages.

One of the main challenges for promoting and using African languages is that local languages are not considered drivers of 'decent' jobs with fair remuneration. For years, local language skills and cultural knowledge have not had an economic value and have been underestimated. Erroneously, there has always been the tendency to consider local languages as minority languages and "ex-colonial" languages as majority languages.

In many Africans' beliefs, knowing an African language limits the youth's potential for professional growth and social mobility. Therefore, the perceived economic value of local languages significantly affects local wealth and development. Multilingualism and cultural fluency practices tend to the development of cross-cultural communication skills. Moleskine Foundation and its Fondazione Aurora are two foundations supporting local communities' development through creativity and job inclusion in Africa. They have launched WikiAfrica Education (WAE), a platform of empowerment that engages young African language speakers to increase knowledge production online. WAE becomes tangible by implementing the Higher Education Initiative and AfroCuration Programs that promote local resources. It amplifies voices from Africa to reflect the continent's rich and valuable history, languages, people, communities, and cultures through creativity and digital platforms. Through the years, WAE has become a non-formal education model that engages African youth, primarily university students and local African communities. WAE can be seen as an innovative approach to education that unlocks youth's unexpressed potential. WikiAfrica aims to foster a state of cross-cultural sensitization and an inclusive climate conducive to new possibilities for Africa by focusing on young Africans.

Multilingualism and cultural fluency in Africa: Endogenous educational and professional resources of the Continent

The African continent is characterized by profound linguistic diversity, reflecting an intricate pluralism of cultures and identities coexisting in the same land. Over 2,000 languages are spoken in Africa, one-third of the total idioms.[426]

Multilingualism in Africa is crucial in preserving cultural heritage and maintaining a sense of identity among diverse communities as features that resisted colonialism. Local languages encapsulate the traditions, customs, and values of different ethnic groups.

African languages are also characterized by their spread of 'transnationality,' as they are spoken in several States. A case in point is Kiswahili, spoken in Tanzania, Kenya, and other areas with fewer

---

[426] Eberhard et al. (2019).

speakers, such as Uganda, Rwanda, Burundi, Southern Somalia, Northern Mozambique, and the Comoros Islands. In 2022, the widespread use of Kiswahili led the African Union to adopt it as a working language officially.[427] Across Africa, interaction is also possible through the "ex-colonial languages" such as English, French, or Portuguese. However, local African languages allow one to explore a country's cultural heritage and beyond. This is an exceptional tool to build strategic alliances and foster an African sense of belonging.

WikiAfrica Education attempts to demonstrate how using local African languages promoted by non-formal education formats can foster young Africans' soft and digital skills—many coming from unserved communities—and make them more competitive in today's professional world.

Multilingualism is an invaluable asset for economic growth in Africa. With the increasing globalization and the interconnectedness of economies, proficiency in multiple languages enhances international trade into a broader range of markets, attracting foreign regional investment and business opportunities.

The gap between recognizing local African languages and ex-colonial languages remains wide. This is a long-standing issue, as recognized by the first President of the African Academy of Languages (ACALAN):[428] "It must be acknowledged that the educational systems inherited from colonization, the linguistic and cultural identities infringed by the relegation of African languages to the background, the low literacy and education levels, to mention only these aspects, could not effectively promote active participation and socio-economic development of our young States."[429]

The stories and the language used reflect the many cultural identities that co-exist in the world. As digital spaces increasingly become the primary repository of knowledge, communities without access to digital tools risk losing language vitality, cultural narratives, and interconnectivity.

---

[427] Wasike Shimanyula (2022).
[428] ACALAN (2019).
[429] Samassekou (2004). p.2-3

Language variety is critical to sustaining cultural uniqueness in how people express their customs. African local languages are used to communicate at home, online, and for familial and intergenerational language transfer.

Multilingualism is linked to multiculturalism. Africa is one of the continents with the most incredible wealth in terms of cultural diversity. Its socio-demographic textures prove that cultural fluency is an innate talent of the continent.

Cultural fluency means fostering understanding, building relationships, and promoting social cohesion. For instance, understanding different African communities' cultural norms and values in business is essential for successful cross-cultural access to market, negotiation, and collaboration. Indeed, Africa is becoming an increasingly critical area for economic growth and inclusive development. AfCFTA (African Continental Free Trade Area) and the breakdown in Regional Economic Communities (RECs) through the African Union are concrete examples of how cultures and languages establish economic cohesion.

Therefore, cultural fluency and multilingualism are pillars of African education that celebrate diverse identities and foster future African professionals.

Why WikiAfrica Education

WikiAfrica Education (WAE) is a platform of empowerment that amplifies voices from Africa to reflect the continent's rich and valuable history, languages, people, and communities on Wikipedia. WAE's vision inspires a new generation of African creative thinkers and doers by increasing production, access, and awareness of contextually and linguistically relevant knowledge resources from Africa. Thus, WAE amplifies African content and narratives on Wikipedia, enhancing the quantity and quality of information available about Africa in the digital realm.

The African continent is a collectively resourceful land and technologically savvy space, but it is not well represented online on a global scale.

The Moleskine Foundation and Fondazione Aurora believe that this initiative contributes to preparing young people for the global professional world. The program enables young Africans to evolve from passive knowledge consumers to active knowledge producers. This transformation also fosters a stronger sense of identity, consolidating international African youth networks and promoting their cultures and identities.

There are several reasons why this program holds particular importance:

1. Identity: The program reflects Africans' knowledge and experiences and promotes social cohesion among individuals interested in learning about Africa's diverse cultures and experiences.
2. Knowledge: Establishing a comprehensive repository of African history and culture empowers Africans worldwide to connect with their cultural heritage, deepen their understanding of themselves, and advocate for their environments on the global stage.
3. Language: The program emphasizes preserving and using African languages, recognizing their vital role in African societies, and promoting their continued existence.
4. Access to African digital knowledge: WAE significantly contributes to addressing the information gap and empowering Africans to actively participate in shaping their narratives.

The framework of WikiAfrica Education

The WikiAfrica Education program involves a range of innovative educational formats. AfroCuration and the Higher Education Initiative are the main ones: the former is more community-based and motivational, and the latter aims to engage university students. Both have in common the goal of co-creating meaningful change in communities by connecting young Africans with educational and work opportunities in the countries. This helps communities face economic and local challenges like resource access and contrasting digital divides.

AfroCuration

AfroCuration is the most popular format launched by the Moleskine Foundation, with the support of Fondazione Aurora, the Wikimedia Foundation (WMF), and several local cultural partners. AfroCuration integrates cultural elements into Wikipedia editing sessions, where participants collaboratively write, improve, and translate articles. This unique event series combines creativity, knowledge, and activism and provides soft skills training for young Africans.

AfroCuration events differ from regular edit-a-thons as they provide a cultural and inspirational experience. Participants are encouraged to create knowledge about their culture and identity and address historical biases. These events can be conducted online, offline, or as a hybrid model, typically spanning two days, allowing Pan-African participation. The AfroCuration event comprises the following elements: a) Introductions by Partners and AfroCuration theme exploration: Introductive talks unpack the significance and relevance of the chosen theme, emphasizing the need for action. Participants engage in understanding and delving into the theme's meaning; b) Inspirational moment: A keynote address by a subject expert or a prominent speaker is designed to inspire participants. This session highlights the ideals of creativity, plurality, and open knowledge as well as the importance of creating knowledge in your language to reconnect with your culture and identity; c) Introduction to Wikipedia and multiple breakout sessions: A practical session is conducted to familiarize participants with editing Wikipedia and its tools. Participants now form groups and engage in collaborative work on articles, with guidance and support from experienced Wikipedians. Here, people experience teamwork and the meaning of working together; d) Cultural reflections and feedback sessions: participants reflect on their cultural experiences and how it feels to create knowledge in their local language and provide feedback on the event.

Since 2021, AfroCuration events have significantly impacted African languages and Wikipedia. These events have led to the creation of over 2,500 articles written in 15 different African languages, enriching the content available on Wikipedia. The high number of views these articles have received, consisting of over 322,736, is a testament to the strong interest in accessing information related to African languages and cultures. Over 400 young individuals have been trained through these events, equipping them with the necessary skills and knowledge to contribute to Wikipedia and actively participate in the digital knowledge-sharing ecosystem. Young Africans are not just participants. They are critical actors in this movement, gaining agency and essential abilities to become tomorrow's professional leaders.

Higher Education Initiative

The Higher Education Initiative (HEI) was launched in December 2020, and since then, it has been managed and supported by Fondazione Aurora. It engages and trains university students who speak and write in African languages to produce digital content on Wikipedia. HEI is designed to provide students with relevant ICT, research, and writing skills. The initiative equips a diverse range of 18-35-year-olds under and post-graduate students with competencies and motivation to be knowledge producers in their communities. The program consists of training sessions delivered digitally and conducted by an experienced Wikimedian professional training manager. Students attend a 2-hour session per week, for a total of 4 lectures per month, in a class of a maximum of 50 participants coming from international backgrounds. The trainings are delivered in English, French, or Portuguese entirely online, permitting the participation of anglophone, francophone, and lusophone students from different African universities.

The outcome of the Higher Education Initiative involved more than 200 students in over ten sessions, resulting in the publication of more than 800 articles written in at least 16 African languages such as Kinyarwanda, Kiswahili, Dagbani, Igbo, Isizulu, Isixhosa, Lologooli, Yoruba, Sepedi, Twi, Amharic, Isixhosa, Emakhwa,

Yemba, Tigrinya, Moore, and others. The articles produced reached more than 1,780,000 individual views.

The project has a significant impact on youth and institutions. Conversely, Fondazione Aurora succeeded in expanding a consistent network of notable stakeholders. Many international institutions recognized the value of the HEI and signed collaboration agreements to further the trusted Project. Among these, African and Italian institutions are included, such as the Italian Ministry of Foreign Affairs and International Cooperation (MAECI), the African Research Universities Alliance (ARUA), South Africa's Constitution Hill, and universities in both Italy and Africa, such as University of Federico II in Naples, University of "Tor Vergata" in Rome, Amref International University, Nairobi University in Kenya and Burkina Institute of Technology.

Covid-19 awareness campaign: The solution will not be televised

In 2020, while the world was engaged in discussions about the Coronavirus, a sizable portion of the global population could not participate in these conversations due to a lack of information in their language. Recognizing this issue, the Moleskine Foundation and Fondazione Aurora partnered with African language writers and African Wikipedia communities to address this language gap and ensure vital content about the pandemic was accessible in local languages. The collaborative effort focused on translating crucial information about COVID-19 into 17 African languages. By making this information available in local languages, it became possible for people to engage in conversation, contribute their insights, and create potentially life-saving responses tailored to their specific contexts. The results of this campaign demonstrated the power of collective action. It involved 410 Movement Members and produced 197 articles that reached 500,000 article views.

This campaign is a powerful example of how global collaboration and volunteerism can address language barriers and ensure that crucial information reaches all corners of the world in local languages.

A joint partnership for education and capacity building by the nonprofit sector: The Moleskine Foundation and Fondazione Aurora

WikiAfrica Education is a youth-focused training proposal from the third sector. The Moleskine Foundation launched it in 2006 and implemented it in partnership with Fondazione Aurora in 2019. The Wikimedia Foundation has also recognized the program.

The foundations are deeply rooted in global society and actively contribute to building collective growth pathways, capturing key drivers of sustainable development that inspire young people.

Moleskine Foundation is a non-profit organization based in Milan (Italy) pursuing a "Creativity for Social Change" mission. Its central belief is that creativity is vital to producing positive change in society and driving our collective future. Its focus is to inspire, empower, and connect young people to transform themselves and their communities. To do so, the Foundation implements unconventional educational programs that unlock creative potential and develop a change-making attitude in youth. The Foundation enables collaborative processes to generate spaces where criticality and imagination can occur. It is done by creating a global platform of cultural and creative partner organizations operating in the field of creativity for social transformation.

Fondazione Aurora is a non-profit organization based in Rome (Italy) committed to scaling up African social impact enterprises. It promotes inclusive and sustainable economic growth, employment, and decent work. It fosters young African entrepreneurs who manage businesses with social impact on their communities. To establish a more inclusive business climate, the Foundation promotes training programs by offering scholarships and internships to young people with a migrant background and international training programs to stimulate the production of digital content on Africa and deconstruct negative stereotypes about Africa.

Combining each WikiAfrica Education promoter's unique characteristics generates a high added value, more significant than they could have achieved individually. The partnership between the

Moleskine Foundation and Fondazione Aurora significantly impacts areas where large and under-represented local communities exist. Coordinated efforts to propose innovative social and educational initiatives can address complex challenges. Moleskine Foundation and Fondazione Aurora intend to be an actual example of a partnership model that can foster collective responsibility and mobilize resources towards common goals while promoting long-term, sustainable solutions that benefit society.

Achievements of WikiAfrica Education

Empowering youth and ensuring knowledge for communities in Africa

WikiAfrica Education has demonstrated its direct and indirect impacts on its target communities, leading to remarkable achievements that cannot be overlooked. Participants reported the benefits of creating content juggling cultural insights, the unexpected motivation of using their language to do further research, and the realization that they are knowledge producers to people far away who often speak only one language. These skills drive value creation: training young people's skills starting from their inner local knowledge improves the quality of the current and future workforce. Some other notable achievements resulting from this collaborative endeavor are:

Expanded Knowledge

WikiAfrica Education has significantly expanded knowledge of African cultures, histories, and languages. Through the collective work of participants, over 14,000 articles have been created and improved, reaching over 4,50 million views and enriching the representation of African narratives through Wikipedia and its related tools.

Enhanced Visibility

The program has played a pivotal role in increasing the visibility of African perspectives and experiences on the global stage. WikiAfrica Education participants have ensured that African knowledge in local languages receives the recognition they deserve. By focusing on African languages, the initiative aims to promote linguistic diversity and ensure that information on Wikipedia is accessible to a broader audience within Africa.

Empowered Communities

WikiAfrica Education has empowered communities by enabling them to take ownership of their digital narratives. By creating and curating content about their own cultures and identities, participants have gained agency and a stronger sense of pride in their heritage – contrasting the mainstream hierarchy of colonial culture.

Language Preservation

The program has made significant strides in preserving African languages by encouraging the creation of knowledge in at least 21 languages, including Emakhuwa, Kiswahili, Shona, Ndebele, Tshivenda, isiXhosa, isiZulu, Igbo, Arabic, Kirwanda, Sesotho, Sepedi, Twi, Wolof, Dagbani, Moore. WikiAfrica Education has contributed to revitalizing and increasing the usage of these languages in the digital sphere to increase accessibility.

Inspiration and Creativity

WikiAfrica Education has been a source of inspiration and a platform for fostering creativity. Through keynote addresses and cultural reflections, participants have been motivated to think critically, explore innovative ideas, reflect on their identity, feel empowered to become change-makers in their communities, and express themselves creatively.

Improving access to development opportunities and business climate from and towards Africa

The continent has already started to reveal its potential; however, the lack of activation and distribution of resources continues to limit the visibility of its growth. Estimates state that today, about 60% of its population is under 25 years old, and 40% (especially in sub-Saharan Africa) is under 15. By 2030, over 40% of the world's youth will be African; by 2050, Africa will represent more than 25% of the global population.[430] On the other hand, the Continent's GDP is expected to grow by 3.8% and 4.2% in 2024 and 2025, respectively. This is higher than the global average of 2.9% and 3.2%. The continent is set to remain the second-fastest-growing region after Asia.[431] This implies that Africa is the continent with the most rapid population growth and the youngest population. Its demographic growth indicates that by 2035, more young Africans will enter the workforce each year than in all other countries combined.[432] This vast pool represents enormous potential for development, but only if everyone has access to adequate educational and training pathways.

Does WikiAfrica Education contribute to a better professional world? The decision to promote training courses such as WikiAfrica is reflected in several crucial factors in the employability landscape.

Creativity

For Africa, creativity can be a powerful strategic lever. The described context explains why it is essential to "think out of the box" for young Africans. Developing creative thinking, which can be defined as the ability to approach situations in innovative and original ways, going beyond conventional boundaries, will be crucial for Africa. In response to the new demands that the demographic increase of multicultural populations will bring, adopting a new perspective and developing a mindset that can overcome the limitations of settled methods will be essential. Diversification through exposure to

---

[430] United Nations (2022).
[431] Anuforo (2024).
[432] Mpemba & Munyati (2023).

diverse backgrounds leads to this highly demanded skill in today's marketplace. However, the potential for developing creative thinking is underestimated. The World Economic Forum describes it as a crucial skill for those who want to innovate, from start-ups to large multinationals, precisely because creative thinking is at the heart of any innovative process.[433] It is a stimulus to creativity to ask young African university students to produce content to express their voices in an accessible way.

Non-formal education

WikiAfrica Education is now among the international training offers for a non-formal education dedicated explicitly to Africa and its growing human capital resources. The benefit of a diverse form of learning is the encouragement of inclusion and participation, reinforcing traditional academic curricula. WikiAfrica Education demonstrated itself as a good practice that induced respect for differences and allowed young people to express themselves. As a tailored form of training, it boosts job placement opportunities.

Digital skills

Today, the general workforce requires digital skills to use technology in daily life and work. Even though digitalization is not occurring at the same rate in all economies and regions, its impact on the demand for skills is felt everywhere. In Africa, the lack of ICT skills prevents businesses from adopting new technologies and, in the worst case, becomes a barrier to individual employability and career progression towards productive, decent jobs in the digital economy. WikiAfrica Education encourages students to hone their online research and publishing skills. Contributing to the world's largest digital encyclopedia means learning digital tools and the responsible use of the Internet.

---

[433] World Economic Forum (2023).

New skills required by enterprises.

Global leading companies require profiles of innovative workers who combine their peculiar personal skills with practical technical skills and transculturality. Cultural fluency and multilingualism add value to today's companies as multilingual people a) show fewer stereotypes and prejudices than monolingual speakers; b) have a better metalinguistic competence as they can juggle unfamiliar cultures that they naturally explore and make them more open-minded; c) are keen to innovation. Diversity is a competitive advantage, not something to be observed out of political correctness: a diversified working environment is more innovative. The benefits of collaborating in a heterogeneous team can be maximized if educational processes like WikiAfrica Education are initiated in the younger generation, promoting intercultural collaboration.

Enhancing African representation through WikiAfrica Education

WikiAfrica Education initiatives have promoted African languages, cultural representation, and knowledge dissemination. By publishing articles, increasing their visibility, and training young Africans, these initiatives have played a crucial role in strengthening the African presence on Wikipedia and empowering individuals to actively participate in shaping the digital information landscape. The WikiAfrica Education case study also illustrates that promoting equality in language dissemination fosters intercultural awareness and mutual respect, which are essential in today's interconnected professional world and beyond.

Fostering lifelong learning and youth exchange

To further enhance the impact of WikiAfrica Education, it is recommended that physical and virtual spaces be promoted where youth from diverse communities can converge, engage in dialogue, and share knowledge. As primary centers of education and youth engagement, universities should be encouraged and involved as partners in addressing social change. Embracing initiatives in non-formal education from social actors committed to sustainable development, as well as social and employment inclusion of young people, and integrating them into educational programs will expand the opportunities students can leverage during their formative years. Additionally, access to acquiring new digital and cross-cutting skills significantly increases the likelihood of securing "decent" employment within shorter periods.

Tapping into the cultural and creative sector to empower and inspire youth

Exploiting the potential of the multicultural diversity of the African continent can uncover the invaluable richness that can inspire young people to create in their local languages. By attracting the cultural organizations on the continent to the various events and unlocking their content onto digital platforms, the youth are inspired to write their digital narrative in their native language and tell stories about the richness of their culture and community. Being empowered by access to the cultural sector in their communities, the youth will develop invaluable skills to shape the digital narrative of our collective future.

Chapter 18 – Multilingualism for all: From dream to reality in public policy

Gabrielle Durana

The linguistic trajectory of Vladimir Nabokov, evolving from a Russian cradle to literary consecration in English, illustrates the multilingual journey and raises a fundamental question about the impact of linguistic environments from an early age. Nabokov's transition from his "rich Russian vocabulary" to a "substitute English" sheds light on the challenges and opportunities of multilingualism, revealing how mastering multiple languages can open vast and varied horizons.

My time at the École Normale Supérieure highlighted an inescapable reality: success in learning foreign languages tends to be the privilege of those exposed to early linguistic immersion or from advantaged backgrounds. This observation raises questions about the equity of access to multilingualism. In this context, we will look at the origins and development of linguistic public policies and the recognition of foreign language acquisition as an essential global competency in our interconnected economies.

While the advent of artificial intelligence promises to remove language barriers, the importance of multilingualism and active language learning persists, offering an irreplaceable window into cultural diversity and a deep mutual understanding. This chapter will explore the principles that can guide the development of effective public policies favoring multilingualism. We will question the place of these policies in the era of artificial intelligence. Together, we will explore how multilingualism, far from being a privilege of the elite, should become a common heritage, enriching our global competence and ability to navigate an increasingly globalized world.

Multilingualism: A persistent ideal of public policy

Integrating multilingualism as a key public policy objective prompts an exploration of significant historical episodes worldwide. Emblematic legislation such as Quebec's Bill 101, the rise of the Language Movement in 1952 in what would become Bangladesh, and the affirmation of Ukrainians against the remnants of Russification all highlight the ongoing struggle to preserve minority languages. These examples illustrate that multilingualism, as a vital aspect of cultural identity, has often been not just a matter of domestic policy but also a symbol of resistance and cultural affirmation.

Towards linguistic uniformity: Ambitions and realities

Abbé Henri-Baptiste Grégoire's 1794 report,[434] advocating the universalization of the French language, embodies a vision where linguistic unity is seen as a vector of progress and linguistic fragmentation as an imperfection to be eliminated through energetic and well-thought-out public policies in the interest of the "beneficiaries." However, the reality is quite different. Sociolinguist Jonathan Pool concludes: "There is virtually no country that is linguistically diverse and prosperous." He cites two exceptions, Switzerland and Singapore, highlighting the importance of linguistic diversity in prosperity.

For some countries, former colonies, multilingualism is a luxury that cannot be afforded because priority must be given to economic development. This decision is significant, as building and administering a single-quality school system is more accessible and less costly. Centralization as a tool for development goes hand in hand with the perception that the country will fare better if "a working solution is generalized." He who tries to do too much does it badly.

Of course, the choice of language to be favored is never neutral. The argument that language selection is strategic was precisely what Pakistan used to promote Urdu over Bengali in East Pakistan, a non-

---

[434] Grégoire (1794).

contiguous territory carved out of Bengal by the British at the time of India's independence in 1947. This strategic language selection was a critical factor in the Movement for the Defense of the Bengali Language, which led to the civil war and the birth of Bangladesh on March 26, 1971.

Public policies and multilingualism: A mosaic of approaches

Multilingualism, reflecting the complexity of collective identities, requires adaptive public policies. Initiatives range from coercive linguistic regimes protecting minority languages to policies encouraging the learning of strategic languages, illustrating the diversity of strategies to promote multilingualism.

The genesis of linguistic policies is rooted in a context of responses to sociocultural and political dynamics. They arise from the need to reconcile national unity and linguistic diversity, marked by debates on the balance between monolingual and multilingual visions of society.

Coercive Linguistic Regimes and Encouragement of Future Languages: Linguistic policies vary from coercive regimes aimed at protecting minority languages to strategies promoting the learning of languages considered helpful for the future. This diversity reflects an awareness of the value of multilingualism as a societal and economic asset.

"Benign Neglect" and Linguistic Inclusion Policies: Approaches such as "benign neglect" in the United States show another facet of linguistic policies. They aim to facilitate access to information and civic participation in various languages, underscoring the importance of language mastery as a global skill in an interconnected world.

What principles underpin public policies on multilingualism?

Van Parijs explains that establishing a territorially differentiated coercive linguistic regime aims to give the weaker language "the same parity of esteem" as the more robust language.[435] In his book *Linguistic Justice for Europe and the World*, he explains that there are

---

[435] Van Parijs (2011).

three good reasons to establish a coercive regime of linguistic protection:

Combating colonialist attitudes: The law avoids creating neo-colonial situations in which speakers of the strong language expect to be served in their language, even if they live permanently in the country. He also invites a reciprocity test: if you expect immigrants to learn the local language, would you do the same if you moved to their country? The argument "I would never move there" is not acceptable.

"The agony of kindness": Under this cryptic expression, Van Parijs designates a situation in which the cohabitation of languages is not hostile. For this very reason, i.e., the multiplication of fruitful and mutually advantageous exchanges, the weaker language finds itself in danger of being ousted by the use of "to be practical" or "to be polite" of the language spoken by the majority, leading to the agony of the weaker language.

"Each language is a queen": Using an artistic metaphor coined by Gellner in 1983,[436] Van Parijs describes scenarios of multilingualism as akin to Kokoshka's paintings, where a tapestry of languages is intricately woven together within the same territory or as resembling Modigliani's artworks, where distinct territories of varying colors are neatly juxtaposed. He explains that in both cases, the rules prevent the weak language from being systematically crushed by giving it reserved spaces, either by territory or by function (school, health, media, and more).

Efficiency – equity, a false debate:

Politics is the science of will. Knowing how to embody action in words is necessary to crystallize a collective project and then find alliances to implement it by expressing the general will. All public policies, including those related to language, are designed to enhance the well-being of those governed.

When Abbé Grégoire proposed annihilating the "patois," he believed he was doing well: French would be a tool for education and

---

[436] Gellner (1983).

emancipation. When a country like South Africa adopts in its new Constitution at the end of Apartheid eleven official languages and adds a twelfth, South African Sign Language, in 2023, the concern for justice and reconciliation dictates that pragmatism dictates a public policy "less practical" than the monolingualism of before 1994, when Afrikaans was the only language of schooling. To achieve reconciliation (principle of efficiency), it is better to advocate multilingualism (principle of equity).

Moreover, the definition of equity varies: the European approach based on teaching from an early age one or more languages considered "useful" with support in post-bac studies is very different from the American philosophy, which is based on a discourse of equalizing the chances of immigrant children, who fell into bilingualism somewhat by accident, and that it should be opened to other students, particularly curious or lucky. As for decolonized countries, does the survival of multilingual school policies perpetuate the subjugation of national culture and languages or offer them a chance to stand out and escape underdevelopment?

What is certain is that public policies in favor of multilingualism have a cost: The European thurifers will choose the figures that justify the "cost of doing democracy," while the Eurosceptics will ridicule the translation of the slightest text from the Commission or Parliament into Maltese.

The question of democratizing access to multilingual education, especially in OECD countries, because these economies generate added value that would finance a costly and ambitious policy, but also in the rest of the world because of the brain drain, deserves to be posed to the voters of each country. Of course, school systems are decentralized in many countries, and there is no magic wand to transform public schools. However, the elite exception system that is the subject of today's multilingual education is a mistake in efficiency (output gap) and an injustice in equity (the rich get richer).

Van Parijs points out a paradox: the more English becomes a common language, the more countries are encouraged to train their citizens in this language. However, this has the perverse effect of favoring the establishment of a global labor market for highly qualified workers that devalues the skills of graduates to the lowest bidder. In other words, France can offer English-language training in higher education. Still, there will always be a Filipino or a Bangladeshi who can do the same job in English, better and cheaper. The response to this vicious circle? According to Van Parijs, public policies must coercively implement linguistic diversity!

Rethinking linguistic policies in the age of AI

As we consider the imminent emergence of generative artificial intelligence, one might wonder if this does not mark the end of an era. If tomorrow's technology can quickly and smoothly translate content at minimal cost, do public linguistic policies become obsolete? With every individual owning a smartphone as a universal translation tool, the struggle to promote acquiring a second language may seem futile, given the fifteen-year effort required to achieve bilingualism.

However, as any multilingual individual understands, a language is more than just a collection of concepts and wordplay. It embodies culture, worldview, and a bridge to understanding others, not as obstacles but as enriching experiences. Moreover, governments must assume the visible role of architects, guiding the dissemination of best practices, ensuring cybersecurity, combating misinformation, and promoting the constructive use of generative artificial intelligence. Without a state to protect our shared resources, we may communicate through our devices and understand each other, but we will not form a cohesive society.

Therefore, as we navigate the transformative landscape of technological advancement, let us not relinquish the essence of language learning and cultural exchange. Instead, let us embrace the evolving role of governments as guardians of digital common goods, ensuring that technology serves as a bridge rather than a barrier to meaningful human connection. In a world where servers may buckle under climate change, our collective resilience and commitment to fostering understanding remain our most precious assets.

Chapter 19 – Multilingualism in Lebanon

Lama Fakih

Often mentioned in travel memoirs about Lebanon, the greeting "Hi, kifak? Ça va?" playfully illustrates the unique trilingual greeting that Lebanese people commonly use. This melding of Arabic, French, and English in a single sentence reflects the local dialect and the widespread ability among the population to communicate in these three languages. The roots of this linguistic blend can be traced to a history of trilingual, and occasionally quadrilingual, education, a solid Armenian community deeply embedded in the country, enduring ties with the diaspora, a cosmopolitan outlook, and an ongoing exploration of identity. These factors have consistently positioned Lebanese individuals advantageously in a competitive job market, where their language skills, academic prowess, and cultural openness distinguish them from their Arab peers. Abroad, particularly in the West and the Middle East, they are often perceived as distinct, enjoying preferential treatment in recruitment and salary (at least until the 2019 economic crisis), especially in the Gulf Cooperation Council states.

What relationship do young Lebanese have with these different languages today? What significance does multilingualism hold in their professional lives? This chapter examines the state of multilingualism in Lebanon, highlighting its benefits and challenges.

Origins of multilingualism in Lebanon

Lebanon's strategic location on the Mediterranean at the crossroads of various continents and civilizations has exposed it to numerous invasions. The Arab-Muslim expansion in the 7th century began a lengthy process of Islamization, leaving a lasting cultural and primarily linguistic imprint. Despite four centuries of Ottoman rule, the local populace retained only a few Turkish words in their dialect, using Arabic increasingly as a tool of resistance against oppression.

By the late 19th century, in response to Turkification policies from Istanbul and Western interference through the Eastern Question, a cultural renaissance known as the Nahda emerged. This renaissance modernized and simplified Arabic, spurring growth in the press and literature.

The 19th century also witnessed the arrival of missionaries, particularly Catholics from France and Protestants from America, who founded numerous educational institutions in Mount Lebanon and Beirut. These included establishing the Syrian Protestant College in 1866 (now the American University of Beirut) and the Saint Joseph University of Beirut in 1875. This era solidified trilingualism among the elite, predating even the formation of the Lebanese state in 1920. The French mandate further elevated the status of French as it became the language of administration, the language of the local aristocracy, and the preferred language in education, including in public schools. Upon independence, one of Lebanon's first acts of sovereignty was to designate Arabic as the official language. At the same time, French retained its status as a lingua franca, and English gradually gained prominence due to increasing American influence. These foreign languages were integrated into the educational system, with institutions often choosing to deliver their entire curriculum in French or English.

French was particularly favored within the Christian communities, not only because of the substantial presence of French Catholic missions but also because France was seen as a "protective mother," ensuring their coexistence with other religious groups. On the other hand, Muslims were more inclined to pursue their studies in English, given Great Britain's historical influence on their regions and the joint economic and political interests. In this case, London and Washington pressured Paris in 1943 to grant independence to Lebanon. Though it is undeniable that (foreign) languages can serve as markers of identity to some degree, the situation is nuanced by the fact that Arabic continues to serve as a unifying factor across all groups, irrespective of their political alignments. These preferences are passed down from generation to generation and influence the linguistic choices of families and individuals in their social, professional, and educational interactions. This also shapes the perception of foreign languages in the country and their role in contemporary Lebanese society.

The evolution of multilingualism within Lebanese society

The early 1990s, marking the end of the Cold War and the Lebanese Civil War, brought significant changes to Lebanon, including accelerating globalization and normalizing English usage. This period ushered in a notable shift: Many young Lebanese, including those from French-speaking educational backgrounds, began to opt for higher education in English-speaking systems. Data from various educational institutions across different socio-economic backgrounds supports this trend.[437]

For instance, students from the prestigious International College (IC), which offers both French and English instruction and the option to obtain a French or International Baccalaureate (IB), increasingly choose English-speaking universities in Lebanon and abroad. Similarly, the Amjad institution, catering to middle- to lower-class students and offering courses in either language, sees most French-speaking students enrolling in more affordable English-speaking universities like the Lebanese International University (LIU). In contrast, students from Carmel Saint Joseph, a Catholic school accredited by the French Ministry of National Education, display more varied educational paths. While previous generations preferred the American University of Beirut (AUB), many now opt for French instruction at Saint Joseph University, where tuition remains comparatively affordable.

According to the orientation service of the French Protestant College of Beirut, part of the AEFE network, most young people who remain in Lebanon for higher education choose American institutions in the capital, such as AUB and LAU, despite their higher tuition fees. These universities are well-regarded internationally and are believed to offer better career prospects, particularly in the Gulf

---

[437] The following pieces of information are from interviews the author has conducted. Please note that we did try to gather data on Lebanese public high-schools but were unsuccessful. They keep no information regarding which university their students chose to enroll at.

Cooperation Council countries. This trend has continued even amidst Lebanon's economic collapse since 2019. Post-2019, there has also been a rise in enrollment at foreign universities, especially in France, primarily among affluent students. The simplified admission processes and the low cost of education in France are particularly appealing during times of crisis. Additionally, there has been an increase in language course enrollments at the French Institute of Beirut, driven by young Lebanese seeking better living conditions in France.[438]

Impact of multilingualism on career development

Proficiency in these languages, which are international, is a competitive advantage for Lebanese individuals in the job market. It opens more opportunities for them, facilitating their recruitment. The career paths of the individuals we have interviewed confirm this hypothesis. They work in Lebanon or abroad across various sectors. However, individuals working in education, psychology, personal development, communication, tourism, hospitality, and catering seem to be the most advantaged. The following section highlights the most revealing examples of the link between multilingualism and employability among young Lebanese.

L.A., a psychologist who graduated from the Saint Joseph University of Beirut, was immediately hired at the medical center of the American University (AUBMC) due to her trilingual proficiency, which proved crucial for communicating with French-speaking patients in an English-speaking environment. Her command of Arabic enabled her to work with NGOs assisting Syrian refugees. Later, she pursued a master's degree in the UK and provided consultations through online platforms, expanding her reach globally. Her multilingualism again proved to be an asset when she was employed by a Parisian organization assisting undocumented migrants suffering from psycho-trauma. Notably, L.A. can also

---

[438] Please note that we did try to gather data on Lebanese public high-schools but were unsuccessful. They keep no information regarding which university their students chose to enroll at.

communicate in Spanish and Persian, enhancing her ability to interact with a diverse clientele without needing interpreters, thereby saving on their often-substantial fees.

L.F., a teacher at a French high school in the capital, was quickly recruited to join the team for the French baccalaureate's international option due to her versatility in teaching both in French and Arabic and her role in developing bilingual vocabulary and contextualized courses. Her skills led to her recruitment by another French school in Europe to teach French programs in English within their American section. L.F. and L.A. exemplify the importance of cultural fluency; beyond linguistic ability, they understand and adapt to various cultural contexts and non-verbal communication cues.

Furthermore, many Lebanese individuals, like L.F., find employment in French schools abroad, especially in the Gulf, due to their qualifications, linguistic skills, and knowledge of foreign educational standards. This trend persists even with the modernization of these regions.

In these countries' broader business worlds, English predominates. M.A., a senior consultant at PWC in Saudi Arabia, communicates primarily in Arabic and English. However, communicating in French could be advantageous with French-speaking clients. Jean-Noël Baléo, Regional Director of AUF Middle East, emphasizes that while English is essential, the ability to communicate in French offers a comparative advantage and broadens business opportunities.

A.F., working in the finance sector in Dubai, uses English exclusively for daily transactions. Despite his fluency in French, he does not view it as a competitive advantage in a city characterized by its globalized digital economy. This perspective contrasts with the significant Lebanese expatriate community in the United Arab Emirates, which grew during the 1980s due to the civil war and the economic boom in the petro-monarchy. Mastery of Arabic and English has been crucial for their mobility.

According to Forbes magazine, influential Lebanese expatriates like Alain Bejjani, CEO of Majid Al Futtaim, and Nabil Habayeb, who leads General Electric in the Middle East, North Africa, and Türkiye, underscore the prominent positions held by Lebanese in the

Gulf. Guita Hourani's study highlights that Lebanese occupy 35% of management positions in the Gulf.

Between 1990 and 2015, around 1.5 million people left Lebanon, contributing to a significant brain drain. Philippe Fargue's study for the United Nations reveals that approximately 52% of this diaspora holds higher education degrees, with limited job opportunities and endemic corruption in Lebanon pushing these multilingual, qualified workers to seek better prospects abroad.

The limits of multilingualism

However, while Lebanese multilingualism undoubtedly offers an advantage in the job market, its limits and challenges must be examined: Is it a source of enrichment, or could it pose a threat in its present form? Are all three languages truly mastered?

In a context where linguistic mixing is becoming the norm, an entire vocabulary tends to disappear and be replaced by terms in French and English, even conjugating foreign verbs in Arabic. This phenomenon concerns the field of computer terminology: *sayyavet* (I saved), *dallatet* (I deleted), and *chayyaket* (I checked), but it is becoming increasingly commonplace.

Furthermore, certain words and expressions commonly used, such as "weekend," "parking," "stress," "meeting," "elevator," or even "hello," "thank you," and "goodbye" are never said in Arabic. As an indicative example, 52% of the 522 words listed in Freiha's dialect dictionary from 1948 are of foreign origin. Others, less commonly used in daily life, are unknown! For instance, in a sample of 20 randomly interviewed people on the street, only one person found the Arabic equivalent of the word "ladybug." On the one hand, this is undoubtedly because most parents prefer to address their children in a foreign language to ensure its transmission even before they join kindergarten.

Additionally, schools often consider the ability to express oneself in a foreign language as a selection criterion for their future students. On the other hand, some pronunciation challenges can be attributed to heavy sounds like ' and q (do'souqa), which younger people increasingly find difficult to articulate. This leads to the deformation of many words, presenting a unique problem.

Communication gaps often arise between Arabic-speaking grandparents and their grandchildren, for whom Arabic has become a foreign language. This issue is particularly concerning, as it impacts not only oral communication but also writing. In the Arab world, language hybridization has given rise to "Arabizi" or "Arabish," a system that uses Latin letters to write dialectal Arabic. Numbers are used to represent certain Arabic letters, simplifying communication but also signaling a shift in traditional language use.

In summary, Lebanon is experiencing a gradual decline in Arabic proficiency, while French and English are not mastered to perfection. Many professionals — including those we interviewed— admit they initially underestimated the importance of Arabic, only recognizing its value often after entering the job market. Furthermore, does mastery of one language not foster a particular discipline when learning another?

While multilingualism offers professional, cultural, and personal advantages, the specific form of multilingualism in Lebanon often leads to an inability to recall words in one language as equivalents quickly replace them in another. This suggests more than just linguistic challenges; it points to a profound identity crisis among a population struggling to define its native language.

Amid broader national crises and the shortcomings of Lebanon's state model, reforming the educational system to align with a renewed political and civic vision is increasingly crucial. Implementing a "School of the Republic," similar to the model in France, could be a viable solution, especially considering the high enrollment in private schools due to the declining quality of public education. A unified national educational project emphasizing language learning and consolidation as essential human capital could provide a solid economic foundation. Additionally, the state could adopt an active communication strategy to educate the population about the importance of multilingualism and position it as a cornerstone of national branding, yielding significant economic benefits.

Chapter 20 – The missing link between global competence education and Chinese laborers' life abroad

Xiaojin Niu

For over four decades, China has been seen as the "workshop of the world," employing hundreds of millions of workers as cheap labor to provide products and services for the global market.[439] In the meantime, it is also one of the biggest countries where labor emigrates abroad. As of early 2022, approximately 573,000 Chinese nationals were working abroad, directly contributing to the labor forces of their host countries.[440] Traditionally, these workers have been drawn to wealthy and developed nations. However, initiatives such as the Belt and Road Initiative (BRI) have increasingly attracted Chinese workers to developing regions as well.[441]

As an international scholar who has lived in the United States for almost ten years, I have met many Chinese workers there – many of them are professional workers who decided to stay in the U.S. after graduating with their post-secondary degrees, while many are service workers who went to the U.S. only for the job opportunities. I often interact with the latter at Chinese restaurants, supermarkets, laundromats, and Chinatown. Unlike Chinese students enrolled in universities or professionals working in offices, they enter the American labor force right after leaving China without getting to know the new country through educational programs. They are more likely to live in or near Chinatowns and continue to use only Chinese languages in their daily communications.

Furthermore, I also had a chance to learn more about Chinese workers' lives in the Global South. During my visit to Papua New Guinea (PNG) in 2022, I saw many Chinese businesses everywhere, from the capital city, Port Moresby, to other middle-sized towns. I

---
[439] Pun (2020).
[440] Ministry of Commerce. (2022).
[441] Song (2018).

also met many Chinese workers at those Chinese-owned department stores, pharmacies, supermarkets, and hotels. They speak Tok Pisin, the local pidgin language, fluently and work with local Papua New Guinean workers. Later, at the airport in Port Moresby, I met a man from China who just arrived there to begin his job as a shopkeeper at a Chinese store. He told me that this was his first time going abroad. At that time, he did not know Tok Pisin or English (another official language of PNG). He decided to go there because of the higher pay compared to his previous work in China and some friends or family members who already worked in PNG for years. He was also looking forward to learning Tok Pisin from the lessons provided by his company. I said goodbye to him when his new colleagues, who were all Chinese, went to pick him up from the airport. Later in that trip, some local Papua New Guinean friends told me they had been used to frequently seeing Chinese people in their country. However, they still felt that Chinese people always kept to themselves and seldom interacted with the locals. This was my observation as well – at the stores I went to, the Chinese shopkeepers rarely chatted with the local people other than doing business, always stayed vigilant to potential shoplifters, and even wore assorted colors of uniforms to distinguish themselves.

Inspired by these experiences, I want to explore how education may affect Chinese workers' lives abroad. In this literature-based chapter, I provide a general picture of the Chinese working class abroad, including the background of its members, the motivation for their migration, and the difficulty they face in another country. More importantly, I argue that there is a missing link between the education they receive and the necessary skills or competence they need to thrive overseas. The education includes both the professional training offered by their employers and the school education they receive back in China when they are young. Drawing from statistics, academic studies, and personal narratives, I aim to provoke readers' attention to this less-known population and advocate for more enriched education opportunities to be provided for this community. Chinese workers' situations represent workers from many other parts of the world, and they are all making significant contributions to globalization, the world economy, and intercultural communication.

Defining the global working-class community

The community being studied is problematic because it constantly expands, shrinks, and changes. Multiple names, such as workers, laborers, or the working class, can describe this community. However, "workers" can also refer to professional employees working in offices. "Laborers" exclude the workers who work for service, sales, trades, or some manufacturing positions. In this sense, I find the term "working class" most appropriate. It is "a social group that consists of people who earn little money, often paid only for the hours or days they work, and usually do physical work."[442] In addition to a definition marked by pay range, I consider two other factors for understanding the working-class group. Firstly, The International Standard Classification of Occupations maps out four skill levels to classify all types of occupations: Skill level 1: elementary; Skill level 2: factory, craft, trades, agriculture/fishery, service and sales, and clerical workers; Skill level 3 and 4: technician, professionals, and managers.[443] The workers spotlighted in this chapter usually offer their skills in the first two levels to earn money. Secondly, employment skill levels are also correlated to education levels. For example, according to Rozelle and Boswell, the low education rate (middle school and lower) satisfied China's industrial and economic growth until the early 2000s. Still, it may have hindered the nation's future development.[444] Therefore, the working class can also be defined as workers who do not need post-secondary or high school education to find suitable jobs.

As the world's economy has been deeply interconnected for over a century, the labor force has also been moving across borders. According to the International Labour Organization's (ILO) estimation, in 2019, there were 169 million migrant workers worldwide who were involved in the labor force in their countries of residence instead of origin. ILO's data also indicate that in the same year, 66.2% of the migrant workers were in services, 26.7% in

---

[442] Cambridge Dictionary.
[443] International Labour Organization (2023).
[444] Rozelle & Boswell (2021).

industry, and 7.1% in agriculture.⁴⁴⁵ Although ILO's report does not specify what percentage of these migrant workers is categorized as working class, at least 30% are likely to be working class workers involved in industry and agriculture. Furthermore, in this post-industrial era, large-scale manufacturing has been relocated to developing countries like China, India, or South Africa from Europe, Japan, and North America, which engendered a generation of "global working class" consisting of migrants from the Global South.⁴⁴⁶ That is why, in 2019, 67.4% of the migrant workers moved to high-income countries.⁴⁴⁷

Chinese working class overseas

As discussed in the Introduction section, the Chinese working-class community that makes a living overseas has been growing for decades. The main destinations for these workers are still in the developed world, in Australia, Europe, and North America.⁴⁴⁸ In the meantime, as China's economy and international standing rise, projects like BRI also diverged the emigration trend. The data published by the Ministry of Commerce of China show that in 2021, China's global foreign direct investment flows reached around 1.7 trillion U.S. dollars, making China the second-largest investing entity in the world. Fifteen percent of this investment flew to the manufacturing industry.⁴⁴⁹

The immense investments stimulated labor mobility, enabling Chinese workers to emigrate to countries participating in BRI. For instance, Papua New Guinea joined the Belt and Road Initiative in 2018.⁴⁵⁰ This inter-governmental relationship brought billions of dollars of investments in agriculture, trading, mining, highways, roads, and airports from China to PNG. Chinese workers who were needed to serve these investments also moved to PNG.⁴⁵¹ Like PNG,

---

⁴⁴⁵ International Labour Organization (2021).
⁴⁴⁶ Ness (2016).
⁴⁴⁷ International Labour Organization (2021).
⁴⁴⁸ Song (2018).
⁴⁴⁹ Ministry of Commerce (2021).
⁴⁵⁰ Wroe (2018).
⁴⁵¹ Silk Road Briefing (2022).

many other developing countries, especially in Africa, are also members of the Belt and Road Initiative. In 2015, the number of Chinese workers in the labor force in Africa peaked at 263,659. This figure later declined significantly due to disruptions caused by the COVID-19 pandemic, yet there were still around 21,000 Chinese workers in Africa by the end of 2021.[452] Therefore, BRI paved the way for capital exchange between China and the partnering countries and built a bridge for many Chinese people to work overseas.

Beyond these statistics, how do these Chinese workers, many from rural villages and provincial areas, navigate their lives abroad? First, some alarming news and events always show the downside of their lives. Worldwide, Chinese workers and their businesses are often targeted for kidnapping, looting, or even homicide.[453] In developed countries, they are constantly pressured by Sinophobia. The Stop AAPI Hate coalition in the U.S. disclosed that over 9,000 anti-Asian attacks were reported between March 2020 and June 2021.[454] In many developing countries, Chinese workers are often exposed to life-threatening violence or anti-Asian riots.[455] They can also easily fall into traps set by illegal contractors and hiring processes, which may force them to engage in exploitative and dangerous working conditions or even human trafficking.[456]

The academic literature that documents the lives of Chinese workers on the ethnographic and personal levels is still scarce. Nevertheless, their stories and feelings while working and living abroad can be found in some news reports and social media posts. For instance, Zheng shared his experiences on a social media platform called Interviews with Real People (2022). Due to limited educational opportunities and a low salary as an auxiliary police officer in China, he relocated to Berlin in 2014. Initially working as a dishwasher in a relative's restaurant, he described his life there as "not as beautiful as imagined." He often worked 15-hour days, leaving him no time to explore Germany or engage with the local

---

[452] China Africa Research Initiative (2023).
[453] Hendrix (2022).
[454] The Associated Press (2021).
[455] Smith (n.d.).
[456] China Labor Watch (2022)

community.⁴⁵⁷ According to a news article by *Zhejiang Daily*, Fang once worked at a clothing factory in Japan to earn more money and improve her family's living conditions. She described her life in Japan as "feeling lost," "missing her son," and "must endure the sufferings to make money."⁴⁵⁸ In other parts of the world, African Chinese workers face different difficulties. Cao claimed that at his company, the Chinese and local workers lived separately to protect the Chinese people. He was not allowed to leave the factory park, guarded by 30 to 40 security guards with guns.⁴⁵⁹

In addition to these objective hardships that the Chinese workers abroad must endure, how do they navigate the local context regarding language and cultural interaction? Fang mentioned that she had received a two-month course in Japanese before her departure, which was far from enough for someone like her who only had a middle-school education.⁴⁶⁰ Cao tried to learn Swahili by noting the commonly used vocabulary, such as "screwdriver," "lazy," or "good job," with Chinese Pinyin pronunciations, to communicate with his team members. Another person who worked in Africa, Shi, mentioned that he respected his local workers because they would protect and help him when in danger only if he treated them well.⁴⁶¹ In Sudan, 24 Chinese workers worked day and night with Sudanese employees. Although they maintained friendly relationships, they stayed within their group daily, including celebrating the Chinese New Year.⁴⁶²

As an educator, these stories triggered my curiosity to investigate their education before going abroad. I focus on education that aims to facilitate multilingual and multicultural fluency. The following sections discuss two types of education: The professional training that prepares the workers to fulfill their job duties and the school education they go through in China.

---

⁴⁵⁷ Interviews of Real People (2022).
⁴⁵⁸ Zhejiang Daily (2011).
⁴⁵⁹ Chen (2023).
⁴⁶⁰ Zhejiang Daily. (2011).
⁴⁶¹ Chen (2023).
⁴⁶² iFeng.com Living Studio (2021).

Professional training for workers

Professional training usually includes both skill training and language education. For many Chinese international students and professional workers going abroad, mastering the language used in the destination countries is usually the primary requirement. When I decided to study in the U.S. many years ago, the first thing I did was to prepare and pass the Test of English as a Foreign Language (TOEFL). Most professionals sent to work abroad can only be selected if they have specific language qualifications. Moreover, Chinese students and professional class also typically grow up in more privileged urban environments where they have been exposed to consistent quality language education at schools long before they go abroad. However, the working class does not need high language proficiency to fulfill their work responsibilities, nor can they access quality language training programs.

According to Ma's study on practical English training for workers going abroad in Tai-an, China, this training exhibits the following traits:
- Workers do not possess sufficient English ability from previous education, which causes learning anxiety and low self-esteem.
- Many tutors do not have standard and professional qualifications.
- The curricula tend to be simple and not tailored to the audience.[463]

Furthermore, since the training is organized and implemented by the companies, the lessons focus only on the most pragmatic usage of the local language and culture to help the employees fulfill their work responsibilities. Although they can be effective in this aspect, they also simultaneously build an exclusive social circle for the workers. Isolating people from local communities can lead to resentment and discrimination within the local environment.

---

[463] Ma (2014).

Global competency in school education

Another critical factor is the Chinese workers' previous school education before going abroad since it shapes their worldview and cultural identity. Most of the Chinese working class overseas are rural residents of China. Therefore, I focus on multilingual and multicultural education in rural areas.

Most Chinese elementary and secondary public schools primarily offer English as the foreign language curriculum, which serves as a window into the cultures of English-speaking countries. Additionally, students gain exposure to diverse world cultures through geography and specific social studies courses. In 2016, the Chinese Ministry of Education published *The Core Competencies for Chinese Student Development* as a guideline for students' holistic growth. This framework includes "International Understanding" as an organic component.[464] Since then, schools nationwide have also been trying to promote multicultural education. However, due to China's dichotomous structure between urban and rural areas, rural schools usually lack quality teachers and resources for multilingual and multicultural education.

According to Chen and Wang, English education in rural Chinese schools has these salient problems: 1) there are not enough qualified teachers who can provide accurate guidance on grammar, pronunciation, and theory; 2) teachers utilize outdated pedagogy that leads to reduced learning outcomes; 3) teachers put low value and attention to English learning; 4) schools cannot afford sufficient materials and equipment; and 5) there is no immersive language environment either at schools or at home.[465] Therefore, as stated earlier, even for those workers who have studied some English at school before going abroad, it is still intimidating to restart learning. Furthermore, multicultural education outside of English classes can often be ignored because it is not a subject that can be tested for students to enter universities. This is particularly true for rural students because they face higher pressure to get high exam scores

---

[464] Core Competencies and Values Research Team (2016).
[465] Chen & Wang (2021).

than their urban counterparts.[466] Outside of schooling, limited by parents' education level and the general provincial context, rural students have fewer opportunities to learn a new language or experience a diverse culture. In contrast, urban students can obtain more resources to learn English or communicate with native English speakers through participating in extracurricular activities, online learning, or simply meeting international travelers on the streets.

Recommendations for enhancing multilingual and multicultural education among Chinese working-class communities abroad

Compared to Chinese students and professionals abroad, working-class communities are less proficient in local languages and culturally more enclosed to their groups. Drawing from the aforementioned personal narratives, the top priorities concerning Chinese overseas workers' lives are income and safety. Because of their occupation, they may not care much about personal communication and diverse experiences on the cultural level. Some may argue that encouraging the working class to obtain more multilingual and multicultural education adds more stress to their lives since it is useless for them. However, these views are trapped in a status quo without imagining the possibility of class mobility and systematic societal change. If the professional class needs more multilingual and multicultural education to prosper, it should be accessible to the working-class community as well.

Therefore, I propose suggestions for fostering multilingual and multicultural education in this community in this section. For professional training, especially language training, in addition to hiring qualified tutors and utilizing updated curricula to encourage students, the companies can organize social and cultural events to connect Chinese workers with local workers. Modeling many study-abroad programs worldwide, professional development for these global working-class employees should also begin to emphasize connection and understanding instead of only efficiency and profit.

---

[466] Wu & Zhang (2018).

For school education, it can be more complicated to change. However, one type of programming feasible for rural schools is having the workers who return from abroad introduce and talk about their experience to the school students in their home village. Their experience and knowledge are the best resources for multicultural education in these areas and should be employed and valued. Last, I also encourage more scholars to pay attention to this group. This chapter, limited by its scope, is only a reflection based purely on a literature review. In the future, empirical studies can be conducted worldwide with Chinese workers and workers from all other countries. Researchers should aim to break the division of social class and go into communities to build equal partnerships and learn from the workers.

Highlighting the Chinese working-class community abroad

Inspired by my experiences, this chapter focuses on the Chinese working-class community living abroad. I begin by defining the population studied and presenting key statistics to outline their situation. Drawing from scholarly studies, news reports, and social media posts, I explore the overseas lives of community members, highlighting the language and cultural barriers they face. I argue that limited professional and educational opportunities in language skills and global competencies have made it difficult for them to overcome these challenges. Finally, I propose several strategies for creating more effective educational programs for working-class communities who move across borders. Although their stories are not thoroughly told and heard, this growing group has played a critical role in today's global labor market. More attention and support should be directed to this population. These communities are not only labels but also formed by individuals who carry their history and stories.

PART 5.
Reflections

Language is the road map of a culture.
It tells you where its people come from and where they are going.
– Rita Mae Brown,
Starting From Scratch: A Different Kind of Writers' Manual

Marylène Fage, Organizational Change Manager at Bosch

My name is Marylène. I was born in the seventies in France to parents who did not speak foreign languages but were always interested in the world. Our first international trip to Spain in the early eighties sparked my passion for exploring diverse cultures. Since then, I have lived in eight countries, traveled to over forty, and learned to speak four languages fluently.

Reflecting on my multicultural experiences, I value the international studies I pursued across three European countries and one in Asia. These experiences exposed me to diverse perspectives, fostering a deep appreciation for cultural differences and shared values. Language, especially English, served as a vital tool for meaningful exchanges.

Working on a project in China was both challenging and rewarding. Despite cultural differences, I approached the experience with an open mindset, embracing teamwork and mutual respect. By fostering trust and equality among colleagues, we achieved success beyond expectations. Similarly, my time in Bangladesh taught me valuable lessons in humility and adaptability, contributing to personal growth.

Multilingualism and cultural fluency in the professional world

Multilingualism and cultural fluency are distinct yet complementary skills. While multilingualism facilitates communication, cultural fluency fosters understanding and collaboration in today's globalized workplace.

The relevance of multilingualism varies depending on the context. For instance, a nurse in Canada may prioritize language skills for patient communication, while an electrician in Germany may not require fluency in the local language. Cultural fluency, however, can enhance integration and collaboration in diverse professional settings.

Multilingualism and cultural fluency reflect both mindset and skillset. While language proficiency demonstrates a learning capacity, cultural fluency requires genuine interest, openness, and empathy toward diverse cultures. The combination of these attributes enriches intercultural interactions.

Organizations can promote multilingualism and cultural fluency through targeted training programs and intercultural workshops. Identifying individuals willing to develop these skills and leveraging internal resources can optimize the effectiveness of such initiatives.

Preparing future professionals involves fostering curiosity, providing exposure to diverse cultures, and offering opportunities for language learning and intercultural experiences. Networking, mentorship programs, and exchange initiatives can further support their development.

Multilingualism and cultural fluency facilitate exposure to diverse perspectives, although actively seeking them may come later. Initially driven by curiosity and interest, individuals gradually recognize the value of embracing cultural diversity for personal and professional growth.

While multilingualism was once a significant competitive advantage, its prevalence in today's global economy has shifted priorities. Mastery of languages like Chinese can still provide a competitive edge in specific contexts, but individuals must seek other unique strengths for differentiation.

While multilingualism may indirectly contribute to economic growth through enhanced communication and collaboration, its impact is not direct. Other factors, such as innovation, infrastructure, and political stability, play more significant roles in driving economic development.

Mastering a heritage language is an asset that demonstrates language proficiency and adaptability. It enhances an individual's capacity for learning additional languages and fosters a deeper connection to cultural heritage.

Cultural fluency is essential for global citizenship, enabling individuals to navigate diverse cultural landscapes with understanding and respect. While multilingualism may complement cultural fluency, it alone does not define global citizenship.

Embracing multilingualism and cultural fluency: Unlocking global perspectives

In closing, I invite you to embrace languages not merely as tools for communication but as gateways to understanding diverse cultures and traditions. Let us cultivate cultural fluency alongside multilingualism, enriching our experiences and fostering deeper connections with the world. As we continue to explore the significance of cultural fluency in global cooperation and performance, may we unlock its full potential and embrace the richness it brings to our lives and workplaces.

I draw inspiration from individuals like Alexandra David-Neel, whose adventurous spirit and cultural fluency set remarkable examples. Additionally, the friendships forged during my international studies continue to inspire me in diverse ways.

The essence of where I live lies not in the location but in the connections with friends from various countries. Reuniting with them to exchange perspectives and grow together would be the ideal scenario, regardless of the geographical setting. As organizations strive for global cooperation and performance, exploring the role of cultural fluency becomes increasingly relevant. Let us delve deeper into this fascinating topic to unlock its full potential.

Alexandra Erman, Chief People Officer at BforeAI

I come from a multilingual family, where my exposure to English started early due to my mother's profession as an English teacher. My childhood travels to England and the U.S. ignited my passion for language and culture. I pursued German and Latin studies and later immersed myself in Spanish during business school. My professional journey led me to work in various multicultural environments, from French to Japanese and American banks, shaping my perspective on language and culture.

My multicultural experiences have been instrumental in my professional growth. Starting at BNP Paribas in New York, I seamlessly navigated French and English, facilitating communication with international clients and colleagues. However, maintaining proficiency in both languages posed challenges over time, primarily as I specialized in certain areas. Adapting to unfamiliar cultural contexts while excelling in my field required continuous adjustment and self-awareness.

Transitioning from a French bank to a Japanese one presented significant challenges. The cultural shift demanded patience, adaptability, and a willingness to reinvent communication strategies. Understanding the nuances of communication and hierarchy in the new environment took time. Immersion in the Japanese culture, including a visit to Tokyo, provided invaluable insights and taught me the importance of observation and patience in cross-cultural interactions.

Relevance of multilingualism and cultural fluency

Multilingualism and cultural fluency have been pivotal in my professional journey. Working across continents and with international clients required language proficiency and an appreciation for diverse cultures. While their relevance depends on the role and company culture, they offer a unique advantage in building connections and navigating global markets.

Multilingualism is indispensable in today's competitive academic and professional landscape. Proficiency in English and other languages opened doors for me, from university admissions to job opportunities. Early exposure to language learning laid a solid foundation for future success in the global marketplace.

Multilingual and culturally fluent individuals exhibit a unique mindset characterized by adaptability, curiosity, and empathy. Their skill set extends beyond language proficiency, including effective communication, cross-cultural understanding, and flexibility in diverse environments.

Early exposure to language learning, immersion programs, and real-world experiences are essential for upskilling professionals in multilingualism and cultural fluency. Resources and support, such as language classes and mentorship programs, can further enhance their development.

Future professionals can benefit from a comprehensive approach to language learning and cultural immersion. Early exposure, supplemented by practical experiences and mentorship, prepares individuals to thrive in multicultural workplaces and global markets.

Multilingualism and cultural fluency naturally broaden one's perspective over time. Language influences thought processes and awareness of cultural nuances, enabling individuals to adapt and empathize across diverse contexts.

Competitive advantage in global economies

Multilingual individuals possess a competitive advantage in global economies due to their ability to adapt, communicate effectively, and navigate cultural barriers. Early exposure to language learning fosters curiosity and a desire for exploration, shaping future success in international markets.

Multilingualism contributes to economic growth by fostering adaptability, efficiency, and collaboration in global settings.

Multilingual individuals drive innovation and create environments conducive to international trade and cooperation.

Mastering a heritage language is beneficial and enriching in the professional world. It is a valuable resource for connecting with diverse communities, sharing experiences, and building credibility in multicultural environments.

While multilingualism and cultural fluency enhance global citizenship, they are not prerequisites. However, they enable individuals to connect with the world deeper, fostering a sense of belonging and appreciation for diverse cultures.

Embracing multilingualism and cultural fluency: A path to global success

In this concluding reflection, I encourage you to continue nurturing your language skills through consistent practice and exposure to diverse cultures. My journey has been shaped by familial influences and firsthand experiences, highlighting the importance of curiosity and open-mindedness.

While I appreciate the opportunities the U.S. provides, my ideal living situation would involve warmer climates while maintaining connections with my French heritage. Finding balance and fulfillment wherever we are is vital to a satisfying life.

For international professionals, embracing multilingualism and cultural fluency is essential for success in today's interconnected world. Individuals are better equipped to thrive in diverse environments and contribute significantly to global economic growth by cultivating curiosity, resilience, and adaptability.

Louise Roussel, Senior Relationship Manager at KeyBank

I was raised in a multilingual family where my mother, an English teacher, often visited England with us. I learned English as a second language and, from an early age, traveled extensively in the US, including a transformative, immersive experience in Cincinnati for three summers. This fully integrated experience with a host family significantly improved my English and deepened my cultural understanding. Additionally, I studied German for 12 years and Spanish in business school, further supported by an academic exchange in South Carolina and internships in the US.

My professional journey began at BNP Paribas in New York, eventually leading me through various roles in international banks, including a Japanese bank and a small investment bank in Boston, and finally to a U.S.-only bank. Throughout these positions, my ability to communicate across cultures, particularly in French and English, was crucial in managing international client relationships and complex financial transactions.

Facing limitations in career advancement at BNP Paribas, where opportunities were often reserved for expatriates despite my French origins, I transitioned to a Japanese bank. This move brought significant cultural and linguistic challenges, requiring two years to adapt to new ways of communication and corporate dynamics. My time in Tokyo was particularly enlightening, allowing me to fully grasp the nuances of Japanese business practices and communication styles.

Multilingualism and cultural fluency in the professional world

In my professional experiences, multilingualism was crucial for direct communication with international clients and colleagues, particularly at a French bank in America. It allowed me to bridge cultural divides within the banking industry effectively. My ability to adapt culturally also facilitated the expansion of professional networks and client bases.

Multilingualism has been a critical asset for both academic and professional success. The capability to switch between languages and understand diverse cultural contexts is increasingly essential in today's global business environment.

Multilingual individuals typically exhibit a mindset and skillset characterized by adaptability, patience, and an appreciation for diverse perspectives, qualities that are indispensable in global business settings.

Achieving multilingual proficiency and cultural fluency involves early language education and real-world exposure through immersive experiences and professional interactions. Continuous self-education and utilization of diverse linguistic environments are also essential to maintaining and improving language skills.

Advice to future multilingual professionals

I advise future multilingual professionals to continually nurture their language skills by engaging with multiple languages through reading, speaking, and cultural immersion to maintain and enhance their fluency.

My global perspective and career path were significantly influenced by my mother, who instilled a love of the English language and encouraged global exploration. My grandfather's adventurous spirit and insights from a business school professor also shaped my professional and personal growth approach.

While I value my experiences in the U.S. and prefer to stay here, I would consider relocating to a warmer state, but I still intend to maintain my connections to French culture and networks.

Navigating multiple languages and cultures requires practical exposure and constant curiosity. Applying these skills in multicultural settings can transform potential challenges into substantial opportunities.

Dave Margulius, Co-founder of Quizlet

I am Dave Margulius, an entrepreneur who has been actively involved in the startup scene for over thirty years. I founded Quizlet, an education software company that now serves over 50 million students per month. I am dedicating most of my efforts to addressing the climate crisis, focusing on accelerating actions to transition away from fossil fuels.

I grew up learning French and spent many of my 20s traveling, often by hitchhiking, across Europe and the U.S. These experiences broadened my worldview, exposing me to various cultures and instilling a sense of openness to new possibilities and positive surprises.

Multilingualism and cultural fluency in the professional world

Understanding different languages and cultures has provided a significant advantage in an increasingly global business environment. However, the context is shifting. Political and social forces are challenging globalization—nationalism, protectionism, and various crises, including environmental ones. These changes alter how businesses operate globally, making interactions more reliant on technology than direct human mediation.

The rise of AI and automation is transforming the landscape of professional skills, making traditional multilingual abilities potentially less valuable. AI technologies can now perform real-time translations and manage cultural nuances, diminishing the need for human intervention in these areas.

Despite the advancements in AI, the need for human cultural fluency remains vital. In a world where individuals are becoming more isolated within their ideological or cultural echo chambers, multilingual and cultural knowledge can help bridge divides and counteract the manipulative capabilities of algorithm-driven platforms.

I advocate for a broader definition of multilingualism, including traditional spoken languages and critical fields such as finance, economics, science, and technology. Understanding these "languages" is essential for navigating our complex global environment and effectively influencing change.

AI is set to redefine what it means to be skilled in the workforce. As AI takes over more routine and complex tasks, the human workforce needs to adapt by enhancing skills that AI cannot replicate—such as emotional intelligence, creative problem-solving, and ethical judgment.

Advice for future multilingual and culturally fluent individuals

My family history inspired my passion for global perspectives. My grandparents were immigrants who valued education and spoke multiple languages. My father, an MIT graduate, traveled extensively for business, interacting with diverse cultures and bringing those experiences home. These influences shaped my understanding of the world and the importance of maintaining a broad, inclusive view.

If I chose a place to live and work other than the Bay Area, I would consider cities known for their quality of life and cultural depth, like Copenhagen, Milan, Lisbon, or London. Each city offers unique opportunities to engage with diverse communities and lifestyles.

The best advice I can offer is to become proficient in asking insightful questions, listening deeply, and interpreting the nuances in communications. Staying abreast of technological advancements and understanding complex systems like finance and human behavior is vital. This knowledge can empower you to navigate and positively impact the world. Embrace the challenges of creating and contributing to society and ensure you live life entirely along the way.

It is increasingly important for multilingual and culturally competent individuals to understand and address global risks. Such individuals can bridge cultural divides and foster a more comprehensive understanding of global issues like climate change, enhancing collaborative efforts to mitigate these challenges.

Although I have not personally managed international teams, the company I started benefits significantly from a diverse global workforce. This diversity enhances innovation and commitment, which are crucial to thriving in a competitive global marketplace.

Conclusion: Embracing multilingualism and cultural fluency – charting the path forward

Mehdi Lazar and Fabrice Jaumont

As we draw this book to a close, it becomes evident that multilingualism and cultural fluency are valuable assets and essential tools for navigating the modern, interconnected world. The various chapters and contributions have explored the transformative power of languages and cultural understanding in diverse professional, academic, or societal contexts. Now, more than ever, individuals and organizations recognize the necessity of fostering these skills to thrive in an increasingly globalized environment.

This volume has shown that multilingualism goes beyond the ability to speak multiple languages; it fosters adaptability, empathy, and resilience in the face of cultural differences. Likewise, cultural fluency extends beyond mere awareness—it is about deeply understanding and navigating the intricacies of diverse cultural landscapes. Together, these skills form the bedrock of a truly global professional identity.

The imperative of multilingualism in the global economy

The role of multilingualism in fostering global cooperation and competitiveness cannot be overstated. In a rapidly evolving global economy, professionals with multilingual skills can easily navigate international markets, build stronger relationships with diverse stakeholders, and enhance their organization's competitive advantage. As we have seen in the chapters discussing various global industries, multilingual professionals are better equipped to manage complex cultural interactions, negotiate across borders, and adapt to the nuances of different markets.

Multilingualism opens doors to diplomatic opportunities, international trade, and enhanced global networking. As the world becomes more interconnected through trade, technology, and migration, the ability to communicate effectively in multiple languages is increasingly seen as a fundamental requirement rather than a luxury.

However, it is also crucial to recognize the broader societal impacts of multilingualism. By promoting language learning from an early age, we prepare future generations to compete in a global economy and foster a more inclusive, empathetic world. The cognitive and social benefits of being multilingual—such as improved problem-solving skills, creativity, and open-mindedness—extend far beyond professional success. They create a more interconnected, harmonious society that values and respects linguistic and cultural diversity.

Cultural fluency: Beyond language proficiency

While multilingualism is a powerful tool for communication, cultural fluency adds another dimension to global success. Cultural fluency involves understanding, respecting, and adapting to different cultural contexts. As explored in this volume, cultural fluency is essential for building trust and fostering meaningful relationships in both professional and personal settings.

The chapters examining cross-cultural management and leadership highlight the need for cultural fluency in navigating the complexities of global teams. Culturally fluent leaders are better equipped to manage diverse workforces, address potential cultural conflicts, and create inclusive work environments where all employees feel valued. In today's globalized workplace, cultural fluency allows leaders to go beyond surface-level cultural differences and foster deep, collaborative relationships that drive innovation and organizational success.

Moreover, cultural fluency is critical in avoiding misunderstandings, leading to miscommunications, damaged relationships, or even failed business ventures. Understanding cultural norms, values, and expectations allows professionals to communicate more effectively, negotiate more strategically, and avoid the pitfalls of cultural misinterpretation. As the chapters discussing Francophone Africa, Silicon Valley, and international educational systems demonstrate, cultural fluency is indispensable in settings where diverse cultures intersect.

Educational implications: Preparing future global citizens

One of this book's core discussions revolves around education's role in fostering multilingualism and cultural fluency. As the global marketplace becomes increasingly interconnected, educational systems must adapt to prepare students for this reality. The chapters dedicated to dual-language programs, international schools, and multilingual education models demonstrate that early exposure to language learning and cultural immersion is critical to building a foundation for future success.

Educational institutions play a pivotal role in shaping future global citizens. By integrating multilingual education and cultural studies into the curriculum early, schools can equip students with the skills they need to succeed in a globalized world. This involves teaching multiple languages and promoting intercultural competence through real-world experiences, such as study abroad programs, exchange opportunities, and partnerships with international institutions.

Furthermore, the importance of lifelong learning cannot be ignored. As the professional world evolves, adults must be given opportunities to develop and refine their language and cultural skills. Organizations that invest in language training and cultural fluency programs for their employees will be better positioned to succeed in a globalized economy. Governments, too, have a role in promoting policies supporting multilingual education and encouraging international collaboration.

The role of technology in multilingualism and cultural fluency

As we look toward the future, technology will undoubtedly play a significant role in shaping how we approach multilingualism and cultural fluency. The rise of artificial intelligence and machine translation tools has transformed the way we communicate across languages, making real-time translation more accessible than ever before. However, while these technologies are valuable, they cannot replace the human element of cultural understanding.

AI may be able to translate words but cannot fully grasp the cultural nuances and emotional subtleties essential to effective communication. This is where cultural fluency becomes critical. As technology advances, the demand for professionals who can navigate cultural contexts and bridge the gap between technology and human interaction will grow.

Technology provides opportunities for language learning and cultural exchange. Digital tools that facilitate language learning, virtual cultural immersion, and global collaboration can help individuals acquire the skills needed to thrive in a multicultural world. However, these tools must be complemented by real-world experiences to develop fully multilingual and culturally fluent professionals.

Further research directions: Expanding the horizon of multilingualism and cultural fluency

While this book has provided a comprehensive exploration of the roles that multilingualism and cultural fluency play in today's professional and educational environments, it has also highlighted several areas that merit further study. The complexity of globalization, cultural exchange, and language acquisition creates fertile ground for new research, particularly as technology and society evolve. Here are several promising avenues for future exploration:

1. The impact of emerging technologies on language acquisition and cultural fluency

While technology has already begun to shape language learning through AI-driven translation tools, mobile apps, and online platforms, there is still much to explore regarding the long-term impact of these innovations on multilingualism and cultural fluency. Future research could focus on:

Effectiveness of AI and Machine Translation Tools: How do these technologies affect the ability to communicate across languages and the understanding of cultural nuances that human translators intuitively grasp? Studies comparing the outcomes of machine translation versus human-mediated language exchange in professional settings would be required.

Virtual Cultural Immersion: With the rise of virtual reality (VR) and augmented reality (AR), researchers could explore the efficacy of these tools in enhancing cultural fluency. How effective are virtual environments in preparing individuals to navigate real-world cultural challenges, and what are the limitations of these technologies compared to in-person immersion?

Technology-Enhanced Language Learning: What are the long-term cognitive and social impacts of using mobile apps, gamified platforms, and online courses to learn languages? Studies could explore how these tools shape learners' understanding of language mechanics and cultural contexts.

2. Multilingualism and neurodiversity: Tailoring language education

One of the more intriguing areas discussed in this book is the intersection of multilingualism and neurodiversity. Future research could investigate how language learning can be tailored to meet the needs of neurodiverse individuals, particularly those with conditions such as autism, ADHD, or dyslexia. Key research directions include:

Cognitive Differences in Language Acquisition: How do neurodiverse learners process and retain multiple languages compared to neurotypical learners? This could involve longitudinal studies tracking language acquisition in neurodiverse individuals, exploring their unique strengths and challenges.

Educational Frameworks for Neurodiverse Multilinguals: More research is needed into effective pedagogical strategies for teaching languages to neurodiverse students. What instructional methods, tools, and supports work best, and how can education systems better integrate these approaches?

Professional Outcomes for Neurodiverse Multilinguals: How does multilingualism intersect with professional success for neurodiverse individuals? Investigating how these individuals leverage multilingual skills in the workplace and whether cultural fluency can be a compensating strength would offer valuable insights for educators and employers.

3. Multilingualism in corporate settings: Enhancing diversity, equity, and inclusion (DEI)

The corporate world is becoming more multicultural, and multilingualism is increasingly recognized as an asset in building diverse teams. However, there is much more to understand about how language and cultural fluency contribute to DEI initiatives. Areas for future research include:

Language as a Barrier or Bridge in DEI: Research could explore how language policies in multinational corporations foster inclusivity or inadvertently create barriers. What language practices most effectively promote equity, and how do they impact team dynamics, employee engagement, and leadership development?

The Role of Language in Reducing Bias: Can multilingualism and cultural fluency reduce unconscious bias and enhance cross-cultural understanding in global teams? Investigating how language learning and cultural education programs influence employees' attitudes toward diversity could reveal new strategies for DEI.

Multilingual Leadership: What traits distinguish leaders who are both multilingual and culturally fluent from those who are monolingual? Studies could examine how these leaders manage diverse teams, resolve conflicts, and foster innovation in multicultural environments.

4. The role of multilingualism in social and political integration

Multilingualism is critical in shaping how societies and nations integrate migrant and minority populations. Understanding how multilingualism supports or hinders social cohesion will be essential as migration patterns evolve. Potential research avenues include:

Language Learning and Social Integration: How do government policies around language education affect the integration of immigrants and refugees? Research could focus on the effectiveness of language acquisition programs in promoting social inclusion, employment opportunities, and civic participation.

Multilingualism and National Identity: As nations become more linguistically diverse, it is essential to understand how multilingualism influences concepts of national identity. Do multilingual policies strengthen or challenge the sense of unity within a nation, and how can countries foster linguistic diversity while maintaining social cohesion?

Language Rights and Policy: Further exploration of multilingualism's political and legal implications is needed, particularly in regions where language rights are contested. Research could focus on the impact of policies aimed at protecting minority languages and promoting linguistic diversity within governmental, educational, and public spheres.

5. Early childhood language learning: Longitudinal studies

While much research has been conducted on the benefits of early exposure to multiple languages, long-term studies still need to track the effects of multilingual education from childhood into adulthood. Specific areas to investigate include:

Cognitive and Social Benefits of Early Language Exposure: Longitudinal studies could explore how early bilingual or multilingual education affects cognitive development, problem-solving abilities, and social skills over time.

Professional Outcomes of Multilingual Individuals: By tracking individuals educated in dual-language or multilingual programs, researchers could examine how these early experiences translate into professional success, adaptability in multicultural environments, and leadership potential in global industries.

Challenges in Language Retention: Research could also focus on how well individuals retain multiple languages learned in childhood, particularly when they are not regularly exposed to those languages in adulthood. Understanding language retention factors could inform more effective long-term language education strategies.

6. The intersection of multilingualism and mental health

Multilingualism's potential effects on mental health, particularly in cross-cultural environments, represent another understudied area. Research could examine the following:

Multilingualism and Mental Resilience: Does speaking multiple languages contribute to mental resilience, particularly in high-stress, cross-cultural work environments? Understanding how multilingual professionals manage stress, adapt to new environments, and maintain mental well-being could provide essential insights for organizations operating in global markets.

Language Barriers in Mental Health Services: How do language barriers impact access to and quality mental health services for multilingual individuals, especially in immigrant and refugee populations? Further research could investigate the effectiveness of culturally and linguistically adapted mental health interventions.

7. AI and its limitations in multilingualism and cultural fluency

Artificial intelligence (AI) has made tremendous strides in language translation and communication, particularly with the rise of machine learning models like Google Translate, DeepL, and natural language processing (NLP) systems. These tools have undoubtedly revolutionized how we interact with different languages, making instant translation accessible to millions. However, despite the advances in AI technology, inherent limitations prevent these systems from fully addressing the complexities of multilingualism and cultural fluency. While AI can facilitate essential communication, it struggles with the nuances of language, cultural contexts, emotional subtleties, and the deeper understanding that humans naturally bring to multilingual and cross-cultural interactions.

The path forward: Embracing multilingualism and cultural fluency

As global interdependence deepens, the need for thoughtful and expansive research into multilingualism and cultural fluency becomes increasingly apparent. The areas outlined here represent only a glimpse of the many topics that future scholars, educators, and policymakers can explore. By delving deeper into these subjects, we can better grasp how language and culture influence individual success and the broader social, economic, and political dynamics shaping our world.

Collaboration between researchers, educators, and practitioners across various fields is essential for understanding the profound impact of multilingualism and cultural fluency. While the challenges are significant, so are the opportunities for innovation and meaningful change. As this field evolves, so will our insights into building a more inclusive, adaptable, and interconnected global society.

In our increasingly connected world, the importance of multilingualism and cultural fluency will only grow. These skills are crucial in business and education and across all aspects of society for fostering cooperation, creativity, and mutual understanding. The contributions in this book offer valuable perspectives on the challenges and opportunities of cultivating a multilingual and culturally fluent world, but this is just the beginning.

A collective effort is needed—from educators, policymakers, business leaders, and individuals alike—to harness the transformative power of languages and cultures. By cultivating a global mindset that embraces diversity, openness, and empathy, we can create a more inclusive world where multilingualism and cultural fluency are recognized as critical pillars of success.

Let us carry the insights gained, commit to nurturing these skills in ourselves and others, and continue championing a world where linguistic and cultural diversity is celebrated and embraced. To further support educators and parents in fostering these essential skills, this book concludes with a dedicated guide: *Fostering Multilingualism and Cultural Fluency in School Communities*. This guide offers practical strategies and actionable insights to help develop language proficiency and cultural awareness in the classroom and at home. Empowering educators and parents with these tools can better prepare the next generation to thrive in an increasingly interconnected and diverse world.

Guide for educators and parents: Fostering multilingualism and cultural fluency in school communities

Introduction

In an increasingly interconnected world, the ability to communicate across languages and understand diverse cultures is not just an asset but a necessity. Multilingualism and cultural fluency open doors to global opportunities, enhance personal growth, and foster a more inclusive society. This guide is designed to support teachers and parents in nurturing these skills and mindsets in students and children.

The resources provided include lists of key mindsets and skillsets characteristic of multilingual and culturally fluent individuals and practical strategies and activities to develop them. These are complemented by discussion questions that stimulate thoughtful classroom and home conversations. The materials are **flexible, adaptable, and tailored to** various educational contexts and individual needs.

How to use this guide

- **Flexible application:** The lists and activities are starting points. Feel free to modify or expand them to suit your teaching environment or your child's interests.
- **Engagement through discussion:** Use discussion questions to encourage critical thinking and personal reflection.
- **Interactive learning:** Incorporate suggested activities to make learning dynamic and experiential.
- **Encourage exploration:** Motivate students and children to explore beyond the materials, fostering a lifelong interest in languages and cultures.

Contents

1. Understanding the mindset and skillset of multilingual and culturally fluent individuals
2. Preparing future professionals to be multilingual and culturally fluent

3. Upskilling professionals to be multilingual and culturally fluent
4. Exploring global citizenship
5. The competitive advantage of multilingualism in global economies

Section 1: Understanding the mindset and skillset of multilingual and culturally fluent individuals

Overview

This section outlines the core mindsets and skillsets that characterize individuals proficient in multiple languages and culturally adept. Understanding these traits can help develop programs and activities that cultivate these qualities in students and children.

Mindset

1. **Open-mindedness**: Exposure to multiple languages and cultures fosters an open-minded approach. These individuals are more likely to embrace different perspectives and ideas and appreciate the diversity of thought and experience.
2. **Adaptability**: Navigating different linguistic and cultural environments requires high adaptability. Such individuals often adjust their behavior and expectations to suit social and professional contexts.
3. **Empathy**: Understanding and communicating across cultures enhances one's ability to empathize with others. This involves recognizing and appreciating the feelings and viewpoints of people from diverse backgrounds.
4. **Curiosity**: A natural curiosity about languages, cultures, and the world is a common trait. This curiosity drives the desire to learn and understand more about people and places.
5. **Cultural sensitivity**: Awareness and respect for cultural differences are central to this mindset. Individuals are mindful of cultural nuances and are careful to act in culturally appropriate ways.
6. **Resilience**: Dealing with language barriers and cultural misunderstandings can be challenging. Multilingual and culturally fluent individuals often develop resilience, learning to navigate and overcome such challenges effectively.

Skillset

1. **Language proficiency**: The most prominent skill is communicating in multiple languages. This includes speaking, reading, writing, and understanding cultural nuances in communication.
2. **Cultural intelligence** involves understanding cultural norms, practices, and expectations and interacting appropriately in various cultural contexts.
3. **Interpersonal skills**: Effective communication, negotiation, and conflict resolution across cultures are key. These individuals are adept at building relationships with people from diverse backgrounds.
4. **Global awareness**: They possess a broad understanding of global issues and dynamics, including knowledge of international politics, economics, and social issues.
5. **Adaptability**: They are skilled in adjusting their communication style to suit distinct cultural expectations, whether in formal business settings or casual social interactions.
6. **Problem-solving and creativity**: Exposure to diverse perspectives can enhance problem-solving abilities and creativity. These individuals often bring innovative approaches to challenges.
7. **Networking skills**: Connecting with a diverse range of people is valuable. They often build and maintain a comprehensive, multicultural professional network.

Activities and questions

Activity: *Cultural exploration project*
- **Description:** Assign students to research a culture different from their own and present their findings through a medium of their choice (presentation, poster, essay, etc.).
- **Objective:** Develop curiosity and cultural sensitivity by exploring and sharing insights about another culture.

Discussion questions:
- *Open-mindedness:* "What surprised you the most about the culture you researched, and how did it change your perspective?"
- *Empathy:* "How do you think people from this culture might view certain global issues differently than we do?"
- *Language proficiency:* "What are some phrases or expressions in the language of the culture you studied that have no direct translation in our language?"

Reflection question:
- How can your own experiences as an individual shape your approach to teaching and interacting with students from diverse backgrounds?

Application questions:
- What specific strategies can you implement in your classroom to leverage your students' linguistic and cultural diversity to enhance their learning experiences?
- What kind of learning experiences can help students develop cultural fluency?

Implications question:
- How can fostering a multilingual and culturally inclusive environment impact students' readiness for a globalized world and their future career opportunities?

Section 2: Preparing future professionals to be multilingual and culturally fluent

Overview

This section provides strategies for educators and parents to prepare students for global professions by developing their language skills and cultural understanding from an early age.

Key strategies

1. **Early language education**: Introduce language learning early when linguistic skills are most easily acquired. This should include significant world languages and less commonly taught languages to broaden the scope of cultural understanding.
2. **Cultural studies in the curriculum**: Integrate cultural studies into the educational curriculum. Through courses in international relations, world literature, and global history, teach students about world histories, traditions, customs, and social norms.
3. **Exchange programs and study abroad**: Encourage participation in exchange programs and study abroad opportunities. These experiences immerse students in unfamiliar cultures, enhancing their language skills and cultural understanding.
4. **Interactive and immersive learning**: Use technology to create interactive and immersive learning experiences. Language learning apps, virtual reality, and online exchange programs can provide engaging exposure to languages and cultures.
5. **Cultural competence workshops**: Conduct workshops and seminars on cultural competence. These should focus on teaching respect for diversity, understanding global issues, and skills for intercultural communication.
6. **Real-world language application**: Promote opportunities for students to use their language skills in real-world settings. This can include internships in multinational companies,

volunteer work in diverse communities, or participation in multilingual events.

7. **Professional development programs**: Offer programs focused on multilingualism and cultural fluency. These programs can be part of continuing education for professionals who wish to enhance these skills.
8. **Mentorship and networking**: Provide mentorship opportunities with multilingual and culturally fluent professionals. Networking events can also help students and young professionals connect with mentors and peers from diverse backgrounds.
9. **Collaborations and partnerships**: Foster collaborations and partnerships with organizations and institutions from different countries. This can expose students and young professionals to diverse business practices and professional cultures.
10. **Encourage critical thinking**: Teach students to critically analyze their cultural biases and understand the relative nature of cultural norms and values. This fosters deeper cultural fluency and sensitivity.
11. **Utilize diverse teaching staff**: Educators from diverse linguistic and cultural backgrounds can provide students with varied perspectives and firsthand insights into unfamiliar cultures.
12. **Promote language and cultural clubs**: Support the formation of language and cultural clubs in educational institutions. These clubs can organize events, language practice sessions, and cultural festivals.
13. **Incorporate global perspectives in all subjects**: Integrate global perspectives across all subjects, not just language and social studies. This helps students see the relevance of cultural fluency in various fields, including science, technology, and business.
14. **Role models and guest speakers**: Invite multilingual professionals and culturally adept individuals as guest

speakers. Their experiences and insights can inspire and inform students.

Activities and questions

Activity: *Language exchange buddy system*
- **Description:** Pair students with peers who speak different languages for regular language practice and cultural exchange.
- **Objective:** Enhance language proficiency and interpersonal skills through peer learning.

Discussion questions:
- *Early language education:* "How does learning a new language at a young age influence how we think and interact with others?"
- *Cultural studies:* "Why is it important to learn about global histories and traditions besides local ones?"
- *Critical thinking:* "How can we challenge our cultural assumptions when learning about others?"

Reflection Question:
- How has your personal experience with language learning and cultural exposure influenced your perspective on the importance of multilingualism and cultural fluency in professional settings?

Application Question:
- What specific strategies or activities can you implement in your classroom to enhance students' multilingual abilities and cultural understanding, preparing them for diverse professional environments?

Implications Question:
- How might integrating multilingual and culturally fluent education impact the future workforce, and what are the potential long-term benefits and challenges for society?

Section 3: Upskilling professionals to be multilingual and culturally fluent

Overview

Acquiring new language skills and cultural competencies can significantly enhance professional career prospects. This section outlines methods to support professionals in their ongoing development.

Key strategies

1. **Language training programs**: Offer language courses tailored to professional needs. These can be in-house training, online courses, or partnerships with language schools. Focus on conversational fluency, industry-specific terminology, and cultural nuances within business contexts.
2. **Cultural competency workshops**: Conduct workshops and seminars on cultural awareness and competence. These should cover topics like cross-cultural communication, understanding cultural biases, and adapting to business etiquette and social norms.
3. **Immersive experiences**: Encourage participation in language immersion programs or cultural exchange opportunities. These could include short-term assignments abroad, participation in international projects, or travel opportunities focused on cultural learning.
4. **Mentorship and language partners**: Pair professionals with language mentors or conversation partners. This could involve matching employees with native speakers within the organization or through external language exchange programs.
5. **Self-directed learning resources**: Provide access to self-directed learning resources such as language learning apps, online tutorials, podcasts, and literature in the target language. Encourage regular practice and engagement with these tools.

6. **Interactive and practical sessions**: Organize interactive language practice sessions or role-playing scenarios that simulate real-life professional interactions in a different language. This can help in applying language skills in practical situations.
7. **Incentives and recognition**: Offer incentives for employees who make considerable progress in language learning or demonstrate high levels of cultural fluency. Recognition could include certifications, awards, or opportunities for advancement.
8. **Cultural events and activities**: Host cultural events, international days, or language-specific activities within the organization. This could involve celebrating cultural festivals, organizing international food days, or setting up language cafes.
9. **Cross-cultural teams**: Create diverse work teams with members from different linguistic and cultural backgrounds. This promotes a natural environment for language practice and cultural learning.
10. **Feedback and continuous learning**: Provide regular feedback on language and cultural learning progress. Encourage a culture of continuous learning and improvement, making it clear that developing these skills is a valued part of professional development.
11. **Networking opportunities**: Facilitate participation in multicultural networking events or professional groups. Networking with professionals from diverse backgrounds can enhance language skills and cultural understanding.
12. **Utilizing technology**: Leverage technology like virtual reality or AI-based language tools for immersive learning experiences. Such technologies can simulate real-life interactions in different languages and cultural settings.
13. **Tailored learning paths**: Recognize that professionals have different learning styles and proficiencies. Offer personalized learning paths that cater to individual needs and goals.
14. **Integration in professional development plans**: Include language and cultural fluency goals within regular professional development plans. This formalizes commitment and integrates these skills into career progression pathways.

Activities and questions

Activity: *Professional role-playing scenarios*
- Description: Simulate business meetings or negotiations in different cultural contexts, requiring participants to navigate language and cultural nuances.
- Objective: Develop adaptability in communication and cultural intelligence in professional settings.

Discussion questions:
- *Cultural competency workshops:* "What are some common cultural misunderstandings in the workplace, and how can we prevent them?"
- *Utilizing technology:* "How can technology assist in overcoming language barriers in international collaboration?"
- *Continuous learning:* "Why must professionals keep updating their cultural knowledge and language skills?"

Reflection Question:
- How has your own journey in learning new languages and engaging with different cultures shaped your leadership style and approach to fostering a multilingual and culturally inclusive workplace?

Application Question:
- What specific programs or initiatives can you implement to support ongoing language learning and cultural competency development among your team members, ensuring they are equipped to thrive in a globalized professional environment?

Implications Question:
- How might investing in multilingual and culturally fluent upskilling programs influence your organization's competitive edge and adaptability in the global market, and what are the potential long-term impacts on employee satisfaction and retention?

Section 4: Exploring global citizenship

Overview

This section delves into the concept of global citizenship and examines whether multilingualism and cultural fluency are essential components. It encourages reflection on what it means to be a responsible and engaged member of the global community.

Key concepts

Advantages of multilingualism and cultural fluency for global citizens:

1. **Enhanced communication:** Knowing multiple languages allows for direct communication with a broader range of people, fostering better understanding and stronger relationships.
2. **Deeper cultural insight:** Language is deeply intertwined with culture. Fluency in a language often brings a deeper appreciation and understanding of the associated cultures, enhancing empathy and reducing cultural misunderstandings.
3. **Broader perspectives:** Exposure to different languages and cultures broadens one's perspective, helping to recognize and value the diverse ways of thinking and living in the world.
4. **Effective advocacy:** Being multilingual can be an asset in advocating for global issues, allowing one to reach and resonate with a more diverse audience.

Aspects of global citizenship beyond language skills:

1. **Awareness of global issues:** Understanding critical global challenges like climate change, human rights, poverty, and health crises and recognizing how these issues are interconnected across nations.
2. **Ethical responsibility:** A sense of ethical responsibility towards people and the environment that transcends national borders.

3. **Informed and engaged:** Being well-informed about international affairs and engaging in discussions, policies, and actions that have global impacts.
4. **Cross-cultural empathy:** The ability to empathize with people from diverse cultural backgrounds, even if one does not speak their language fluently.
5. **Advocacy and action:** Taking action on global issues can range from local community involvement to international advocacy.
6. **Respect for diversity:** Valuing and respecting cultural diversity, including but not limited to linguistic diversity.
7. **Lifelong learning:** A commitment to continuous learning about the world and its diverse inhabitants.

Activities and discussion questions

Activity: *global issues debate*
- Description: Organize debates on pressing global issues, encouraging students to consider multiple cultural perspectives.
- Objective: Foster global awareness, critical thinking, and respectful discourse.

Discussion questions:
- *Defining Global Citizenship:* "In your opinion, what qualities make someone a global citizen?"
- *Language and Communication:* "Can we fully understand a culture without speaking its language?"
- *Advocacy and Action:* "What actions can we take locally that have a global impact?"

Reflection Question:
- How do your personal experiences and understanding of global citizenship influence your approach to teaching and fostering a sense of global responsibility among students?

Application Question:
- What specific classroom activities or projects can you design to help students actively engage with and understand global issues, promoting a sense of global citizenship?

Implications Question:
- How might integrating global citizenship education into the curriculum impact students' perspectives on diversity, inclusion, and their roles in a global society, and what are the potential long-term benefits for their personal and professional development?

Section 5: The competitive advantage of multilingualism in global economies

Overview

This section highlights how proficiency in multiple significant languages can give individuals a competitive edge in global markets and explores the tangible benefits in various professional contexts.

Key points

1. **Enhanced communication**: Proficiency in major world languages like English, Mandarin, Spanish, or French, for instance, facilitates communication with a large segment of the global population. This is particularly beneficial in international business, diplomacy, and global networking.
2. **Broader market reach**: Knowing most languages allows professionals to engage directly with larger markets. They can effectively market products, negotiate deals, and provide services in these languages, thus expanding the reach and impact of their business or organization.
3. **Cultural insight**: Language skills also come with a deeper understanding of the cultures associated with those languages. This insight is crucial for navigating different regions' social and business norms, enabling more effective cross-cultural interactions and decision-making.
4. **Networking opportunities**: Multilingualism opens doors to a broader range of networking opportunities. Professionals can connect with peers, partners, and clients worldwide, enhancing international collaboration and business opportunities.
5. **Employment prospects**: Many global companies prioritize hiring individuals who can communicate in multiple major languages. This skill set makes candidates more attractive for roles that require interaction with international clients or travel to different countries.

6. **Global mobility**: Multilingualism can increase an individual's chances of being selected for international assignments, global leadership programs, or expatriate roles, offering a pathway to a global career.
7. **Competitive edge in specific industries**: Language skills are precious in tourism, international trade, diplomacy, and global media. They enable professionals to operate more effectively in these global fields.
8. **Improved cognitive skills**: Research suggests that multilingual individuals often have enhanced cognitive abilities, such as problem-solving, multitasking, and creative thinking, which are highly valued in the global economy.
9. **Crisis management and adaptability**: Multilingual individuals are often more adaptable and practical in crisis management, especially in situations that involve coordination across different countries and cultures.
10. **Enhanced customer service**: In customer-facing roles, speaking the customer's language can significantly improve service quality and customer satisfaction, which is vital in a globalized market.

Activities and discussion questions

Activity: *market expansion simulation*
- **Description:** Students develop a plan to expand a business into a new country, considering language and cultural factors.
- **Objective:** Apply language and cultural knowledge to real-world business scenarios.

Discussion questions:
- *Employment Prospects:* "How does being multilingual make you more attractive to potential employers?"
- *Global Mobility:* "What are the personal and professional benefits of being able to work in different countries?"
- *Cognitive Skills:* "In what ways does learning another language enhance problem-solving abilities?"

Reflection Question:
- How has multilingualism personally benefited your professional interactions and career growth in the global economy?

Application Question:
- What initiatives or programs can be implemented to encourage and support multilingual education and training within your organization or community?

Implications Question:
- How might widespread multilingualism influence global economic competitiveness and collaboration, and what are the potential long-term impacts on workforce development and international relations?

Additional resources

- Downloadable guides for school leaders, teachers, parents, and students, as well as online resources.
- Recommended reading: books and articles on multilingualism, cultural fluency, and global citizenship.
- Professional development, webinars, experts, and speakers.

Conclusion

Developing multilingualism and cultural fluency is a journey that enriches individuals and communities. By fostering these skills and mindsets, we prepare students and professionals to navigate and contribute positively to our diverse world. This guide is a roadmap, offering practical steps and thought-provoking questions to inspire action and reflection.

Feedback and continuous improvement

We welcome your feedback on this guide. Please share your experiences, suggestions, and any additional resources that could enhance these materials. You can reach us at editors-ac@calec.org. Together, we can continue to support the growth of globally competent individuals.

References

References

Abbott, A., Austin, R., Mulkeen, A., & Metcalfe, N. (2004). The Global Classroom: Advancing Cultural Awareness in Special Schools Through ICT Collaborative Work. European Journal of Special Needs Education, 19(2), 225–240.

ACALAN (2019). ACALAN Plans to Use African Languages in the International Forum. Addis Ababa: UA.

ACTFL (2019). Making Languages Our Business: Addressing Foreign Language Demand among U.S. Employers.

Agirdag, O. (2013). The Long-Term Effects of Bilingualism on Children of Immigration: Student Bilingualism and Future Earnings. The International Journal of Bilingual Education and Bilingualism, 17(4), 449–464.

Alabi, T., Kazeem, A. A., & Babatope, J. (2022). Lexical Variation between English and Ogu: Cultural Implications for Language Learning and Translation. International Journal of Language and Literary Studies, 4(1), 304–316.

Albrecht, S. F. and Joles, C. (2003). Accountability and Access to Opportunity: Mutually Exclusive Tenets Under a High-Stakes Testing Mandate. Preventing School Failure: Alternative Education for Children and Youth, 47(2), 86–91.

Al-Dossary, S. (2016). Psychometric Properties of the Cultural Intelligence Scale in a Saudi Arabian Context. International Journal of Selection and Assessment, 24(4), 305–311.

Aleksander, K. (2008). When You Shouldn't Go Global. Harvard Business Review.

Alphonso, C. (2020, October 17). Pandemic worsens French-Immersion Teacher Shortage. Retrieved from The Globe and Mail.

Altbach, P. G., Reisberg L., & Rumbley, L. E. (2010). Trends in Global Higher Education: Tracking an Academic Revolution. Brill Publication, 23–35.

Amaro-Jimenez, C. (2012). Service Learning: Preparing Teachers to Understand Culturally and Linguistically Diverse Learners Better. Journal of Education for Teaching, 38(2), 211–213.

American Councils for International Education. (2021). 2021 Canvass of Dual Language and Immersion (DLI) Programs in U.S. Public Schools.

American Psychological Association (2003). Guidelines on Multicultural Education, Training, Research, Practice, and Organizational Change for Psychologists. American Psychologist, 58(5), 377–402.

Ang, S., Van Dyne, L., & Koh, C. (2006). Development and Validation of the CQS: The Cultural Intelligence Scale. In: P. C. Earley & S. Ang (Eds.), Handbook of Cultural Intelligence: Theory, Measurement, and Applications (34–56). Routledge.

Ang, S., Rockstuhl, T., & Tan, M. L. (2015). Cultural Intelligence and Competencies. International Encyclopedia of the Social and Behavioral Sciences, 2(5), 433–439.

Ang, S., Van Dyne, L., Koh, C., Ng, K. Y., Templer, K. J., Tay, C., & Chandrasekar, N. A. (2007). Cultural Intelligence: Its Measurement and Effects on Cultural Judgment and Decision Making, Cultural Adaptation and Task Performance. Management and Organization Review, 3(3), 335–371.

Angouri, J. (2014). Multilingualism in the Workplace: Language Practices in Multilingual Contexts. Multilingua, 33(1-2), 1–9.

Antón, E., Carreiras, M., & Duñabeitia, J. A. (2019). The Impact of Bilingualism on Executive Functions and Working Memory in Young Adults. PLOS ONE, 14(2).

Anuforo, E. (2024). Africa Dominates List of the World's 20 Fastest-Growing Economies in 2024—African Development Bank Says in Macroeconomic Report. African Development Bank Group.

Appiah, K. A. (2006). Cosmopolitanism: Ethics in a World of Strangers. Norton & Company.

Arnett, K., & Mady, C. (2017). Core or Immersion? Canadian French-Second Language Teacher Candidates' Perceptions and Experiences of the Best and Worse Program Options for Students with Learning Difficulties and English Language Learners. Exceptionality Education International, 27(1), 17–37.

Association canadienne des professionnels de l'immersion. (2021, October 15). The Shortage of French Immersion and French as a Second Language Teachers. Retrieved from Association canadienne des professionnels de l'immersion.

Aureli, S. (2020). Cross-Cultural Management. In: S. Idowu, R. Schmidpeter, N. Capaldi, L. Zu, M. Del Baldo, & R. Abreu (Eds) Encyclopedia of Sustainable Management. Springer, Cham.

Arnett, R. (2023). How to Bring Your Cultural Identity to Work. Knowledge at Wharton.

Asención Delaney, Y. (2012). Research on Mentoring Language Teachers: Its Role in Language Education. Foreign Language Annals, 45(S1), S184–S202.

AUF (2023). Le français, langue de l'emploi ? les grands employeurs répondent.

Bacon, N. A., Kischner, G. A. (2002). Shaping Global Classrooms. Educational Leadership, 10, 48–51.

Baker, C. (2014). A Parents' and Teachers' Guide to Bilingualism (4th Ed.). Multilingual Matters.

Baker, W. (2012). From Cultural Awareness to Intercultural Awareness: Culture in ELT. ELT Journal, 66(1), 62–70.

Barkley, R. (2011). The Important Role of Executive Functioning and Self-Regulation in ADHD. Burnett Lecture.

Barner-Rasmussen, W., Ehrnrooth, M., Koveshnikov, A., & Mäkelä, K. (2014). Cultural and Language Skills are Resources for Boundary Spanning within the MNC. Journal of International Business Studies, 45(7), 886–905.

Barrère, A., Delvaux, B. (2017). La fragmentation des systèmes scolaires nationaux. Revue internationale d'éducation de Sèvres, 76, 39–50.

Baudelaire, C. (1855). L'exposition universelle de 1855. Michel Lévy Frères.

———— (1869). L'art romantique. Flammarion.

Baylis, W. (2015). Global Education Through IB. Principal Leadership, 15(7), 60–62.

BBC News. (2019). Why the Future of French Is African.

Beelen, J., Jones, E. (2015). Redefining Internationalization at Home. In: A. Curaj, L. Matei, R. Pricopie, J. Salmi, & P. Scott

(Eds), The European Higher Education Area. Springer, Cham: 59–72.

Bennett, M. J. (1986). A Developmental Approach to Training for Intercultural Sensitivity. International Journal of Intercultural Relations, 10(2), 179–196.

―――――― (2004). Becoming Interculturally Competent. In: J.S. Wurzel (Ed.), Toward Multiculturalism: A Reader in Multicultural Education. Intercultural Resource Corporation.

Bennis, W., & Nanus, B. (1985). Leaders: Strategies for Taking Charge. Harper & Row

Berken, J., Gracco, V., & Klein, D. (2017). Early Bilingualism, Language Attainment, and Brain Development. Neuropsychologia, 98, 220–227.

Bernardo, A., Presbitero, A. (2018). Cognitive Flexibility and Cultural Intelligence: Exploring the Cognitive Aspects of Effective Functioning in Culturally Diverse Contexts. International Journal of Intercultural Relations, 66, 12–21.

Bialystok, E. (1999). Cognitive Complexity and Attentional Control in the Bilingual Mind. Child Development, 70(3), 636–644.

Bialystok, E., Senman, L. (2004). Role of Inhibition of Attention and Symbolic Representation. Child Development, 75(2), 562–579.

Bialystok, E., Martin M. M. (2004). Attention and Inhibition in Bilingual Children: Evidence from the Dimensional Change Card Sort Task. Developmental Science, 7(3), 325–339.

Bialystok, E., Craik, F., & Luk, G. (2008). Cognitive Control and Lexical Access in Younger and Older Bilinguals. Journal of Experimental Psychology: Learning, Memory, and Cognition, 34, 859–873.

Bialystok, E., Craik, F., & Freedman, M. (2010). Delaying the Onset of Alzheimer Disease: Bilingualism as a Form of Cognitive Reserve. Neurology, 75(19), 1726–1729.

Bialystock, E., Craik, F., & Luk, G. (2012). Bilingualism: Consequences for Mind and Brain. Trends in Cognitive Sciences, 16(4), 240–250.

Bialystok, E., Hawrylewicz, K., Wiseheart, M., & Toplak, M. (2016). Interaction of Bilingualism and Attention-

Deficit/Hyperactivity Disorder in Young Adults. Biling (Camb Engl), 20(3):588–601.

Bialystok, E. (2017). The Bilingual Adaptation: How Minds Accommodate Experience. Psychological Bulletin, 143(3), 233–262.

Black, J. S., & Mendenhall, M. (1989). Cross-Cultural Training Effectiveness: A Review and a Theoretical Framework for Future Research. the Academy of Management Review, 15(1), 113–136.

Black, J. S., Morrison, A. J., & Gregersen, H. B. (1999). Global Explorers: The Next Generation of Leaders. New York: Routledge.

Black, D. (2007). We Are Becoming Bilingual and Biliterate! An Ethnographic Study on How a Dual-Language Program in Florida Contributes to the Literacy Development of English-Language Learners [Doctoral Dissertation, the University of Central Florida].

Blom, E., Boerma, T., Bosma, E., Cornips, L., & Everaert, E. (2017). Cognitive Advantages of Bilingual Children in Different Sociolinguistic Contexts. Frontiers in Psychology, 8, 552.

Bogliotti, C., Puissant-Schontz, L., & Marshall, C. (2017). Atypies langagières de l'enfance à l'âge adulte. In : Bogliotti, Isel et Lacheret-Dujour (Ed.), Atypies langagières de l'enfance à l'âge adulte. Apports de la psycholinguistique et des neurosciences cognitives. De Boeck Supérieur. 75–114.

Borgonovi, F. et al. (2022), "The environmental sustainability competence toolbox: From leaving a better planet for our children to leaving better children for our planet", OECD Social, Employment and Migration Working Papers, No. 275, OECD Publishing, Paris.

Boroditsky, L. (2018). Language and the Construction of Time Through Space. Trends in Neurosciences, 41(10), 651–653.

Boudou, B. (2001). Italian Ugliness according to Henri Estienne. In: Propos sur la laideur et les muses : figurations et défigurations de la beauté. Revue de l'Université de Paris X-Nanterre. Littérales. No. 28. 143–156.

Bourbaki, N. (1971). General Topology. Hermann.

Bourdieu, P. (1986). The Forms of Capital. In: J. C. Richardson, (Ed.), Handbook of Theory and Research for the Sociology of Education. New York: Greenwood Press.

Bowen, H. R. (1953). Social Responsibilities of the Businessman. University of Iowa Press.

Brimm, L. (2015). How to Embrace Complex Change. Harvard Business Review.

_____ (2018). The Global Cosmopolitan Mindset: Lessons from the New Global Leaders. Springer.

_____ (2016). What the Best Cross-Cultural Managers Have in Common. Harvard Business Review.

Buchanan, J., Widodo, A. (2016). Your Place or Mine? Global Imbalances in Internationalisation and Mobilisation in Educational Professional Experience. Asia Pacific Education Review, 17, 355-364.

Byram, M. (2012). Language Awareness and (Critical) Cultural Awareness – Relationships, Comparisons, and Contrasts. Language Awareness, 21(1-2), 5–13.

Cambridge Dictionary (N.D.). Working Class. In: Cambridge Dictionary.com dictionary. Retrieved August 9, 2023.

Canadian Charter of Rights and Freedom. (1982). S 23, Part 1 of the Constitution Act. Being Schedule B to the Canada Act 1982.

Canadian Heritage. (2018, February). Some facts on the Canadian Francophonie. Retrieved March 2024, from Official Languages Branch.

Canadian Teachers' Federation. (2021, November 2021). Canadian Teachers' Federation Board tackles teacher retention and recruitment.

Caravolas, J. A. (2009). Comenius (1592-1670) and Plurilingualism. Documents pour l'histoire du français langue étrangère ou seconde. 43. 25–39.

Cabrera, Á., & Unruh, G. (2013). Join the Global Elite. Harvard Business Review.

Cabrera, Á. (2019). Éducation inclusive et politiques prioritaires : regards croisés entre le Chili et l'Europe. Éducation et Sociétés.

Carstens, S. (2015). Bilingual Education for Global Citizenship: Creating an Integrated Language/Culture Curriculum for

Mandarin/English Students. Human Organization, 74(1), 16–26.

Castañeda v. Pickard, 648 F.2d 989 (5th Cir. 1981).

Cenoz, J., Gorter D. (2023). Multilingualism at School and Multilingual Education. International Encyclopedia of Education (4th Ed.), 188–194.

Centre for the New Economy and Society. (2023). Future of Jobs Report 2023. World Economic Forum.

Cere, R. C. (2012). Foreign Language Careers for International Business and the Professions. In: Global Advances in Business Communication, 1(1), Article 6.

Chastel, A. (1993). Introduction to French Art History. Flammarion.

Chen, G. M., Starosta, W. J. (2000). The Development and Validation of the Intercultural Sensitivity Scale. Human Communication, 3, 1–15.

Chen, G. M. (2010). The Impact of Intercultural Sensitivity on Ethnocentrism and Intercultural Communication Apprehension. Intercultural Communication Studies, 19(1), 1–9.

Chen, J. (2023). 中国夫妻殒命非洲：淘金圣地的诱惑与枪声 [Chinese Couples Lost Their Lives in Africa: The Seduction and Gunshots in the Gold Mining Heaven]. Southern Weekly.

Chen, S. (2010). Multilingualism in Taiwan. International Journal of the Sociology of Language, 2010(205), 79–104.

Chen, Y.-Z., Hélot, C. (2018). The Notion of Plurilingual and Pluricultural Competence in Teaching Foreign Languages in France. Language Education and Multilingualism, 1., 168–187.

Chen, X., Wang, H. (2021). 中国农村小学英语教育面临的问题及对策 [The Problems and Solutions for English Education in Chinese Rural Elementary Schools]. Overseas English, 23, 208–209.

Cheng, Y., Wang, R., Chen, J., Chao, Y., Maimaitili, A., & Zhang, H. (2023). Context-Based AI Translation from a Globalization Perspective: A Case Study of ChatGPT. Sino-US English Teaching, 20(9), 370–380.

China Africa Research Initiative (2023). Data: Chinese Workers in Africa [Database].

China Labor Watch (2022). Trapped: The Belt and Road Initiative and Its Chinese Workers.

Chomsky, N. (1965). Aspects of the Theory of Syntax (50th ed.). The MIT Press.

Chomsky, N. (2011). Language and Other Cognitive Systems. What is Special about Language? Language Learning and Development, 7(4), 263–278.

Church-Morel, A., Louzir-Ben Hassine, A., Sacco, S.J., and Vigier, M. (2023, May 14). Workplace Language Dynamics in the Highly Multilingual Contexts of Tunisia, Senegal, and Mauritania: Groundwork for Future Research. [Conference Session]. ISIT, Paris.

Clark, D. (2008). Global Teams and the Cultural Paradigm. Communication at the 9th IFSAM Conference in Shanghai.

Clayton J. (2020). Multiculturalism. International Encyclopedia of Human Geography (2nd Ed.), 211–219.

Coady, M.R. (2020). The Coral Way Bilingual Program. Multilingual Matters.

Cohen, A. (1975). A Sociolinguistic Approach to Bilingual Education: Experiments in the American Southwest, Rowley, Mass. Newbury House.

Combs, M. C. (2012). Everything on Its Head: How Arizona's Structured English Immersion Policy Re-Invents Theory and Practice. In: M.B. Arias & C. Faltis (Eds.), Implementing Educational Language Policy in Arizona: Legal, Historical, and Current Practices in SEI. Multilingual Matters, 59–85.

Commission on Teacher Credentialing. (2008). Bilingual Authorizations (CL-628b). Special Education Credentials. Ca.gov.

Contini, R. M., Maturo, A. (2010). Multi-Ethnic Society and Cross-Cultural Perspectives in the School. Procedia – Social and Behavioral Sciences, 5, 1537–1545.

Coquery, E. (2023). Vincent Van Gogh, les dernières lettres. Hazan.

Council of Ministers of Canada, Canada. (2024). French First-Language Learning in a Minority Setting. Retrieved March 2024, from Council of Ministers of Canada

Council of Ministers of Education, Canada. (2001). The Development of Education in Canada. Retrieved March 2024, from Council of Ministers of Education, Canada

Courrier de l'UNESCO, Le. (1957). Jean Amos Comenius, Apostle of Modern Education and World Understanding. UNESCO.

Couteau, J., & Breguet, G. (2014). Time, Rites, and Festivals in Bali. BAB Books.

Core Competencies and Values Research Team. (2016). 中国学生发展核心素养 [Core Competencies and Values for Chinese Students' Development]. Journal of Chinese Society of Education, 10, 1-3.

Crépin, A. (2004). When the English Spoke French. Comptes rendus des séances de l'Académie des inscriptions et belles-lettres. 148(4). 1569–1588. Académie des inscriptions et belles-lettres.

Crose, B. (2011). Internationalization of the Higher Education Classroom: Strategies to Facilitate Intercultural Learning and Academic Success. International Journal of Teaching and Learning in Higher Education, 23 (3), (2011): 388–395.

Crowne, K. (2008). What Leads to Cultural Intelligence? Business Horizons, 51(5), 391–399.

———— (2009). The Relationships Among Social Intelligence, Emotional Intelligence, and Cultural Intelligence. Organization Management Journal, 6, 148–163.

Cummins, J. (1984). Wanted: A Theoretical Framework for Relating Language Proficiency to Academic Achievement Among Bilingual Students. In: C. Rivera (Ed.), Language Proficiency and Academic Achievement. Clevedon, England: Multilingual Matters.

———— (2000). Language, Power, and Pedagogy: Bilingual Children in the Crossfire. Clevedon, England: Multilingual Matters.

Cushner, K. (2007). The Role of Experience in the Making of Internationally Minded Teachers. Teacher Education Quarterly, 34(1), 27–39.

D'Iribarne, P. (1998). Culture et mondialisation, gérer par-delà des frontières. Seuil.

D'Iribarne, P., Chevrier, S., Henry, A., Segal, J.-P., & Tréguer-Felten, G. (2020). Cross Cultural Management Revisited – A Qualitative Approach. Oxford University Press (OUP).

Davis, R., Fletcher-Watson, S., & Digard, B. G. (2021). Autistic People's Access to Bilingualism and Additional Language Learning: Identifying the Barriers and Facilitators for Equal Opportunities. University of Edinburgh, Edinburgh, UK.

De Costa, P. (2016). Constructing the Global Citizen: An ELF Perspective. Journal of Asian Pacific Communication, 26(2), 238–259.

De Lissovoy, N. (2011). Pedagogy in Common: Democratic Education in the Global Era. Educational Philosophy and Theory, 43(10), 1119–1134.

De Staël. (1813). De l'Allemagne. Nicolle.

Deardorff, D. K. (2004). The Identification and Assessment of Intercultural Competence as a Student Outcome of Internationalization at Institutions of Higher Education in the United States. (Doctoral Dissertation). North Carolina State University Library.

────── (2006a). Assessing Intercultural Competence in Study Abroad Students. Languages for Intercultural Communication and Education, 12, 232.

────── (2006b). Identification and Assessment of Intercultural Competence as a Student Outcome of Internationalization. Journal of Studies in International Education, 10(3), 241–266.

────── (2009). The SAGE Handbook of Intercultural Competence. Thousand Oaks, CA: Sage.

────── (2020). Manual for Developing Intercultural Competencies: Story Circles. UNESCO/Routledge.

DeBoer, F. (2023). Pick a Practical Major, Like French. New York Magazine.

Delbridge, A., Helman, L. (2016). Evidence-based Strategies for Fostering Biliteracy in any Classroom. Early Childhood Education Journal, 44(4), 307-316.

Della Chiesa, B., Scott, J., & Hinton, Ch. (Eds.) (2012). Languages in a Global World-Learning for Better Cultural Understanding. OECD.

Derey, J.-C. (2016). Fordlandia. Paris, Editions Payot Rivages.
Dewey, J. (1934). Art as Experience. New York: Perigee Books.
Diercks, M., Sacco, S. J. (2023). Creating an Interdisciplinary Francophone African Curriculum for K-16 Educators and Students. [Grant Proposal]. U.S. Department of Education, International Research and Studies Program.
Digard, B. (2020). Bilingualism in Autism: A Neurocognitive Investigation of the Influence of Bilingualism on Perspective-Taking in Autistic Adults. PhD Dissertation, University of Edinburgh.
Drobot, I.A. (2022). Multilingualism and Awareness of Cultural Differences in Communication. Intech Open (Edited by Xiaoming Jiang).
Du Bellay, J. (1549). La deffence et illustration de la langue francoyse. Arnoul l'Angelier.
Dubois, J. (2017). L'enseignement des langues étrangères sous la troisième république : des disciplines en prise avec les relations internationales. ENS Editions. Revue Française de Pédagogie, 199, 23–37.
Dubos, R., Ward, B. (1972). Nous n'avons qu'une terre. The report, Stockholm World Conference on the Environment.
Dubuisson, M. (1981). Vtraque Lingua. L'Antiquité classique, 50(1-2), 274–286.
Durrleman, S. (2021). Autism Research. Universités de Genève, Cambridge & Thessalie.
Earley, P. C., Mosakowski, E. (2004). Cultural Intelligence. Harvard Business Review, 82(10), 139–146.
Earley, P. C., & Peterson, R. S. (2004). The Elusive Cultural Chameleon: Cultural Intelligence as a New Approach to Intercultural Training for the Global Manager. Academy of Management Learning & Education, 3(1), 100–115.
Eberhard, D., Simons, G., & Fennig, C. (Eds) (2019). Ethnologue: Languages of the World. SIL International (22nd Ed).
Morin, E. (2015). Penser global : l'humain et son univers, Robert Laffont, Paris.
Edsall, T. (2022). There's a Reason There Aren't Enough Teachers in America. Many Reasons, Actually. The New York Times.

Esposito, E. G., Baker-Ward, L. (2013). Dual-Language Education for Low-Income Children: Preliminary Evidence of Benefits for Executive Function. Bilingual Research Journal, 36, 295–310.

European Commission (EU). European Education Area: Quality Education and Training for All.

Fargues, P. (2006). International Migration in the Arab Region: Trends and Policies. United Nations Expert Group Meeting on International Migration and Development in the Arab Region, United Nations Secretariat, Beirut.

Fattal, A. B. (2023). Teacher Prep Program to Support "English Learners" in Public School System. Florida International University.

Fédération nationale des conseils scolaires francophones. (2019). L'éducation en langue française au Canada, un passeport vers... Retrieved from www.fncsf.ca

Feely, A., & Harzing, A. W. (2003). Language Management in Multinational Companies. Cross-Cultural Management, 10(2), 37–52.

Flores, M. A. (2017). Practice, Theory, and Research in Initial Teacher Education: International Perspectives. European Journal of Teacher Education, 40(3), 287–290.

Forbes Middle East. (2018). 50 Most Influential Expats in the UAE.

Frame, A., & Sommier, M. (2020). Penser les tensions interculturelles en organisation. Communication et Organisation, 58, 11-24.

Freiha, A. (1948). Dictionnaire des termes en dialecte libanais. Liban Publisher.

Fritz, W., Graf, A., Hentze, J., Möllenberg, A., & Chen, G. M. (2005). An Examination of Chen and Starosta's Model of Intercultural Sensitivity in Germany and the United States. Intercultural Communication Studies, 14 (1), 53–64.

Fumaroli, M. (2001). Quand l'Europe parlait français. Éditions de Fallois.

Gándara, P. (2014). Is There Really a Labor Market Advantage to Being Bilingual in the U.S.? (Princeton, NJ: Educational Testing Service.

Garcia Mathewson, T. (2023). Students With Disabilities Often Left Out of Popular 'Dual-Language' Programs. Hechinger Report. May 31, 2023.

García, O., Wei, L. (2014). Translanguaging: Language, Bilingualism, and Education. Palgrave Macmillan.

García, O., Johnson, S. I., & Seltzer, K. (2017). The Translanguaging Classroom: Leveraging Student Bilingualism for Learning. Caslon.

García, O., Angel M., & Lin. Y. (2017). Introduction. In: O. García, M. Angel, Y. Lin, & S. May (Eds), Bilingual and Multilingual Education. Springer International (3rd Edition).

Gardin, B. (1976). Pour un enseignement du français aux travailleurs immigrés. Langue Française, 29, 3–16.

Garritsen, M., Nickerson, C. (2009). BELF: Business English as a Lingua Franca. In: F. Bargiela-Chiappini (Ed.), The Handbook of Business Discourse. Edinburgh: Edinburgh University Press, 180-93.

Gaumont, M.-F. (2023). Issues Related to Recruitment in University Education Programs and Possible Solutions to Increase the Pool of New FSL Teachers: Strategic Review and Survey Report.

Geddes, P. (1915). Cities in Evolution. London: William, p. 397

Geeslin, K. L., Schmidt, L. B. (2018). Study Abroad and L2 Learner Attitudes. In: The Routledge Handbook of Study Abroad Research and Practice. Routledge, 385–405.

Gellner, E. (1983). Nations and Nationalism. Ithaca: Cornell University Press.

Girault de Coursac, P. (1995). L'éducation d'un roi : Louis XVI. François-Xavier de Guibert.

Goh, M. (2012). Teaching with Cultural Intelligence: Developing Multiculturally Educated and Globally Engaged Citizens. Asia Pacific Journal of Education, 32(4), 395–415.

Gohard-Radenkovic, A. (2004). Communicating in a Foreign Language: From Cultural Competence to Linguistic Competence. Peter Lang.

Goldstein, S. B. (2022). A Systematic Review of Short-Term Study Abroad Research Methodology and Intercultural Competence

Outcomes. International Journal of Intercultural Relations, 87, 26–36.

Gomez, L. (2019). Bill to Repeal Arizona's English-Only Law Moves Forward. The Arizona Mirror.

Gomez, L. (2021). Lawmakers Will Once Again Consider Repealing English-Only.

Gordin, M. D. (2015). How Did Science Come to Speak Only English? Aeon.

Government of British Columbia. (2022). Language education policy. Retrieved March 2024.

Government of Canada. (2018). Investing in our future 2018-2023: Action plan for official languages. Retrieved March 2024.

Grandin, G. (2009). Fordlandia: The Rise and Fall of Henry Ford's Forgotten Jungle City. Metropolitan Books.

Grégoire, H.B. (1794). Rapport sur la nécessité et les moyens d'anéantir les patois, et d'universaliser l'usage de la langue française [Report on the Necessity and Means to Annihilate the Patois and to Universalize the Use of the French Language]. Presented to the National Convention on June 4, 1794.

Grey, S., Sanz, C., Morgan-Short, K., & Ullman, M. T. (2017). Bilingual and Monolingual Adults Learning an Additional Language: ERPs Reveal Differences in Syntactic Processing. Bilingualism: Language and Cognition, 21(5), 970–994.

Grosjean, F. (1982). Life with Two Languages: An Introduction to Bilingualism. Harvard University Press.

——————— (1998). Studying Bilinguals: Methodological and Conceptual Issues. Bilingualism: Language and Cognition, 1(2), 131–49.

——————— (2010). Bilingual: Life and Reality. Harvard University Press.

——————— (2021). Life As a Bilingual: Knowing and Using Two or More Languages. Cambridge University Press.

Gupta, A. K., Govindarajan, V., & Wang, H. (2008). The Quest for Global Dominance: Transforming Global Presence into Global Competitive Advantage. (2nd Ed.).

Hall, E. T., Hall, M. R. (1990). Understanding Cultural Differences: Germans, French and Americans. Intercultural Press, Boston.

Hall, E. T. (1983). The Dance of Life: The Other Dimension of Time. Anchor Books, Doubleday.
Hall, E. T. (1976). Beyond Culture. Anchor Books, Doubleday.
Hampden-Turner, C., Trompenaars, F. (2004). Riding the Waves of Culture. Nicholas Brealey International (3rd Ed.).
Hammer, M. R. (2015). Intercultural Competence Development. In: J. M. Bennett, (Ed.), The SAGE Encyclopedia of Intercultural Competence. Thousand Oaks, CA: SAGE Publishing, Inc., 483–486.
Harford, T. (2012). Messy: How to Be Creative and Resilient in a Tidy-Minded World, Little Brown.
_____ (2017). Fifty Things That Made the Modern Economy, Little Brown.
Harveston, P. D., Kedia, B. L., & Davis, P. S. (2000). Internationalization of Born Global and Gradual Globalizing Firms: The Impact of the Manager. Advances in Competitiveness Research, 8(1), 92–99.
Haug, D. T. T. (2007). Greek Dialects in Homer. GAIA. Revue Interdisciplinaire sur la Grèce Ancienne. 11. 11–24. Université Stendhal-Grenoble 3.
Havard, G. (2019). L'Amérique Fantôme : Les Aventuriers Francophones du Nouveau Monde. Flammarion.
Harveston, P. D., Kedia, B. L., & Davis, P. S. (2000). Internationalization of born global and gradual globalizing firms: the impact of the manager. Journal of Competitiveness, 8(1), 92–99.
Haworth Jacobs, J. (2019). Education (Next Volume 19), Cambridge.
Hayden, M. & Thompson, J. (1995). International Schools and International Education: A Relationship Revisited. Oxford Review of Education, 21(3), 327–345.
_____ (2010). International Schools: Growth and Influence. UNESCO.
Hegel, G. W. F. (1830). Encyclopedia of Philosophical Sciences in Abridged Form (§462). Johann Friedrich Cotta.
Heidar, D. M., Shahsavari, A., Afghari, A., & Mohammadi, E. G. (2012). Intercultural Complexities: Translation as a Process of

Cultural Decoding, Recoding, and Encoding. January 2012, 2(12), 13101–13106.

Helios Educational Foundation (2023). What We Do: Arizona Latino Student Success Strategy. Helios Educational Foundation.

Heineke, A. J. (2017). Restrictive Language Policy in Arizona: English Learners in Arizona. Multilingual Matters.

Henderson, I., Palmer, D.K. (2020). Dual Language Bilingual Education: Teacher Cases and Perspectives on Large-Scale Implementation. Multilingual Matters.

Hendrix, C. S. (2022). Chinese Nationals Have Become Targets for Violence as China Deepens its International Reach. Peterson Institute for International Economics.

Heng, L., Quinlivan, K., & Du Plessis, R. (2019). Exploring the Creation of a New Initial Teacher Education (ITE) Programme Underpinned by Inclusion. International Journal of Inclusive Education, 23(10), 1017–1031.

Henson, R. (2016). The Challenges of Global Leadership. In: Successful Global Leadership. Palgrave Macmillan

Heyward, M. (2002). From International to Intercultural, Redefining the International School for a Globalized World. Journal of Research in International Education, 1(1), 9–32.

Higgins Averill, O., & Rinaldi, C. (2011). Multi-tier system of supports (MTSS). District Administration, 48(8), 91-95.

Hill, I. (2015). What is an International School? Part One. International Schools Journal. 25. 60–70.

――――― (2016). What Is an International School? Part Two. International Schools Journal, 35, 9–21.

Hofstede, G. (1980). Culture's Consequences: International Differences in Work-Related Values. Beverly Hills, CA: Sage Publications.

――――― (1983). Culture's Consequences: International Differences in Work-Related Values. Administrative Science Quarterly. Johnson Graduate School of Management. Cornell University.

――――― (2010). The GLOBE Debate: Back to Relevance. Journal of International Business Studies. Sage Publications.

Hofstede, G., Hofstede, G. J., & Minkov, M. (2010). Cultures and Organizations: Software of the Mind. McGraw-Hill Professional (3rd Ed.).

Hofstede, G. (2011). Dimensionalizing Cultures: The Hofstede Model in Context. Online Readings in Psychology and Culture, 2(1), 8.

Holliday, A. (2006). Native-Speakerism, ELT Journal, 60(4), 385–387.

Holon IQ (2023). U.S. International Education in 2030. 6 Charts, Top 20 Source Countries and Preliminary Forecast, New York, NY, United States.

Horace (23 BC). Odes, I, 11. Bibliotheca Teubneriana.

Hossain, K. I. (2024). Reviewing the role of culture in English language learning: Challenges and opportunities for educators. Social Sciences & Humanities Open, 9, 1–10.

Hourani, G. (2010). Lebanese Migration to the Gulf (1950–2009). Washington, DC: Middle East Institute.

House of Commons. (2018, October 17). Language Committee Report. Retrieved from French as a second language learning programs in Western Canada: Enhancing availability.

House, R. J., Hanges, P. J., Javidan, M., Dorfman, P. W., & Gupta, V. (2004). Culture, Leadership, and Organizations: The GLOBE Study of 62 Societies. Sage Publications.

Hyun, J., Conant, D. (2019). 3 Ways to Improve Your Cultural Fluency. Harvard Business Review.

iFeng.com Living Studio. (2021). 年在异乡·24位中国打工人在非洲过年实录 [New Year in the Other Land: Documentation of 24 Chinese Workers Celebrating Chinese New York in Africa]. Peng Pai.

Igarashi, H., & Saito, H. (2014). Cosmopolitanism as Cultural Capital: Exploring the Intersection of Globalization, Education and Stratification. Cultural Sociology, 8(3), 222–239.

Ingersoll, M. L. (2014). Leaving Home, Teaching Abroad, Coming Home: A Narrative Journey of International Teaching. Queen's University (Canada).

Institut du Monde Arabe. Qu'est-ce que l'Easy Arabic ou Arabizi ?

Institute of Governance (2023). Development, and International Studies (IGDIS).

International Labour Organization (2021). ILO Global Estimates on International Migrant Workers: Results and Methodology. International Labour Office Geneva.

——— (2023). Labour Force Statistics (LFS, STLFS, RURBAN Databases).

Interview with Robert Voyer (2017). Le Monde, Blog Orientation.

Interviews of Real People. (2022). 我为高薪出国务工，一天工作15小时，月薪900欧，没有想象中美好 [I Work Abroad for High-Income, 15-Hour Work Days, 900 Euro per Month, Not as Beautiful as Imagined]. Baidu.com. December 22.

Jaime, H. (2022). Plurilingualism and Scientific Creativity. In: J.-C. Beacco (Ed.), La gouvernance linguistique des universités et établissements d'enseignement supérieur. European Observatory of Plurilingualism, 59–67.

Jakobson, R. (1982). Einstein and the Science of Language. Débat, (20), p. 132. Gallimard.

James, K. (2005). International Education: The Concept and Its Relationship to Intercultural Education. Journal of Research in International Education, 4(3), 313–332.

Jancovitch, J. M., Blain, C. (2023). Un monde sans fin. Oblomov Edition.

Jang, S. (2018). The Most Creative Teams Have a Specific Type of Cultural Diversity. Harvard Business Review.

Janssens, M., Steyaert, C. (2014). Re-Considering Language Within a Cosmopolitan Understanding: Toward a Multilingual Franca Approach in International Business Studies. Journal of International Business Studies, 45(5), 623–639.

Jaumont, F. (2017). The Bilingual Revolution. The Future of Education is in Two Languages. TBR Books, CALEC.

Jaumont, F. (2020). French-speaking population, according to the U.S. Census Bureau. fabricejaumont.net.

Javidan, M. (2010). Bringing the Global Mindset to Leadership. Harvard Business Review.

Jeannet, J. P. (2000). Managing With a Global Mindset. Financial Times Prentice Hall.

Jezer-Morton, K. (2020, January 9). Canada's "Founding Mothers" of French Immersion. Retrieved March 2024, from The Canadian Encyclopedia.

Jhingran, D. (2019). Early Literacy and Multilingual Education in South Asia. United Nations Children's Fund Regional Office for South Asia, Kathmandu, 1–120.

Joint Venture Silicon Valley (2022). Institute for Regional Studies, Silicon Valley Index 2022, San Jose, CA, United States.

Kabir, A. H., Chowdhury, R. (2021). The Privatization of Higher Education in Postcolonial Bangladesh the Politics of Intervention and Control. Routledge, Taylor & Francis, 1–153.

Katz, J. J. (2006). A Hypothesis about the Uniqueness of Natural Language. Annals of the New York Academy of Sciences, 280(1), 33–41.

Kaur, A. (2023). The Best Languages to Learn for Your Job, According to CEOs. Study International.

Kelly, N. (2019). 5 Ways to Foster a Global Mindset in Your Company. Harvard Business Review.

Keysar, B., Hayakawa S., & Sun Gyu A. (2012). The Foreign-Language Effect: Thinking in a Foreign Tongue Reduces Decision Biases, Sage Journal.

Khan, M. M., Rahman, S. M. T., & Islam, S. T. A. (2011). Online Education System in Bangladesh During COVID-19 Pandemic. Creative Education, 12(2), 441–452.

King, L. (2018). The Impact of Multilingualism on Global Education and Language Learning. Cambridge Assessment English Language Assessment, 1–40.

Kitamura, Y. (2015). Expansion and Quality in Bangladesh. International Higher Education, Boston College University Libraries.

Kluckhohn, F. R., Strodtbeck, F. L. (1961). Variations in Value Orientations. Row, Peterson.

Korine, A. (2008). When You Shouldn't Go Global. Harvard Business Review.

Korzilius, H., Bücker, J., & Beerlage, S. (2017). Multiculturalism and Innovative Work Behavior: The Mediating Role of Cultural Intelligence. International Journal of Intercultural Relations, 56, 13–24.

Kotter, J. P. (2001). What Leaders Really Do. Harvard Business Review, 79(11), 85–96.

Kraft, M. A., & Lyon, M. A. (2022). The Rise and Fall of the Teaching Profession: Prestige, Interest, Preparation, and Satisfaction Over the Last Half-Century. Edworkingpapers.com: 22–679. Annenberg Institute at Brown University.

Kroll, J. F., Rossi, E. (In Press). Bilingualism: A Cognitive and Neural View of Dual Language Experience. Oxford Research Encyclopedia of Psychology.

North Carolina Department of Public Instruction (NC DPI) (2022). Language Diversity in North Carolina.

Kramsch, C. (1993). Context and Culture in Language Teaching. Oxford University Press.

Kramsch, C. (2014). Teaching Foreign Languages in an Era of Globalization: Introduction. The Modern Language Journal, 98(1), 298–311.

Krogstad, J. M., Passel, J. S., & Noe-Bustamante, L. (2022). Key Facts About U.S. Latinos for National Hispanic Heritage Month. The Pew Research Center.

Lean, D. (Director). (1962). Lawrence of Arabia [Film]. Horizon Pictures.

Le Goff, J. (2010). La Doctrine de la RSE Est-elle socialement responsable ? ESKA, Revue Internationale de Psychosociologie et de Gestion des Comportements Organisationnels, 38, XVI, 275-291

Le Pichon, E., de Swart, H. E., Vorstman, J.A.S., & Van Den Bergh, H. (2013). Emergence of Patterns of Strategic Competence in Young Multilingual Children Involved in French International Schools. In: International Journal of Bilingual Education and Bilingualism, 16(1), 42–63.

Leitch, A. (2017, December). Indigenous Public Service Leadership and Issues of Cultural Fluency. Australian Journal of Public Administration, 76(4), 403–405.

Leone, H. H. (2024). The Post-Pandemic Repositioning of a Canadian Bilingual Offshore School in the Paris Region: The Value-Added of Purpose, Presence, and Place. Policies and Pedagogies of Canadian Offshore Schools: Geopolitical Dynamics, Internationalization and New Modalities of Coloniality. 137–153.

Lequesne, C. (2021). Diversité linguistique et langue française dans les institutions européennes. Rapport du groupe de personnalités indépendantes.

Levy, O. (2005). The Influence of Top Management Team Attention Patterns on Global Strategic Posture of Firms. Journal of International Business Studies, 36(5), 593–614.

Lévi-Strauss, C. (1952). Race and History. UNESCO.

Li, M., Mobley, W., & Kelly, A. (2016). Linking Personality to Cultural Intelligence: An Interactive Effect of Openness and Agreeableness. Personality and Individual Differences, 89, 105–110.

Lies S. (2022). Internationalization at Home as a Factor Affecting Intercultural Competence. A Study Among Belgian University Students. European Journal of Higher Education.

Lies, S. (2023). Internationalization at Home and the Development of Intercultural Competence Belgian University Students' Views. European Education, 55(1), 1–15.

Linton, A. (2004). Learning in Two Languages: Spanish-English Immersion in U.S. Public Schools. International Journal of Sociology and Social Policy, 24(7/8), 46–74.

Liu Y., & Luo S. (2022). The Non-equivalence of Language-Value between Chinese and American Cultures Based on the Sapir-Whorf Hypothesis. Scholars International Journal of Linguistics and Literature, 5(5), 185–190.

Livermore, D. (2015). Leading With Cultural Intelligence. Amacom (2nd Ed.).

Lo Bianco, J. (2010). The Importance of Language Policies and Multilingualism for Cultural Diversity, International Social Science Journal, 61(199), 37–67.

Long, M. H., Adamson, H. D. (2012). SLA Research and Arizona's Structured English Immersion Policies. In: M. Beatriz Arias, &

C. Faltis (Eds.), Implementing Educational Language Policy in Arizona: Legal, Historical, and Current Practices in SEI. Multilingual Matters, 39–55.

Lønsmann, D. (2014). Linguistic Diversity in the International Workplace: Language Ideologies and Processes of Exclusion. Multilingual, Journal of Cross-Cultural and Interlanguage Communication, 33(1), 89–116.

Lüdi, G., Meier, K., & Yanaprasart, P. (Eds.) (2016). Managing Plurilingual and Intercultural Practices in the Workplace, John Benjamins Publishing Company.

Ma, X. (2014). 出国务工人员实用英语培训的现状和策略研究——基于对泰安的调查与研究 [A Study on the Current Situation and Strategy of the Practical English Training for Workers Abroad: Based on Investigation and Research in Tai'an]. Science and Technology Vision, 190.

Macnab, B., & Worthley, R. (2010). Individual Characteristics as Predictors of Cultural Intelligence Development: The Relevance of Self-Efficacy. International Journal of Intercultural Relations, 36(1), 62–71.

Mahoney, K., Lillie, L., Dubois, N., Rolstad, K., Macswan, J., & Haladyne, T. (2022). Castañeda's Third Prong Redux: The Achievement of Arizona's English Language Learners After Proposition 203. The International Journal of Bilingual Education and Bilingualism, 25(9), 3199–3123.

Mangez, E., Bouhon, M., Delvaux, B., & Cattonar, B. (2017). "Faire société" dans un monde incertain. Quel rôle pour l'école ? Les cahiers de recherche du GIRSEF.

Marrou, H.-I. (1948). History of Education in Antiquity. Sheed and Ward.

Masterson, V. (2023). Future of Jobs 2023: These Are the Most In-Demand Skills Now – and Beyond. World Economic Forum, Geneva, Switzerland

Mbugua, T. (2010). Fostering Culturally Relevant/Responsive Pedagogy and Global Awareness Through the Integration of International Service-Learning in Courses. Journal of Pedagogy, 1(2), 87–98.

Mead, R. (2013). International Management: Cross-Cultural Dimensions, Blackwell.

Merchant, S. J.-N. (2023, May 8). School Districts' Assessment of the French Language Proficiency Perspective FSL Teachers. Canadian Journal of Educational Administration and Policy, 202, 128–140.

Meyer, E. (2014). The Culture Map: Breaking Through the Invisible Barriers of Global Business. Public Affairs

_____ (2014). Leading Across Borders Takes More Than a Multicultural Background. Harvard Business Review.

_____ (2015). When Culture Doesn't Translate: How to Expand Abroad Without Losing Your Company's Mojo. Harvard Business Review, 93(10), 66–72.

_____ (2016). The Culture Map, Decoding How People Think, Lead, and Get Things Done Across Cultures. Public Affairs.

_____ (2017). Being the Boss in Brussels, Boston, and Beijing: If You Want to Succeed, You'll Need to Adapt. Harvard Business Review, 95(4), 70–77.

Michael, J. (2014). A Heteronímia de Fernando Pessoa: Literatura Plurilíngue e Translacional. Cadernos de Tradução, 2 (Especial), 160.

Ministry of Commerce. (2021). 2021 Statistical Bulletin of China's Outward Foreign Direct Investment. China Commerce and Trade Press.

_____ (2022). Brief Statistics of China's Overseas Labor Service Cooperation, January – February 2022.

Mitchell, C. (2019). "English-Only" Laws in Education on the Verge of Extinction. Education Week.

Mokyr, J. (2016). A Culture of Growth – The Origins of Our Modern Economy, Princeton University Press.

_____ (1990). The Levers of Riches: Technological Creativity and Economic Progress, Oxford University Press, New York.

Molinsky, A. (2013). Global Dexterity: How to Adapt Your Behavior Across Cultures Without Losing Yourself in the Process. Harvard Business Review Press.

Molinsky, A., Hahn, M. (2024). Forging Bonds in a Global Workforce: Build Rapport, Camaraderie, and Optimal Performance No Matter the Time Zone. Mcgraw Hill.

Montaigne, M. De. (1580). Essais. Simon Millanges.

——————— (1588). Les Essais (Édition de Pierre Villey). Paris: Presses Universitaires de France, 1922.

Moore, S. C. K. (2021). A History of Bilingual Education in the US: Examining the Politics of Language Policymaking. Multilingual Matters.

Mpemba, C., & Munyati, C. (2023). How Africa's Youth Will Drive Global Growth. World Economic Forum.

Mundi, L. (2017). Why Is Silicon Valley so Awful to Women? The Atlantique.

Murtha, T. P., Lenway, S. A., & Bagozzi, R. P. (1998). Global Mind-Sets and Cognitive Shift in a Complex Multinational Corporation. Strategic Management Journal, 19(2), 97–114.

Naccarato, L. (2024, March 25). Many Ontario Schools Facing Daily Staff Shortages, Data Suggests. Retrieved from CBC/Radio-Canada

Nahavandi, A. (2002). The Art and Science of Leadership (3rd ed.). Pearson College Div.

NCES. See under U.S. Department of Education's Institute of Education Sciences.

Neeley, T. (2012). Global Business Speaks English. Harvard Business Review.

——————— (2014). The Language of Global Management. In: M. Vodosek & D. Den Hartog (Eds), Wiley Encyclopedia of Management, Volume 6: International Management (3rd Ed.). John Wiley & Sons.

——————— (2015a). Getting Cross-Cultural Teamwork Right. Harvard Business Review (Website).

——————— (2015b). Global Teams That Work. Harvard Business Review, 93(10), 74–81.

Neeley, T., Dumas, T. (2016). Unearned Status Gain: Evidence From a Global Language Mandate. Academy of Management Journal, 59(1), 14–43.

Neeley, T. (2017). The Language of Global Success: How a Common Tongue Transforms Multinational Organizations. Princeton, NJ: Princeton University Press.

───────── (2021). Remote Work Revolution: Succeeding From Anywhere. New York: Harper Business.

Ness, I. (2016). Southern Insurgency: The Coming of the Global Working Class. Pluto Press.

New American Economy. (2016a). Language Diversity and the Workforce: The Growing Need for Bilingual Workers in Arizona's Economy.

───────── (2016b). Demand for Bilingual Workers Increasing in Florida

───────── (2017a). Demand for Bilingual Workers More than Doubled in 5 Years, New Report Shows.

───────── (2017b). Not Lost in Translation: The Growing Importance of Foreign Language Skills in the U.S. Job Market.

Ng, K., Van Dyne, L., & Ang, S. (2009). From Experience to Experiential Learning: Cultural Intelligence as a Learning Capability for Global Leader Development. Academy of Management Learning & Education, 8(4), 511–526.

Nietzsche, F. (1873). Philosophy in the Tragic Age of the Greeks. Henry Holt and Company.

───────── (1874). Unzeitgemässe Betrachtungen. Zweites Stück: Vom Nutzen und Nachtheil der Historie für das Leben. E. W. Fritzsch.

Nisbett, R. E. (2003). The Geography of Thought: How Asians and Westerners Think Differently ... and Why. Free Press.

Oberg, K. (1960). Cultural shock: Adjustment to New Cultural Environments. Practical Anthropology, 7(4), 177–182.

Office of the Commissioner of Official Languages. (2019). Accessing Opportunity: A Study of Challenges in French-as-a-second Language Education Teacher Supply and Demand in Canada.

Organization for Economic Co-operation and Development (OECD). (2022). The Environmental Sustainability Competence Toolbox: From Leaving a Better Planet for our Children to Leaving Better Children to our Planet. OECD Publishing, Paris.

―――――― (2023a). Codebook for Global Student Learning Outcomes, Companion to Successfully Educating Tomorrow's Global Citizens. July 5, 2023. OECD, Paris.

―――――― (2023b). OECD Skills Outlook 2023. OECD, Paris.

―――――― (2019). Raising the Bar, Better Policies for a Better Life. OECD, Paris.

―――――― (2018). PISA 2018 Global Competence. OECD, Paris.

Organisation Internationale de la Francophonie (OIF). (2005). Charte de la Francophonie. Paris: Organisation Internationale de la Francophonie.

O'Rourke, P., Zhou, Q., & Rottman, I. (2016). Prioritization of K–12 World Language Education in the United States: State Requirements for High School Graduation. Foreign Language Annals, 49(4), 789–800.

Otoiu, A., Titan, E. (2017). Trends Among Native- and Foreign-Origin Workers in U.S. Computer Industries. Monthly Labor Review, U.S. Bureau of Labor Statistics, Washington DC, United States.

Pajević, M. (2017). Humboldt's 'Thinking Language': Poetics and Politics. Forum for Modern Language Studies, 53(1), 95–107.

Pak, S., Lee, M. (2018). 'Hit the Ground Running': Delineating the Problems and Potentials in State-Led Global Citizenship Education (GCE) Through Teacher Practices in South Korea. British Journal of Educational Studies, 66(4), 515-535.

Paradis, J., Nicoladis, E. (2007). The Influence of Dual Language Exposure on Bilingual Preschoolers' Executive Functioning. Bilingualism: Language and Cognition, 10(1), 1-11.

Pauwels, Y. (2002). L'architecture au Temps de la Pléiade. Presses Universitaires de Rennes.

Pavlenko, A. (2016). Whorf's Lost Argument: Multilingual Awareness. Language Learning, 66(3), 581-607 (Fachportal Pädagogik - Startseite).

Pécastaing, S. (2011). Baudelaire's Translation of Poe, or Fidelity to the Word as Freedom of Expression. In: C. Lapeyre-Desmaison, I. Poulin, & J. Roger (Eds.), Sens de la Langue. Sens du Langage (1-). Presses Universitaires de Bordeaux.

Pfanner, E. & Martin, A. (2015). Rakuten Touts English in Its Growth Push. Wall Street Journal.

Pigott, I. M. (1992). SYSTRAN Development at the EC Commission: 1976 to 1992. Report for the Commission of the European Communities.

Poarch, G. J., Bialystok, E. (2015). Bilingualism as a Model for Multitasking. Developmental Review: DR. 35. 113–124.

Presbitero, A. (2017). It's Not All About Language Ability: Motivational Cultural Intelligence Matters in Call Center Performance. The International Journal of Human Resource Management, 28(11), 1547–1562.

Pufahl, I., Rhodes, N. C. (2011). Foreign Language Instruction in U.S. Schools: Results of a National Survey of Elementary and Secondary Schools. Foreign Language Annals, 44(2), 258–288.

Pun, N. (2020). The New Chinese Working Class in Struggle. Dialectical Anthropology, 44, 319–329.

Rabelais, F. (1532). Pantagruel, Livre Deuxième. Claude Nourry.

―――――― (1534). Gargantua. François Juste.

Ramos, G., Schleicher, A. (2016). Global Competency for an Inclusive World, OECD: Paris.

―――――― (2018). Preparing Our Youth for an Inclusive and Sustainable World: the OECD Global Competence Framework, OECD: Paris.

Reichard, R. (2019). How Miami's Coral Way School Paved the Way for Bilingual Education in the US. Remezcla.

Reiche, B. S. (2021). Research Handbook of Global Leadership: Making a Difference. J Int Bus Stud 52, 1425–1428.

Ren, W. (2018). Developing L2 Pragmatic Competence in Study Abroad Contexts. In: The Routledge Handbook of Study Abroad Research and Practice. Routledge, 119–133.

Renault Trucks (2006). Progress Report 2006. Direction des relations extérieures.

Resnik, J. (2012). The Denationalization of Education and the Expansion of the International Baccalaureate, Comparative Education Review, 56(2), 248–269.

——— (2018). All Against All Competition: The Incorporation of the International Baccalaureate in Public High Schools in Canada, Journal of Education Policy.

Reyes, B. (2021). Dual Language Effectiveness to Narrow Achievement Gaps: A Quantitative Correlational Study. Journal of English Learner Education 12(1).

Richardson, R. C. (1968). *A Study of the Coral Way Bilingual Elementary School: The First Two Years, 1963–1965* (Doctoral dissertation). University of Miami, Coral Gables, FL.

Ricoeur, P. (1990). Soi-même comme un autre. Éditions du Seuil.

Roberts, G., Leite, J., & Wade, O. (2018). Monolingualism is the Illiteracy of the Twenty-First Century. Hispania 100(5), 116-118.

Rodrik D. (2012). The Globalization Paradox: Democracy and the Future of the World Economy. W. W. Norton & Company.

Rolbin, C. & Della Chiesa, B. (2010). We Share the Same Biology... Cultivating Cross-Cultural Empathy and Global Ethics Through Multilingualism. Mind, Brain and Education, 4(4), 196-207.

Ronsard, P. De. (1578). Sonnets pour Hélène. Mamert Patisson.

Rosado, C. (1996). Toward a Definition of Multiculturalism.

Rozelle, S., Boswell, M. (2021). Complicating China's Rise: Rural Underemployment. The Washington Quarterly, 44(2), 61–74.

Ruhani, R. A. (2017). UGC Report: Foreign Students Losing Interest in Bangladeshi Public Universities. Bangla Tribune.

Rumbaut, R. G. (2014). English Plus: Exploring the Socioeconomic Benefits of Bilingualism in Southern California. In: R.M. Callahan & P.C. Gándara (Eds.), The Bilingual Advantage: Language, Literacy, and the Labor Market (p. 1-23). Multilingual Matters.

Russell, A., Vinsel, L. (2016). Hail the Maintainers, Aeon.

Sacco, S. J. (2017). Challenging the Myth of English as a Lingua Franca in International Business. Global Advances in Business Communication, 6(1), Article 3.

——— (2019). Multilingual Franca: Workplace Language Use Within Multinational Corporations in French West Africa. Global Advances in Business Communication, 7(1), Article 5.

Sacco, S. J., & de Koffi, S. (2022). a Case Study of Workplace Language Use Within Micro, Small, Midsize, and Large

Companies: Insights from Language School Students in Abidjan, Côte d'Ivoire. Global Advances in Business Communication, 9, Article 3.

Sacco, S. J., Ohin-Traoré, C. (2022). 'Englishization' in Francophone Africa? Insights From a Study Investigating Workplace Language Use Among 'Women in Logistics-Africa.' Global Business Languages, 14, Article 3.

Samassekou, A. (2004). Approches globales en faveur d'une éducation plurilingue : la perspective africaine. Strasbourg: Conseil d'Europe.

Sapir, E. (1985). Culture, Language, and Personality: Selected Essays (Vol. 342). University of California Press.

Sassen, S. (2000). The Need to Distinguish Denationalized and Postnational, Indiana Journal of Global Legal Studies, 7.

Saussure, F. (1966). Course in General Linguistics. Cours de linguistique générale. New York: McGraw-Hill.

Schippling, A. (2018). Researching International Schools: Challenges for Comparative Educational Research. Revista Lusofona de Educacao. 41. 193–204.

Schlägel, C., Sarstedt, M. (2016). Assessing the Measurement Invariance of the Four-Dimensional Cultural Intelligence Scale Across Countries: A Composite Model Approach. European Management Journal, 34(6), 633–649.

Schmitt, J., Decourcy, K. (2022). The Pandemic Has Exacerbated a Long-Standing National Shortage of Teachers. Economic Policy Institute.

Schneider, S. (2014). Managing Across Cultures, Prentice Hall.

Schwab, K. (2019). Globalization 4.0: Shaping a New Global Architecture in the Age of the Fourth Industrial Revolution. World Economic Forum.

Schwartz, S. H. (1992). Universals in the Content and Structure of Values: Theoretical Advances and Empirical Tests in 20 Countries. In: M.P. Zanna (Ed.), Advances in Experimental Social Psychology. Academic Press, 25, 1–65.

Sea, H. (2020). Becoming a Leader as a First-Generation Immigrant. Doordash Blog.

Senez, D. (1994). Developments in SYSTRAN. In: Proceedings of Translating and the Computer 16, London, UK: Aslib.

Shimanyula, A. W. (2022). African Union Adopts Swahili as Official Working Language. Anadolu Agency. February 10, 2022.

Shohel, M. M. C., Roy, G., Ashrafuzzaman, M., & Babu, R. (2022). Teaching and Learning in Higher Education in Bangladesh During the COVID-19 Pandemic: Learning from the Challenges. Education Sciences, 12, 857.

Shoichet, C. (2023). Where Immigrants Come from and Where They Go After Reaching the US. CNN.

Siddiqui, M. S. (2023). State of Multilingual Education in Bangladesh. The Business Post.

Sieck, W., Smith, J., Rasmussen, L., Chiu, C., Lonner, W., Matsumoto, D., & Ward, C. (2013). Metacognitive Strategies for Making Sense of Cross-Cultural Encounters. Journal of Cross-Cultural Psychology, 44(6), 1007–1023.

Silk Road Briefing (2022). A Potential China-Papua New Guinea Free Trade Agreement.

Simon, F. (2020). La République des Lettres (XVIIe-XVIIIe Siècles). Encyclopedia of European Digital History.

Singmaster, H., Manise, J. (2019). Global Diplomas: Academic Programs that Develop Skills for Work and Productive Lives in an Interconnected World. School Administrator, 76(1), 21.

Smith, M. (2023). Despite Big Layoffs, It's Still a Great Time to Work in Tech, Experts Say: 'I've Seen Bad Job Markets… This Is Not It'. CNBC.Com.

Smith, G. (N.D.). Dreams of Prosperity in Papua New Guinea. The China Story Project.

Social Enterprise UK. (2022). Auticon – Changing the Conversation on Neurodiversity. socialenterprise.org.uk

Sobol, K., Cleveland, M., & Laroche, M. (2018). Globalization, National Identity, Biculturalism, and Consumer Behavior: A Longitudinal Study of Dutch Consumers. Journal of Business Research, 82, 340–353.

Song, L. (2018). 当前中国四大移民潮：问题与对策 [The Four Biggest Emerging Migration Trends: Problems and Solutions].

Journal of Hehai University (Philosophy and Social Sciences), 20(1), 1–7.

Sorge, G., Toplak, M., & Bialystok, M. (2017). Interactions between Levels of Attention Ability and Levels of Bilingualism in Children's Executive Functioning. Developmental Science, 20(1), e12408.

Speroni, S. (1542). Dialogo Delle Lingue. Gabriel Giolito De' Ferrari.

Standing G. Basic Income: and How We Can Make It Happen. Pelican/Penguin.

Stanlaw, J., Adachi, N., & Salzmann, Z. (2018). Language, Culture, and Society: An Introduction to Linguistic Anthropology. Routledge (7th Ed.).

Statistics Canada. (2024). Languages reference guide, census population 2021. Retrieved March 2024.

Statistics Canada. (2024, February 28). Participation in French Immersion, Bilingualism and the Use of French in Adulthood, 2021. Statistics Canada. Ottawa: Statistics Canada.

Steger, M. B. (2020). Globalization: A Very Short Introduction (5th ed.). Oxford University Press.

Steiner-Khamsi, G. (2015). Standards Are Good (for) Business: Standardized Comparison and the Private Sector in Education, Globalisation, Societies and Education.

Stern, H. H. (1963). Foreign Languages in Primary Education: The Teaching of Foreign or Second Languages to Younger Children; Report on an International Meeting of Experts, 9-14 April 1962. UNESCO Institute for Education.

Sternberg, R. (1985). Beyond IQ: A Triarchic Theory of Human Intelligence. Cambridge University Press.

Stewart, J. H. (2005). Foreign Language Study in Elementary Schools: Benefits and Implications for Achievement in Reading and Math. Early Childhood Education Journal, 33, 11–16.

Stiglitz, Joseph E. (2002). Globalization and Its Discontents. New York: W.W. Norton & Company.

Suetonius (C. 120). Lives of the Twelve Caesars: Julius Caesar. Harvard University Press.

Sutcher, L., Darling-Hammond, L., & Carver-Thomas, D. (2016). A Coming Crisis in Teaching? Teacher Supply, Demand, and Shortages in the U.S. Learning Policy Institute.

Tafaroji Yeganeh, M. (2013). Repeated Reading Effect on Reading Fluency and Reading Comprehension in Monolingual and Bilingual EFL Learners. Procedia – Social and Behavioral Sciences, 70, 1778-1786.

Tang, Q. (2014). Global Citizenship Education: Preparing Learners for the Challenges of the 21st Century. Paris: UNESCO.

Taras, V., Baack, D., Caprar, D., Jiménez, A., & Froese, F. (2021). How Cultural Differences Can Impact Global Teams. Harvard Business Review.

Terence. (Circa 163 BC). The Executioner of Oneself. Harvard University Press.

Tiven, M. B., Fuchs, E. R., Bazari, A., Wilhelm, M., & Snodgrass, G. (2023). Codebook for Global Student Learning Outcomes. New York, NY: Bloomberg Philanthropies and the Organisation for Economic Co-operation and Development.

The Associated Press. (2021). More than 9,000 Anti-Asian Incidents Have Been Reported Since the Pandemic Began. NPR.

The University Grants Commission of Bangladesh (UGC-Bangladesh).

Thomas, D., Elron, E., Stahl, G., Ekelund, B., Ravlin, E., Cerdin, J., Lazarova, M. (2008). Cultural Intelligence: Domain and Assessment. International Journal of Cross-Cultural Management, 8(2), 123–143.

Thomas, D. C., Peterson, M. (2017). Cross-Cultural Management: Essential Concepts. New York, NY: Sage (4th Edition).

Thomas, T. G. (2007). New and Veteran Teachers' Perspectives About Delivering Multicultural Education. Curriculum and Teaching Dialogue, 9(1/2), 113–129.

Tochon, F. V. (2009). The Key to Global Understanding: World Languages Education—Why Schools Need to Adapt. Review of Educational Research, 79(2), 650–681.

Toomey, B. (2024). Personal Interview.

Turner, C. & Cohen, N. (2023). 6 Things to Know About U.S. Teacher Shortages and How to Solve Them. NPR.

UNESCO (2001), Universal Declaration of Cultural Diversity, UNESCO, Paris.

―――――― (2007). Guidelines on Intercultural Education, UNESCO, Paris.

―――――― (2013). Intercultural Competences: Conceptual and Operational Framework, UNESCO, Paris.

―――――― (2014a). Global Citizenship Education: Preparing Learners for the Challenges of the 21st Century, UNESCO, Paris.

―――――― (2014b). Learning to Live Together: Education Policies and Realities in the Asia-Pacific, UNESCO, Paris. UNESCO (2014c), Teaching Respect for All, UNESCO, Paris.

―――――― (2015). Global Citizenship Education: Topics and Learning Objectives, UNESCO, Paris.

―――――― (2016). Global Education Monitoring Report, UNESCO, Paris

United Nations (2022). World Population Prospects 2024, United Nations, Department of Economic and Social Affairs.

U.S. Department of Education. (2022). Addressing the Teacher Shortage with American Rescue Plan Funds.

U.S. Department of Education's Institute of Education Sciences (IES), National Center for Education Statistics (NCES). (2020). Data Point.

―――――― (2022). U.S. Schools Report Increased Teacher Vacancies Due to COVID-19 Pandemic, New NCES Data Show.

U.S. Department of Education's Institute of Education Sciences (IES), National Center for Education Statistics (NCES). (2023a). English Learners in Public Schools.

―――――― (2023b). School Pulse Panel.

University of Central Florida Department of Modern Languages and Literatures. (N.D.). Haitian Creole.

Van Gaalen, A., and Gielesen, R. (2014). Internationalizing Students in the Home Country- Dutch Policies. International Higher Education. 78 (Special Issue), 10–12.

Van Parijs, P. (2011). Linguistic Justice for Europe and for the World. Oxford University Press.

Van Troyer, G. (1994). Linguistic Determinism and Mutability: The Sapir-Whorf Hypothesis and Intercultural Communication. JALT Journal, 16(2), 163–178.

Vanhove, J. (2013). The Critical Period Hypothesis in Second Language Acquisition: A Statistical Critique and a Reanalysis. PLOS ONE, 8(7), E69172.

Vaz, D. (2023). Exploring the Applications and Advancements of Artificial Intelligence in Computational Linguistics. Tuijin Jishu/Journal of Propulsion Technology, 44(3), 2774–2782.

Wagner, W., Hansen, K., & Kronberger, N. (2014). Quantitative and Qualitative Research Across Cultures and Languages: Cultural Metrics and Their Application. Integr. Psych. Behav. 48, 418–434.

Walker, G. (2000). International Education: Connecting the National to the Global. In: M. Hayden & J. Thompson (Eds) International Schools and International Education: Improving Management, Teaching and Quality. London: Kogan Page, 193–203.

Wasike Shimanyula, A. (2022). African Union Adopts Swahili as Official Working Language. Anadolu Ajansı.

Weenink, D. (2007). Cosmopolitan and Established Resources of Power in the Education Arena, International Sociology 22(4), 492–516.

Whorf, B. L. (1956). "Language, Thought, and Reality: Selected Writings of Benjamin Lee Whorf." MIT Press.

Wismann, H. (2014). Penser Entre les Langues. Albin Michel.

Wittgenstein, L. (1921). Tractatus Logico-Philosophicus. Kegan Paul, Trench, Trubner & Co

Wohlsen, M. (2013). Japan's Answer to Jeff Bezos Sets Sights on Amazon. Wired.

Wong, A. (2023). Amid Crippling Teacher Shortages, Some Schools Are Turning to Unorthodox Solutions. USA Today.

World Trade Organization (WTO) and International Labour Organization (ILO). (2017). Investing in Skills for Inclusive Trade. Geneva: WTO and ILO

Wroe, D. (2018). Looking North: PNG Signs on to China's Belt and Road Initiative. The Sydney Morning Herald.

Wu, Y., Zhang, Y. (2018). 玩耍中的阶层区隔——城市不同阶层父母的家庭教育观念 [The Class Segregation in Play: The Family Education Values of Parents From Different Urban Classes]. Journal of Research on Education for Ethnic Minorities, 2016, 5, 61–68.

Yang, L., & Shan, L. (2022). The Non-equivalence of Language-Value between Chinese and American Cultures Based on the Sapir-Whorf Hypothesis. Scholars International Journal of Linguistics and Literature, 5(5), 185–190.

Yildirim, S., Tezci, E. (2016). Teachers' Attitudes, Beliefs and Self-Efficacy About Multicultural Education: A Scale Development. Universal Journal of Educational Research, 4(N12a), 196–204.

Young, C., Haffejee, B., & Corsun, D. (2017). The Relationship Between Ethnocentrism and Cultural Intelligence. International Journal of Intercultural Relations, 58(C), 31–41.

Yourcenar, M. (1951). Mémoires d'Hadrien. Plon.

Zentella, A. C. (2009). San Diego's Multilingual Heritage: Challenging Erasure. (Report). Southwest Journal of Linguistics, 28(1), 103–129.

Zhejiang Daily. (2011). 农民出国务工"水土不服",高收入也带来高风险 [Rural People Who Seek Jobs Abroad Fail to Adapt; High Income Comes with High Risk]. ChinaNews.com.

Zolfaghari, A., Sabran, M. S., & Zolfaghari, A. (2009). Internationalization of Higher Education: Challenges, Strategies, Policies and Programs. US-China Education Review, 6(5), 1–9.

About the authors

Sergio Adrada-Rafael, Ph.D., is an Associate Professor of Spanish and Applied Linguistics at Fairfield University, where he also serves as the Director of the Spanish language program's elementary levels. In addition to teaching courses on the Spanish language, he has taught advanced courses on Bilingualism, Spanish linguistics, Spanish for specific purposes, and Psycholinguistics. His main research interests encompass the fields of Second Language Acquisition, psycholinguistics, Spanish for the professions, and Spanish as a heritage language. His publications have appeared in journals like Applied Psycholinguistics, The International Journal of Applied Linguistics, and Languages.

Dina Rosa Agyemang, Fondazione Aurora ETS, Italian Non-Profit Organisation, Rome, Italy. She is an Italian-Ghanaian Economics and International Relations graduate with a strong passion for social inclusion and innovation. She is driving her expertise in fostering access to opportunities for all, particularly for youth with diverse backgrounds, including disabilities and multiculturalism. She is responsible for the Educational and Cultural projects of Fondazione Aurora, a private Italian organization committed to supporting young African entrepreneurs with a positive impact on local communities and changing narratives towards Africa.

Gaspard Belhadj is a 17-year-old International School of Boston senior actively contributing to his school community. He is fluent in English and French, proficient in Spanish, and plays a leading role in the student council to enhance student life and leadership. Gaspard is also deeply involved in the Air Force Auxiliary's cadet program, collaborating with peers on leadership, aerospace, and emergency services training. An avid athlete, he participates in golf, volleyball, and ice hockey and has captained his school's Varsity Volleyball team for the past three years.

Françoise Bougaeff, the Head of School at Lycée International de Calgary, is a trilingual dual citizen of France and Canada with over 20 years of experience in French-accredited schools. Her unique background provides valuable insights into multicultural and multilingual school environments. Françoise has led numerous professional development initiatives and is involved with the work of the Collectif d'interpellation du curriculum. She is passionate about fostering critical thinking, empathy, collaboration, and creativity in students, preparing them to become engaged and informed global citizens.

Laurence Champomier is a dynamic educator with a passion for multilingualism. She embarked on her journey with studies in German literature and civilization. Equipped with a multiple-subject teaching credential, she honed her craft in the vibrant classrooms of Parisian suburbs for six years, engaging students of all ages. Upon relocating to the Bay Area, she spent twelve enriching years at an international school, where she taught and served as program coordinator, ensuring coherence across subjects and levels. Driven by her commitment to bilingual education, Laurence assumed the role of Director of Dual Language Immersion (DLI) at a public charter school in Oakland for six years. There, she spearheaded innovative language programs and embraced leadership as the Principal of TK-2, fostering a nurturing and inclusive learning environment for all students. She is the Assistant Principal of the French Lycée of San Francisco primary school and the Director of its Sausalito campus. Her unwavering commitment to excellence in education earned her the prestigious Chevalier of the Academic Palms title, recognizing her outstanding contributions to education and multilingualism.

Victorien Coquery teaches French and Ancient literature at the International School of Boston. While studying at the École Normale Supérieure (2010-2015), he obtained a bachelor's degree in history and art history at the University of Paris Sorbonne. He wrote his master's thesis on "The Philosophy of Colors in Lucretia's De Rerum Natura" under the direction of Carlos Lévy. After the agrégation, his teaching experience in Los Angeles, Paris, Montpellier, Longwy, and

Boston led him to explore innovative pedagogies such as the setting up of an interactive exhibition on Tocqueville or the creation of karaoke videos in Latin or ancient Greek.

Fatou Alhya Diagne, Moleskine Foundation Italian Non-Profit Organisation, Milan, Italy. She is an Afro-Canadian cultural manager from Milan, Italy, and is associated with the Moleskine Foundation, an Italian non-profit organization. Her expertise fosters the growth and development of African-based creative industries, with a specialized focus on the fashion and textile sectors. As the program manager for the Moleskine Foundation, Diagne plays a role in their vital mission to inspire and empower a new generation of creative thinkers and doers.

Megan Diercks is Executive Director of the American Association of Teachers of French (AATF) and Officier in the Ordre des Palmes Académiques. Megan taught at the high school level for ten years when living in Texas and was named the University of North Texas Foreign Language Department Honored Alumna in 2008. After moving to Colorado in 2010, Megan revived the French program at Colorado School of Mines after a 10-year hiatus. In 2022, Megan initiated a program to expand the study of Francophone Africa within U.S. French programs. Funding from federal and foundation grant programs will support this critical initiative.

Gabrielle Durana is an economist and the President of Education Française Bay Area (EFBA), a non-profit dedicated to promoting French language education in the San Francisco Bay Area. In addition to her leadership role at EFBA, Gabrielle has authored several publications, including *"Bitcoin: bulle ou révolution?"* which appeared in *Esprit* in June 2015. Her work at EFBA reflects her dedication to bilingual education, fostering cross-cultural understanding, and supporting the French-speaking community in California.

Lama Fakih is a doctor in contemporary history and international relations. She has been a lecturer-researcher at Saint Joseph

University in Beirut since 2015, teaching courses on contemporary Middle Eastern history and current events. The Arabian Peninsula, Lebanon, and Hezbollah are her principal areas of expertise. In addition, she has also been a professor in two international sections of the French Baccalaureate. First, in Beirut, where she taught history and geography in Arabic and participated in developing programs and a bilingual lexicon. Then, in Romania, she taught English as part of the American section. More broadly, her mastery of French, Arabic, and English and her excellent knowledge of Spanish constitute a considerable asset in her research and writing activity.

Isabelle Finger is a certified Leadership and Career Strategy Coach who helps global citizens develop cross-cultural leadership skills and embrace change. With experience in major companies in Europe and North America, she has coached clients worldwide in English, German, and French for over four years. Previously, Isabelle led a multinational team at Coursera and was the founding Director of the INSEAD San Francisco Hub for Business Innovation. She also has a background in companies like Dell and Bain & Company across multiple countries. In addition to coaching, she advises EdTech start-ups and volunteers with various organizations in Silicon Valley. Isabelle holds an MBA from INSEAD and has lived with her family in Silicon Valley since 2013.

Tobechukwu Precious Friday, Moleskine Foundation Italian Non-Profit Organisation, Milan, Italy. She is the co-founder and Executive Director of Igbo Wikimedia Organization, a Nonprofit focusing on Open Knowledge. A Wikimedian in Residence at Moleskine Foundation and Wikitongues, a US-based Non-profit. She is a member of the Wikimedia Foundation's Language Committee and a board member at Wiki in Africa, a South African-based non-profit.

Michele Gerring, Ph.D. in French and Francophone Studies, has taught French at Allegheny College, the State University of New York at Fredonia, Grove City College, Ohio State University, and Bowling Green State University. She has also taught online classes in English as a Second Language. Dr. Gerring's other research interests are Maghrebi-French Studies, Quebec Studies, Franco-American relations, and 19th-century French literature. For one year, she lived in Jupiter, Florida, where she became familiar with the wide variety of dual-language and bilingual education programs in that state.

Eric Hertzler is a global educator with degrees in Economics and Management from École Normale Supérieure Paris Saclay and Law from University Aix-Marseille, Panthéon-Assas, and Leiden University. He serves as Vice Dean of International Relations and co-program director of the International MBA at IAE Paris-Est, University Paris Est Créteil (UPEC). With 20 years of teaching experience in Law, Economics, and Management, he has worked in Brazil, Belgium, and California and mentored students in top global companies. His expertise spans International Education, Global Management, Corporate and IP Law, and Cross-Cultural issues. He has also been a visiting scholar at UC Berkeley and has taught at universities worldwide.

Fabrice Jaumont is a scholar-practitioner, award-winning author, non-profit leader, and education advisor based in New York. He is President of the Center for the Advancement of Languages, Education, and Communities, a nonprofit publishing organization based in New York and Paris. He has published nine books on bilingualism and education, philanthropy, and higher education, including *The Bilingual Revolution: The Future of Education is in Two Languages* and *Conversations on Bilingualism.*

Md. Zubair K. Khan, LLB (Hons), Master of Comparative Laws (IIUM, Malaysia), LLM in International Criminal Laws and Human Rights (Bangor University, UK), Master of Public Administration with specialization in Policy Analysis and Evaluation (Baruch College, USA). He is a benefits opportunity specialist at NYC-DSS, NY. He has previously worked as a research fellow for the Malaysian Ministry of Education and as a law lecturer at Chittagong Independent University.

Joanna Greer Koch is an associate teaching professor at the College of Education at NC State University in Raleigh, North Carolina, USA. Additionally, Dr. Koch serves as the Multilingual Education Program Coordinator for the Master of Arts in Teaching (MAT) program. At NC State, Dr. Koch teaches education courses at the undergraduate and graduate levels. She also supervises MAT student teachers in K-12 NC public schools. Before joining NC State in 2012, she was an elementary public-school teacher. Her educational degrees include a Ph.D. from the University of Georgia, an M.A. from Columbia University, Teachers College, and a B.A. from James Madison University.'

Elena Korzhenevich, Moleskine Foundation Italian Non-Profit Organisation, Milan, Italy. She is a co-founder and Program Director of the Moleskine Foundation and has been in charge of the foundation's educational programs for the last ten years. She is committed to unlocking the creative potential of young people from marginalized communities worldwide and transforming themselves and the communities around them through creativity.

Mehdi Lazar is the Academic Director at the International School of Boston in Cambridge, Massachusetts. A graduate of ESCP Business School, he holds a Ph.D. in Geography from Panthéon-Sorbonne University and is completing a Doctor of Business Administration at TBS Education. His doctoral research focuses on school leaders' competencies in the United States and France. Mehdi Lazar has authored six books, including a two-part series on the globalization of higher education and three books focusing on the MENA region. His work sits at the intersection of human resources management and sociology, with a focus on leadership, school leadership, and the development of intercultural competence. Mehdi is also a member of the Harvard Business Review Advisory Council.

Hélène H. Leone earned her Ph.D. in Education from the University of Ottawa and her master's degree from Simon Fraser University. Her work focuses on teacher training and professional development, educational leadership and administration, and minority language education. Dr. Leone has been a researcher for the Office of the Commissioner of Official Languages, the *Fédération culturelle canadienne-française*, and Canadian Heritage. She is a lecturer at the University of British Columbia Faculty of Education and the lead researcher for the Global Governance in Village Schools project in Burkina Faso, Cameroon, and Morocco. Dr. Leone founded the Canadian Bilingual School of Paris, certified by the British Columbia Global Education Program under the Ministry of Education. She is also a member of the United Nations Education Stakeholders Group.

Xiaojin Niu, Ed.D., is an educator, researcher, and theatre artist. She has extensive experience as an instructor, drama teacher, and curriculum developer at universities, schools, and organizations in New York City and China. Xiaojin's research focuses on drama in education pedagogy, equity, and international students' experiences. Her writings and studies have been featured in educational theatre journals and presented at various international conferences, and she serves as an editorial board member of the Teaching Artist Journal. In addition to teaching and research, Xiaojin has been involved in multiple theatre productions as a creator, director, and actor. After graduating from New York University, Xiaojin has taught at a Los Angeles school.

Armineh Petrossian, a seasoned plurilingual elementary school educator at the International School of Boston, is a dedicated lifelong learner. With a distinguished career in education, she earned an Ed.D. in Curriculum, Teaching, and Leadership from Northeastern University, complementing her MBA from Bentley University. With over 20 years of experience spanning French, American, and international educational systems, Armineh also serves as an accreditation evaluator and actively participates in the AIWA Scholarship Program.

Steven J. Sacco is a French professor and co-director emeritus of San Diego State University's U.S. Department of Education-funded Center for International Business Education and Research (CIBER) Program. Sacco is the international leader in workplace language use research within multinational corporations in Francophone Africa. His research began in a Northern California rice mill when he discovered then that English is far from claiming the crown as the nation's workplace language even in the U.S. Sacco's research in Francophone Africa demonstrates that French will continue to serve as the continent's dominant workplace language for decades to come.

Marta Sachy, Fondazione Aurora ETS, Italian Non-Profit Organisation, Rome, Italy. She is an Italian-Mozambican anthropologist and development expert. She worked for NGOs and multilateral organizations in several countries, mainly Brazil and Mozambique. Since 2018, she has been the CEO of Fondazione Aurora, a private Italian organization committed to supporting young African entrepreneurs with a positive impact on local communities and changing narratives towards Africa.

An innovative educator and researcher, **Pascal Vallet** explores AI's impact on language, culture, and education. He developed custom AI systems and smart automation, harnessing technology for student-centered learning and school operations enhancement while considering its broader implications. With experience in international schools in Seoul, Bali, San Francisco, and at UNIS, Pascal's multilingual skills and commitment to ethical AI integration position him as a leader in shaping the future of education and human understanding. Inspired by Marshall McLuhan's insight, "We shape our tools, and after that, our tools shape us," Pascal focuses on the ethical integration of AI in education.

About TBR Books

TBR Books is a program of the Center for the Advancement of Languages, Education, and Communities. We publish researchers and practitioners seeking to engage diverse communities on education, languages, cultural history, and social initiatives. We translate our books into various languages to further expand our impact.

BOOKS IN ENGLISH

Myths and Facts about Multilingualism by J. Franck, F. Faloppa, T. Marinis.
Mosaic of Tongues: Multilingual Learning for the Arabic-speaking World by C. Allaf, F. Jaumont, and S. Tahla Jebril
A Bilingual Revolution for Africa by A.C. Hager M'Boua, F. Jaumont
Bilingual Children: Families, Education, Development by Ellen Bialystok
The Heart of an Artichoke by Linda Ashour and Claire Lerognon
French All Around Us by Kathleen Stein-Smith and Fabrice Jaumont
Navigating Dual Immersion: by Valerie Sun
Conversations on Bilingualism by Fabrice Jaumont
The Hummingbird Project by Vickie Frémont
One Good Question by Rhonda Broussard
Can We Agree to Disagree? by Sabine Landolt and Agathe Laurent
Salsa Dancing in Gym Shoes by T. Oberg de la Garza and A. Lavigne
Beyond Gibraltar; The Other Shore; Mamma in her Village by M. Lorch
The Clarks of Willsborough Point by Darcey Hale
The English Patchwork by Pedro Tozzi and Giovanna de Lima
Peshtigo 1871 by Charles Mercier
The Word of the Month by Ben Lévy, Jim Sheppard, Andrew Arnon
Two Centuries of French Education in New York by Jane Flatau Ross
The Bilingual Revolution by Fabrice Jaumont

BOOKS FOR CHILDREN (available in several languages)

The Adventures of Zenzi and the Talking Bird by Fadzai Gwaradzimba
Biscotte and The New Kid by K. Cohen-Dicker and A. Angeles
Lapin is Hungry by Tania & Olivier Czajka
Uniquely You! by Bertrand Tchoumi
Franglais Soup e by Adrienne Mei
Morgan; Rainbows, Masks, and Ice Cream by Deana Sobel Lederman
Korean Super New Years with Grandma by Mary Kim, Eunjoo Feaster
Math for All by Mark Hansen
Rose Alone by Sheila Decosse
Uncle Steve's Country Home; The Blue Dress; The Good, the Ugly, and the Great by Teboho Moja
Immunity Fun!; Respiratory Fun!; Digestive Fun! By D. Stewart-McMeel
Marimba by C. Hélot, P. Velasco, A. Kojton

Our books, such as paperback and e-book, are available on our website and in all major online bookstores. Some of our books have been translated into over twenty languages. For a listing of all books published by TBR Books, information on our series, or our submission guidelines for authors, visit our website at:

www.tbr-books.org

About CALEC

The Center for the Advancement of Languages, Education, and Communities (CALEC) is a nonprofit organization that promotes multilingualism, empowers multilingual families, and fosters cross-cultural understanding. The Center's mission aligns with the United Nations' Sustainable Development Goals. Our mission is to establish language as a critical life skill by developing and implementing bilingual education programs, promoting diversity, reducing inequality, and helping to provide quality education. Our programs seek to protect world cultural heritage and support teachers, authors, and families by providing the knowledge and resources to create vibrant multilingual communities.

The specific objectives and purpose of our organization are:

- To develop and implement education programs that promote multilingualism and cross-cultural understanding and establish an inclusive and equitable quality education, including internship and leadership training. [SDG # 4, Quality Education]
- To publish and distribute resources, including research papers, books, and case studies that seek to empower and promote the social, economic, and political inclusion of all, focusing on language education and cultural diversity, equity, and inclusion. [SDG # 10, Reduced Inequalities]
- To help build sustainable cities and communities and support teachers, authors, researchers, and families in advancing multilingualism and cross-cultural understanding through collaborative tools for linguistic communities. [SDG # 11, Sustainable Cities and Communities]

- To foster solid global partnerships and cooperation, mobilize resources across borders, participate in events and activities that promote language education through knowledge sharing and coaching, empower parents and teachers, and build multilingual societies. [SDG # 17, Partnerships for the Goals]

SOME GOOD REASONS TO SUPPORT US

Your donation helps:
- Develop our publishing and translation activities so that more languages are represented.
- Provide access to our online book platform to daycare centers, schools, and cultural centers in underserved areas.
- Support local and sustainable action in favor of education and multilingualism.
- Implement projects that advance dual-language education.
- Organize workshops for parents, conferences with large audiences, meet-the-author chats, and talks with experts in multilingualism.

DONATE ONLINE

For all your questions, contact our team by email at contact@calec.org or donate online on our website:

www.calec.org

www.ingramcontent.com/pod-product-compliance
Lightning Source LLC
Chambersburg PA
CBHW021142160426
43194CB00007B/656